# Machiavelli in the Spanish-Speaking Atlantic World, 1880–1940

Edinburgh Studies in Comparative Political Theory & Intellectual History
Series Editor: Vasileios Syros

*Edinburgh Studies in Comparative Political Theory & Intellectual History* welcomes scholars interested in the comparative study of intellectual history/political ideas in diverse cultural contexts and periods of human history and Comparative Political Theory (CPT).

The series addresses the core concerns of CPT by placing texts from various political, cultural and geographical contexts in conversation. It calls for substantial reflection on the methodological principles of comparative intellectual history in order to rethink some of the conceptual categories and tools used in the comparative exploration of political ideas. The series seeks original, high-quality monographs and edited volumes that challenge and expand the canon of readings used in teaching intellectual history and CPT in Western universities. It will showcase innovative and interdisciplinary work focusing on the comparative examination of sources, political ideas and concepts from diverse traditions.

**Available Titles:**
Simon Kennedy, *Reforming the Law of Nature: The Secularisation of Political Thought, 1532–1689*
Lee Ward, *Recovering Classical Liberal Political Economy: Natural Rights and the Harmony of Interests*
Evert van der Zweerde, *Russian Political Philosophy: Anarchy, Authority, Autocracy*
Haig Patapan, *Modern Philosopher Kings: Wisdom and Power in Politics*
Leandro Losada, *Machiavelli in the Spanish-Speaking Atlantic World, 1880–1940: Liberal and Anti-Liberal Political Thought*

**Forthcoming:**
Filippo Marsili and Eugenio Menegon, *Translation as Practice: Intercultural Encounters between Europe and China and the Creation of Global Modernities*
Vassilis Molos, *The Russian Mediterranean: Shaping Sovereignty and Selfhood on the Island of Paros, 1768–1789*
Miguel Vatter, *Machiavelli and the Religion of the Ancients: Platonism and Radical Republicanism*

# Machiavelli in the Spanish-Speaking Atlantic World, 1880–1940

Liberal and Anti-Liberal Political Thought

LEANDRO LOSADA

EDINBURGH
University Press

Edinburgh University Press is one of the leading university presses in the UK. We publish academic books and journals in our selected subject areas across the humanities and social sciences, combining cutting-edge scholarship with high editorial and production values to produce academic works of lasting importance. For more information visit our website: edinburghuniversitypress.com

© Leandro Losada, 2023, 2024

Edinburgh University Press Ltd
13 Infirmary Street
Edinburgh EH1 1LT

First published in hardback by Edinburgh University Press 2023

Typeset in 11/15 Adobe Sabon by
IDSUK (DataConnection) Ltd

A CIP record for this book is available from the British Library

ISBN 978-1-3995-1535-1 (hardback)
ISBN 978-1-3995-1536-8 (paperback)
ISBN 978-1-3995-1537-5 (webready PDF)
ISBN 978-1-3995-1538-2 (epub)

The right of Leandro Losada to be identified as the author of this work has been asserted in accordance with the Copyright, Designs and Patents Act 1988, and the Copyright and Related Rights Regulations 2003 (SI No. 2498).

# Contents

Acknowledgements vi

Introduction: Machiavelli in the Spanish-Speaking Atlantic World – An Open Question 1

1. The First Phase: Machiavelli's Reception Between 1880 and 1914 13
2. Machiavelli and Political Realism 51
3. Machiavelli and Anti-Liberalism 82
4. Machiavelli and Freedom 122
5. The Hispanic and North American Reception of Machiavelli in Comparative Perspective 154

Epilogue and Overview: Machiavelli in Spanish-Speaking Political Thought 191

Bibliography 198
Index 216

# Acknowledgements

This book is dedicated to Paula Bruno.

This research has been supported by a Wallace Fellowship from The Harvard University Center for Italian Renaissance Studies (Villa I Tatti, Florence, Italy), by a François Chevallier Fellowship from Casa de Velázquez–Madrid Institute for Advanced Studies (Madrid, Spain), and by the Project "La democracia y sus enemigos (1918–1931): España, la primera posguerra, la dictadura de Primo de Rivera y sus articulaciones con Italia, Portugal y Argentina," Ministerio de Ciencia e Innovación de España. Programas estatales de generación de conocimiento y fortalecimiento científico y tecnológico I+D+I. Code: PID2020-112800GB-C22.

# Introduction: Machiavelli in the Spanish-Speaking Atlantic World – An Open Question

This is a book about the history of liberal and anti-liberal political thought in the Spanish-speaking Atlantic world between 1880 and 1940 from the perspective offered by allusions to, and reflections on, Niccolò Machiavelli (1469–1527). The notion of the Spanish-speaking Atlantic world alludes to a space formed by Spain and its former colonies, which became independent nations during the nineteenth century and are usually referred to collectively as "Hispanic America."[1] Considering this scenario, the book's inquiry takes Argentina as its main case and proposes dialogues and interpretative relations between authors from Spain and Hispanic American countries.

The figure of Machiavelli is familiar to us all and yet is also shrouded in controversy. It is not necessary to have read *The Prince* (1532) or the *Discourses on Livy* (1531) to know what we mean when we call someone "Machiavellian" or "Machiavellic," or refer to certain behavior in this way. His name resonates far beyond the frontiers of the academic world and has become synonymous with a set of manipulative attitudes and behaviors; it is frequently used as a descriptive metaphor in colloquial language (Sigmund Freud might be considered a similar example).

In fact, since his books began to circulate in sixteenth-century Europe, Machiavelli has courted controversy and censorship. Associated with the validation of immoral and self-serving attitudes of the most reprehensible kind, ranging from cruelty to tyranny, from hypocrisy to violence, Machiavelli puts the unspeakable into words and preaches the art of lying and deception. An author of exceptional frankness, his writing is free of euphemisms and displays an innate mastery of simulation. For both of these reasons, he could be considered as much an accomplice of power as an advocate for freedom: his advice to the prince was both a "textbook for tyrants" and an explicit warning to the people to be on their guard against arbitrary governments.

In the academic field, his work was and still is intensely disputed. Controversies have raged around its essential core and the problems it raises, and sundry debates have been held about the doctrinal affiliation of his ideas. In the historiography of the last decades, significant attention has been paid to Machiavelli and his work, thanks to the classic volume by John Pocock, published in 1975, which established Machiavelli as a republican.[2]

This research has contributed essential knowledge within a broader field of studies, focused on revisiting political traditions in the English-speaking Atlantic world.[3] Thanks to this review, a new field of discussion has opened up on the prevalence of liberalism with an emphasis on the important role played by republicanism, taking Machiavelli as a key author in this context. Historical research into Machiavelli and his relationship with republicanism has, in turn, been linked to the political theory and philosophy devoted to the author of *The Prince* and has even wielded a certain influence on them. It is not unreasonable to note that the principles and characteristics of republicanism, as well as its relation to liberalism and democracy, are weighty and important aspects of a controversial issue (as this book will show) that have been prevalent during the philosophical and theoretical production of the last decades, to which leading historians on Machiavelli and republicanism, such as Quentin Skinner,[4] have made a significant contribution.

Nevertheless, in contrast to developments in the English-speaking Atlantic world, little is known about how Machiavelli's work has been received in the Spanish-speaking Atlantic world. Such research might be considered useless or irrelevant because there have been unwavering characterizations of Machiavelli as not being a relevant author for Spanish and Hispanic American political thought, or because his work has been the target of prejudice and rejection rather than attentive and passionless reflection. The main argument behind these claims is that there was a historically determined way of understanding Machiavelli, the roots of which could be traced back to the sixteenth century. According to this conception, his work was basically synonymous with evil in all its possible broad meanings (tyranny, immorality, arbitrariness, and so on).⁵ The "anti-Machiavellian" tradition would, in turn, be a manifestation of the relevance of Catholic thought, a long-lasting feature of Spanish and Hispanic American intellectual traditions.⁶

In addition, the historiography on Hispanic American republicanism underscores two aspects supporting the view of Machiavelli as a target of prejudice or even ignorance in Spain and Hispanic America. For one thing, there was an intellectually superficial understanding of republicanism, notwithstanding the republican configuration of most Hispanic American nations after their colonial break with Spain. In other words, there was a distinction between the adoption of the republic as a political system (based, in the nineteenth century, mainly on liberal principles) and the knowledge of republicanism as a political and doctrinal tendency. In this sense, it has been pointed out that the doctrinal sources of republicanism, unlike what happened in the English-speaking Atlantic world, would not have recognized significant influences of the Italian republicanism of the Renaissance. The general portrait resulting from all this is that rejection and disapproval would define the reception of Machiavelli in the Spanish-speaking Atlantic world.⁷

This book revisits and discusses this type of claim. Throughout the following pages, it will be shown that, in fact, the way in which Machiavelli was associated with all things evil, with generally superficial invocations and with the influence of Catholic thought, was very relevant to how he was read and understood. But the book also stresses that these were neither the only aspects nor the most important ones coloring the way his work was received. On the contrary, the topics and features addressed by his thought which were relevant for the English-speaking Atlantic world were similarly addressed and studied in Spanish-speaking Atlantic countries. Machiavelli was read with interest by intellectuals and scholars alike, whether liberal or anti-liberal. For this reason, rejection or praise was not the exclusive preserve of any particular political or ideological perspective.

Machiavelli was quoted or invoked by those claiming to justify authoritarianism and limitless power, imperialism, war, or Nazi Fascism. But his work was also studied in the context of deliberations about the rule of law and its epistemological impact on disciplines such as Political Science and History. His thought was identified and even defined as republican, and his republicanism was hailed as a platform for considering and discussing liberalism and democracy. In this more scholarly context, Machiavelli was considered a decisive figure of modernity in the Western world, and it also can be seen why Catholic intellectuals and scholars made key contributions towards this interpretation of his work. This book aims to show that the evidence from this historical research raises considerations about the thought of the author of the *Discourses* which differ from those underpinning contemporary discussions on political theory and philosophy; thus, they could be contributions and inputs to be taken into account in that field of intellectual production.

The book explores these key themes through a leading case, Argentina, and compares the results obtained for this country with authors and works from other intellectual spaces of the Spanish-speaking Atlantic world, primarily Spain.[8] The reasons for this choice are given below.

Argentina has been defined within the Hispanic American context as a "country which was born liberal."[9] This means a country where liberalism gained a firm foothold, a broad and long-lasting consensus, from the beginning of the country's independent life in the 1810s to at least the 1930s. At that moment, and in line with much of what was happening in the rest of the Western world, with a swell of voices criticizing liberalism and challenging the liberal model of the nation state, represented in Argentina by the 1853–60 Constitution, the tide began to turn and anti-liberal tendencies gained strength. These tendencies were, however, more successful in the spheres of thought and culture than in politics; the crisis of liberal democracy in Argentina spanned the entire twentieth century but did not bring about a consolidation of any long-lasting anti-liberal authoritarian experiences. Argentina has nothing that could be compared to Fascism, the Estado Novo of Antonio de Oliveira Salazar in Portugal, or the regime of Francisco Franco in Spain, which lasted nearly four decades. However, the rift in the consensus on liberalism was a major turning point in Argentine intellectual and political history, considering the broad and sweeping hold that liberalism had had over the country initially.[10]

For the purposes of this book, the scenario may be described as having the following characteristics. It features a historically marginal influence on traditionalist or reactionary leanings, and comparatively less weight wielded by Catholic thought when measured against other Hispanic American nations (or, in any case, where Catholicism had a liberal influence until well into the twentieth century). There is also an important current of liberal thought followed by the growth of increasingly radical anti-liberalism, subject to ideological renewal (thanks to the influence of the interwar European experiences). All this sets the scene and presents a pertinent and relevant opportunity to inquire into and question Machiavelli's reception. The Argentine case opens up opportunities to contemplate certain interpretations differing from the anti-Machiavellian tradition that bears a Catholic stamp, such as critical readings based on arguments other than those proffered by Catholicism, and positive receptions from both liberal and anti-liberal perspectives.

Spain, in addition to its obvious cultural influence in the Spanish-speaking Atlantic world, is important because it is the main reference for an anti-Machiavellian tradition of a Catholic hue. But it also has, in its political culture, a long-standing republican tradition (more due to the monarchy than in spite of it) and a widespread presence of anti-liberalism, especially since the 1920s and the 1930s. This anti-liberal current was renewed in doctrinal terms to span a horizon that was far broader than its traditional Catholic basis.[11] The role played by anti-liberalism found its best expression in the Francoist regime, which followed on from the 1936–9 Civil War and lasted well into the 1970s.[12] For these reasons, which differ from those in Argentina, Spanish political thought also encourages a contemplation of whether the anti-Machiavellian tradition of Catholic doctrine was an exclusive or excluding way of receiving Machiavelli's work.

This book, then, aims to question this assumption and tries to show whether it is sufficient to reconstruct Machiavelli's readings, or whether these possibilities conclude in the Spanish-speaking Atlantic world.[13] As already anticipated, the exploration enables us to state that the reception of Machiavelli's work went far beyond the traditional topics covered by Catholic anti-Machiavellianism, which considered that he was an author of evil and limitless power. Besides the various positive, non-critical appropriations, it may be seen that, in any case, an argument of this nature was not formulated from a Catholic perspective only. A point the book emphasizes is that the positive or negative appropriation of Machiavelli cannot be linked to one specific ideological or doctrinal view. Both praise and rejection were forthcoming from liberals and anti-liberals alike.

Apart from that, it should be noted that, by proposing a study of reception in the Spanish-speaking Atlantic world, the book posits a concrete methodological argument. Instead of analyzing a wide variety of authors from different countries, the decision was to undertake a profound study into a national case defined by certain peculiarities within the Spanish-speaking Atlantic world (Argentina). This approach is combined with an attention to texts and authors from the intellectual space that distinguishes this context, whose features also raise questions about the readings and reception of Machiavelli´s work (Spain). Ultimately, the choice has been to select cases whose relevance is not based on representativeness in a statistical sense of the expression (that is, as testimonies which can be generalized, at least *a priori*), but on their singularity. As a result, these cases offer a pertinent opportunity to inquire into the distinctive forms of reading Machiavelli in the Spanish-speaking Atlantic world.

Two other clarifications are needed. One refers to the notion of "reception" used in this work. Its object is both the systematic readings of Machiavelli and the ways in which his work has been evoked in different circumstances. This decision is based on the fact that it cannot be said for sure that, behind each allusion to Machiavelli, there was a detailed reading of his texts. As is suggested in the case of Jean-Jacques Rousseau, the association of different thinkers with certain political or doctrinal positions was frequently as common as knowledge of their works, or even more common. For this reason, even if such stances were influenced more by prejudice or certain biases, it does not, however, mean that they were completely nonsensical, nor that they had no relation to what had been suggested in other intellectual spheres.[14]

Since the interest of this book focuses on readings and invocations of Machiavelli, the corpus studied includes texts and authors who explicitly refer to him, regardless of how frequently they quote him and their reasons for doing so. Thus, it goes beyond scholarly and specialized studies and includes writings whose allusion to Machiavelli was as much instrumental as it was political. Arguments or authors whose proposals or concepts could be attributed to Machiavelli, although he is not explicitly mentioned, are not considered here. There has been no attempt, either, to identify topics or issues that could be attributed to tacit appropriations of his works. There will be references to translations and different editions, even though these are not the main area of analysis.

A second clarification has to do with chronology. The period chosen runs from 1880 to 1940, permitting the exploration of an era that saw the rise of a political and intellectual affirmation of liberalism in the Spanish-speaking Atlantic world, followed by its decline. Consolidation of the states based on liberal principles took place at the beginning of this period. Despite their different stories and circumstances, this happened in Argentina, with the consolidation of the national State in 1880, and in Spain, during the Bourbon Restoration initiated in 1875. The end of the period saw a challenge posed to these forms of State administration, as well as to liberal democracy and universal suffrage, in the context of the growth of anti-liberalism after the First World War. In both of the cases chosen here, the situation was reflected in changes and ideological renovations, in military coups in Argentina (1930 and 1943), and in a civil war followed by the establishment of an authoritarian government that would last for almost four decades in Spain.[15] A second reason, related to intellectual history, is that the specialization, professionalization, and renewal of the intellectual and university sphere constituted an important phenomenon throughout this period. This was colored by one key aspect, as will be seen, which had a bearing on the increased study of Machiavelli: the appearance and strengthening of Political Law as an academic field.

The book has five chapters and an epilogue. Chapter 1 addresses the readings of Machiavelli between 1880 and the outbreak of the First World War. It will be seen there that the most frequent invocation up until then – his association with evil, tyranny, and immorality (otherwise considered the essential expression of the anti-Machiavellian tradition) – began to be replaced by two other ideas: Machiavelli as the author of the modern State, and Machiavelli as the model for imperialism and militaristic nationalism. The first of these meant that he stopped being exclusively associated with the acquisition of personal and arbitrary power and became a foundational author for the power of the State. The second topic, conversely, condensed two aspects. For one thing, condemnatory opinion was perpetuated by Machiavelli being insistently portrayed as the intellectual father of two tendencies considered harmful and even alarming at the turn of the twentieth century: imperialism and militarism. This interpretation was presented as a frequent and recurring topic: the idea of Otto von Bismarck's Germany as the contemporary version of "Machiavellianism." The second aspect associating Machiavelli with imperialism and militarism is the familiarity of the intellectual output of the Spanish-speaking Atlantic world with contemporary debates and controversies under way in other intellectual geographies, since Machiavelli, the author of imperialism, was an especially prevalent subject of debate in the English-speaking Atlantic world. Through this avenue of analysis, Chapter 1 reveals another process of metamorphosis at play in the understanding of Machiavelli and his work: the transition from his classification as an outdated author (along with the consideration that he was the author of evil) to his conception as a contemporary and valid thinker.

Chapter 2 addresses the understanding of what is held to be the most important and, at the same time, most controversial contribution of his thinking: political realism. It will be shown that this aspect of Machiavelli was related to three important topics. First, it was connected to an idea of politics that legitimized reprehensible phenomena and behaviors such as war or authoritarianism. However, it will be emphasized that realism could also be seen in other ways, more along the lines of a humanist approach, in the sense that, by removing the external (transcendent, moral, and material) conditionings from politics, this would throw the capacity of agency into relief and, with that, human freedom. A second area of discussion around realism had to do with the separation of politics from morals: that is, whether this element of his thought justified immorality or merely implied a recognition of the ethical neutrality of certain political behaviors. A third axis involved epistemological implications, meaning the kind of knowledge offered by Machiavelli's political realism. Politics seen either as science or as art was the preference in that respect.

Chapter 3 studies anti-liberal readings of Machiavelli. It will be seen that, from these perspectives, he was read in three different ways: as the inspiration and intellectual father of Fascism, as a key figure for an anti-liberal and even anti-democratic form of republicanism, and as a decisive figure of modernity and liberalism. Consequently, this chapter highlights at least two aspects: the diversity of readings and doctrinal and ideological appropriations existing within the same anti-liberal field (typical of their political stances and, thus, of the tensions existing between them, as well as the short-circuits), and the fact that anti-liberalism (mostly of a Catholic kind) was decisive in portraying Machiavelli as a liberal. This means that the Catholic form of anti-Machiavellianism during the period under study condemned him principally for being a leading author for liberalism, rather than for being synonymous with authoritarianism (which was the view taken by other expressions of anti-liberalism, particularly those enamored of Fascism, who accordingly were supportive in their praise).

Chapter 4 studies liberal readings of Machiavelli. Through these, it will be shown that there was a change in mindset at this time. Liberalism, until the end of nineteenth century, had enjoyed its own version of anti-Machiavellianism, having considered Machiavelli an enemy of individual freedoms and a defender of tyranny. By contrast, during the first decades of the twentieth century,

Machiavelli was associated with phenomena and tendencies linked to liberalism, from the rule of law to republicanism. Machiavelli's liberalism was, therefore, picked up as much by liberal authors as by the anti-liberal ones studied in Chapter 3.

Republicanism was, in turn, the object of controversy. Machiavelli's ideas were invoked to support the portrayal of a liberal form of republicanism, as well as an anti-liberal republicanism. Neither option was exclusive to certain ideological positions. Thus, the liberal republicanism attributed to Machiavelli was identified by liberal authors as a cause for praise and by anti-liberal ones as a reason for rejection. The same occurred with the tensions visible between republicanism and liberalism, underscored by liberal intellectuals and anti-liberal authors alike. At all events, Machiavelli and republicanism – that is, his portrayal as a republican (either with authoritarian or liberal leanings) – was a familiar subject among the cognoscenti, and was furthermore one of the axes sparking the most attention, especially during the first half of the twentieth century.

Chapter 5 takes a more systematically comparative dimension. In Chapters 1–4, the contrasts, parallelisms, and even influences between Argentine, Hispanic American, and Spanish readings, and the comparison between these and readings from other intellectual geographies, are mentioned and annotated. In Chapter 5, however, there is a closer examination of the readings made in Spain between 1880 and 1940, which tests the similarities and differences with the examples examined in the Argentine case. This exercise allows us to identify distinctive topics in each case (it will be pointed out that it was the State in Spain and republicanism in Argentina), and accordingly, some hypotheses are proposed, linked to the political and intellectual history of both countries. A second consideration may be drawn between the readings made in the Spanish-speaking Atlantic world, as they can be characterized on the basis of the Argentine and Spanish evidence, and those in English-speaking Atlantic countries. On this topic, it will be argued that, even though differences exist as to topics and issues, it is not possible to conclude that the readings in the Spanish-speaking Atlantic world were less important or more superficial than those in English-speaking countries. Finally, the chapter proposes a dialogue between the findings obtained by this research and contemporary theoretical discussions on Machiavelli, indicating that the historical evidence provided herein reveals themes or problems which have hitherto been avoided or are not particularly visible in political theory and political philosophy.

The Epilogue, in turn, draws up a general balance sheet of the subjects covered in the book. In this sense, and so as to leave the matter settled from the outset, it should be noted that the premise of this research is that the readings and invocations of Machiavelli are not only an object of study, but also a means to a more general end: the history of liberal and anti-liberal political thought in the Spanish-speaking Atlantic world. This decision stems from the fact that the simultaneous study of both perspectives is not frequent in historiography (at least, not in Hispanic American historiography). An inquiry into these characteristics through the readings of Machiavelli allows us to identify points in common that appear, at first glance, to be surprising when we examine political and ideological opposites. Also visible is the treatment of certain political topics and issues that would be less so if the doors to liberal and anti-liberal thought were different from those offered by Machiavelli's thought. Among the topics that are particularly visible is, precisely, the nature of politics: that is, what is understood by politics when it is taken as something autonomous and independent of any other human or transcendent dimension. In this sense, the book posits a dialogue between history and theory, both because of the indispensable tools that the latter offers for the historical study of political thought, and because of the clues provided by historical research to theoretical elaboration, in showing specific historical versions of discussions and theoretical and conceptual proposals.

## Notes

1. John H. Elliot, *Empires of the Atlantic World: Britain and Spain in America, 1492–1830*, New Haven, CT, and London, Yale University Press, 2006; David Armitage, "Tres conceptos de historia atlántica," *Revista de Occidente*, 281, 2004, pp. 7–28.
2. John G. A. Pocock, *The Machiavellian Moment: Florentine Political Thought and the Atlantic Republican Tradition*, Princeton, NJ, Princeton University Press, 1975.
3. Daniel T. Rodgers, "Republicanism: The Career of a Concept," *The Journal of American History*, 79, 1992, pp. 11–38.
4. Quentin Skinner, *La libertad antes del liberalismo*, Mexico, Taurus-CIDE, 2004.
5. José Antonio Maravall, *Estudios de historia del pensamiento español*, Madrid, Ediciones Cultura Hispánica, 1983; Helena Puigdomenech, *Maquiavelo en España: presencia de sus obras en los siglos XVI y XVII*, Madrid, Fundación Universitaria Española, 1988; Juan Manuel Forte and Pablo López Álvarez, *Maquiavelismo y antimaquiavelismo*

*en la cultura española de los siglos XVI y XVII*, Madrid, Biblioteca Nueva, 2008; Keith David Howard, *The Reception of Machiavelli in Early Modern Spain*, Woodbridge, Tamesis, 2014.

6. Robert Bireley, *The Counter-Reformation Prince: Anti-Machiavellianism or Catholic Statecraft in Early Modern Europe*, Chapel Hill, University of North Carolina Press, 2018; J. A. Fernández-Santamaría, *Razón de estado y política en el pensamiento español del Barroco (1595–1640)*, Madrid, Centro de Estudios Constitucionales, 1986; Anthony Pagden, *The Uncertainties of Empire: Essays on Iberian and Iberoamerican Intellectual History*, Great Yarmouth, Variorum, 1994; Frank Safford, "Politics, Ideology and Society in Post-Independence Spanish America," in Leslie Bethell (ed.), *The Cambridge History of Latin America, Vol. III: From Independence to c. 1870*, Cambridge, Cambridge University Press, 1985. The validity of this tradition has had a relatively recent test in the academy, specifically on the occasion of the Spanish translation of Pocock's book. It was translated as *El momento maquiavélico: el pensamiento político florentino y la tradición republicana atlántica* (Madrid, Tecnos, 2008). The choice of wording generated some controversy and the reason to justify it was that "maquiavélico" (Machiavellian) was the only word related to the author recognized by the Real Academia Española (RAE). For this reason, there was a proposal to include in RAE's dictionary the word "maquiaveliano," to modify the meaning of "maquiavelismo" and to distinguish both terms from "maquiavélico." See Marcelo Barbuto, "El momento maquiaveliano: propuesta de un nuevo vocablo para el Diccionario de la Lengua Española (DRAE)," *Desafíos*, vol. 25, 2, 2013, pp. 15–33. Similar issues, by the way, have been seen in other Latin languages. See Sandra Bagno, "'Maquiavélico' versus 'maquiaveliano' na língua e nos dicionários monolíngües brasileiros," *Cadernos de Tradução*, vol. 2, 22, 2008, pp. 129–50.
7. José Antonio Aguilar and Rafael Rojas (eds), *El republicanismo en Hispanoamérica: ensayos de historia intelectual y política*, Mexico, Fondo de Cultura Económica, 2002; J. A. Fernández-Santamaría, *Natural Law, Constitutionalism, Reason of State and War*, New York, Peter Lang, 2006; Bireley, *The Counter-Reformation Prince*.
8. I made a first attempt at these problems and issues in Leandro Losada, *Maquiavelo en la Argentina: usos y lecturas, 1830–1940*, Buenos Aires, Katz Editores, 2019.
9. Tulio Halperin Donghi, "Argentina: Liberalism in a Country Born Liberal," in Joseph Love and Nils Jacobsen (eds), *Guiding the Invisible Hand: Economic Liberalism and the State in Latin America*, New York, Praeger, 1988.
10. Tulio Halperin Donghi, *La República Imposible (1930–1945)*, Buenos Aires, Ariel, 2004.
11. Ismael Saz Campos, *España contra España: los nacionalismos franquistas*, Madrid, Marcial Pons, 2003.

12. Stanley G. Payne, *El régimen de Franco, 1936–1975*, Madrid, Alianza Editorial, 1987.
13. A similar review has taken place in the study of the Spanish political thought of the sixteenth and seventeenth centuries, specifying that the rhetorical rejection of Machiavelli blended with the appropriation of his ideas even in Catholic thought – for example, through the figure of the "Christian prince" – as well as the idea of reason of State: Howard, *The Reception of Machiavelli in Early Modern Spain*.
14. Jorge Myers, "Prólogo. El teórico de la libertad natural del hombre en el laberinto de la revolución americana," in Gabriel Entin (ed.), *Rousseau en Iberoamérica: lecturas e interpretaciones entre monarquía y revolución*, Buenos Aires, SB, 2018, pp. 9–23. More generally and regarding circulations, mediations, and appropriations in Latin American political thought, Charles Hale, *La transformación del liberalismo en México a fines del siglo XIX*, Mexico, Fondo de Cultura Económica, 2002.
15. This sequence, with the corresponding national singularities, could be extended to the whole of Hispanic America: António Costa Pinto, *Latin American Dictatorships in the Era of Fascism: The Corporatist Wave*, London and New York, Routledge, 2020.

Chapter 1

# The First Phase: Machiavelli's Reception Between 1880 and 1914

Throughout the nineteenth century, conceptions of Machiavelli took a drastic turn. During the first half of that century, he was an object of disdain (so much so that it is not possible to identify any texts or authors analyzing his writings) and rejection, a symbol of evil incarnate. Machiavelli was invoked or referred to (it is more difficult to assert for sure whether he was effectively read) as a benchmark when vilifying conducts and people. This is a starting point that must be taken into account, because it was formulated by the leading public figures and intellectuals of nineteenth-century Argentina, the "founding fathers" of the country as a modern nation, and also because it was an opinion that stemmed from a liberal perspective. Argentine foundational liberalism blacklisted Machiavelli, as is visible not only in the fact that, as an author, he does not seem to have been either particularly read or consulted, but also in the fact that his name was invoked in the context of censoring certain forms of behavior and public figures.

Then, starting in 1880, such considerations began to change. Tellingly, in parallel with the consolidation of the national State, a complex process whose organization spanned three decades between the adoption of the Argentine Constitution in 1853 and the 1880s, Machiavelli began to be seen as an author with vision, who had suggested ground-breaking principles such as the need for political union and the State. This shift in perspective (to put it briefly, going from an author of "evil" to an author of the State) did not necessarily involve a transition from negative judgements to positive opinions. In tune with a controversy that went beyond Argentina's borders, the author of *The Prince* continued to be the object of criticism, largely because he was taken as a key intellectual figure, almost a precursor, of tendencies considered disturbing in international politics at the turn of the twentieth century, such as militarist nationalism and imperialism.

The persistence of such a critical assessment, however, stemmed from a significant disconnect. The topics and phenomena associated with his work had changed (regarding the State and nationalism, not tyranny or despotism), as did the perception of its relevance. Towards the end of the century, Machiavelli came to be recognized as a relevant author, despite the gap of several centuries, because he had pinpointed certain features and behaviors that were long-lasting and even universal, as well as alarming and dangerous. From this point of view, the readings of Machiavelli were a sign of prudence, if not of a certain sense of foreboding about the achievements of civilization and progress in politics in the Western world.

## Machiavelli's Reception in the First Half of the Nineteenth Century

Until well into the nineteenth century, Machiavelli's ideas were usually referred to in Argentine political thought in connection with tyranny or despotism, frequently juxtaposed with the concept of the writer as an individual who legitimized immorality. In other words, not only had he consecrated certain ways of exercising power, but also, by separating politics from morals, he had provided political justification for morally abject behaviors such as lying, violence, or even killing.

This kind of invocation (it is difficult to conclude whether it arose from a direct reading of his texts) may be defined as an Argentine version of one particular way of understanding Machiavelli whose roots reached all the way back to the sixteenth century, soon after his major writings were published in Europe. This reading tradition has been defined as "Machiavellianism," and according to it, the name Machiavelli is synonymous with "evil," a polysemic notion which can be used to allude to immorality, hypocrisy, falsehood, violence, arbitrariness, absolutism, tyranny, and atheism. These are moral, political, or cultural phenomena, which depend on the intentions and arguments of the person doing the invoking (Catholics, Protestants, or humanists, for instance).[1] Although "Machiavellianism" was, similarly, a scholarly or literary term used to define the reception given to the work by the author of the

*Discourses*, the word was bandied about in contexts of political controversy which also had manifestations in popular culture.[2]

In fact, "Machiavellianism" had significant roots in the Hispanic world, in both Europe and America. It should be stressed, for example, that the circulation and reception of his work featured some unique characteristics between the sixteenth century and the time of the American revolutions in the name of independence which began at the outset of the nineteenth century. The Church had prohibited his texts in 1559, including them in its *Index* at the time of the Counter-Reformation and the Council of Trent, almost thirty years after the *Discourses on Livy* and *The Prince* were published in Italy, in the early 1530s.[3]

In Spain, prohibition came later, in 1583, a development which was attributed to the House of Habsburg's interest in Machiavelli's work. In fact, Charles V bestowed his approval on a translation of the *Discourses* in 1552, and had the work dedicated to his son, Philip II. Nevertheless, its circulation seems to have taken place mainly in non-Spanish editions, since, regardless of some manuscript translations between the sixteenth and the eighteenth centuries (one of them addressed to Charles II), *The Prince* was published in its first Spanish edition only in 1821, followed by a second in 1842. This was not the case with the *Discourses*, which, as mentioned earlier, had been published in Spanish back in the sixteenth century. The lack of translations did not, however, hinder circulation of the work, since the Tuscan language was known in the Spanish academic world, and there were close ties with Italy due to the Spanish political presence in that country.[4]

Spanish political thought was, however, generally condemnatory of Machiavelli's works. He was associated with the separation of politics and religion, even between the State and the Church, and as a key author writing about the reason of State. As a reaction to this, Spanish "anti-Machiavellianism" took shape, espoused by lawyers, philosophers, and theologians alike: mainly Jesuits, who attempted to reverse the division. They set the impious reason of State, attributed to Machiavelli, against the "good" or "true" reason of State, invoking a Christian approach that reconciled religion and politics.[5] This argument implied criticism of an immanent monarchical absolutism, but not necessarily of the figure of a "prince" concentrating power. Pedro Ribadeneyra, an exemplary exponent of Spanish anti-Machiavellianism, put up a "Christian prince" against the Machiavellian prince.[6] At the same time, there were "pactist" notions of monarchy, coming from scholastic sources associated with the works of Francisco Suárez or Juan de Mariana, which were brought back into the arena during the eighteenth century to be wielded against Bourbon Regalism, understood as an expression of Machiavellianism. In Spain, thus, Machiavelli was associated with monarchical absolutism, although Catholic anti-Machiavellianism also had "Machiavellian" ingredients inasmuch as it proposed a "good" reason of State.[7]

According to the twists and turns of events in the Hispanic world of the early nineteenth century, the name of Machiavelli could be associated equally with Bourbon absolutism or with some guidelines of Catholic thought. Without ignoring the crucial issue of the relation between religion and politics, both repertoires fostered claims in favor of the concentration of power, the figure of a "prince," and the reason of State. In addition, in Spanish political thought, Machiavelli continued to be associated with *The Prince*, which was, for his critics, tantamount to immorality and arbitrariness. In other European countries (Britain, France, Italy, and Germany) at the end of the eighteenth century, however, another reading tradition was already entrenched which focused on a republican Machiavelli identified with freedom.[8] Finally, it should not be forgotten that, in the Hispanic American colonies, the authorities (in connivance with the Inquisition) had censored his works and done everything possible to prevent or restrict their circulation, including confiscating and burning his books, along with texts from other authors, from the *Encyclopedia* to Montesquieu, at least until the end of the 1700s.[9]

To summarize, if we look at the tradition of reading or, at least, the reception or invocation of Machiavelli prevalent in the Hispanic American world, knowledge of the Florentine author by the mid-nineteenth century in the Río de la Plata may be defined as fragmentary, imperfect, and largely negative, either because of the difficulties underlying the revolutionary and post-revolutionary scenario in terms of the circulation of and access to foreign literature and culture, or because of the more entrenched versions of his works (meaning "Machiavellianism").

Therefore, there are sufficient reasons to suggest that the Argentine reception in the nineteenth century serves as a model of how Machiavelli was read in the Spanish-speaking Atlantic world, or of the traditions and ways of reading and invoking him that had prevailed in this space since the sixteenth century. The interesting point is that these continued, despite the deliberate search to break with the past and with Hispanic traditions and legacies.

In fact, the "Machiavellianism" school of thought may be observed in the first generation of intellectuals in Argentina, the so-called Generation of 1837. The key figures of this movement were men such as Juan Bautista Alberdi (1810–84, "intellectual father" of the Argentine Constitution that was adopted in 1853) and Domingo Faustino Sarmiento (1811–88, President of Argentina between 1868 and 1874). These intellectuals sought nothing less than the construction of Argentina as a nation after the period of institutional instability and civil war that had spread throughout the Río de la Plata region since the wars seeking independence from Spain in the 1810s. The desire to shake off the plethora of Hispanic legacies may be seen in the multitude of theoretical and intellectual references, romantic socialism, and French doctrinal liberalism, historicist modulations and illuminist gestures, North American federalism, and Anglo-Saxon classical liberalism (from Adam Smith to Herbert Spencer), for example.[10]

These intellectuals did not specifically write about the study of Machiavelli's work. Instead, they mentioned him in writings whose main goal was to contribute to the political debates which opened up after dissolution of the colonial bond with Spain. As indicated above, these discussions were a response to the difficulty involved in achieving constitutional organization (finally reached in 1853, more than forty years after breaking with Spain), against a background of armed conflicts and troubled political life. Even when governed by the rules, institutions, and proceedings similar to the republican ones that had replaced those of the Old Regime after the North American and French revolutions of the late eighteenth century, daily political life was threatened by violence and authoritarianism. Juan Manuel de Rosas, governor of the Province of Buenos Aires and undoubtedly the key political figure of the first half of the nineteenth century, was a paradigmatic example of the type of leadership that flourished in this scenario. His was the warlord approach or *"caudillismo,"* with a personal style based on charisma and an unanimist conception of power, as well as a sense of impunity and arbitrariness, which included the persecution and even killing of opponents and dissidents.[11]

Sarmiento and Alberdi, opponents of Rosas, invoked Machiavelli as a way of portraying the Rosas administration and the public figure in precise fashion, as the governor was the best example of Machiavellianism in nineteenth-century Río de la Plata. Sarmiento, in his seminal work *Facundo*, published in 1845 (and whose title referred to Facundo Quiroga, *caudillo* of one of the provinces of north-western Argentina, La Rioja), wrote what is probably the best-known profile of the man:

> Facundo, provincial, barbaric and valiant, audacious, was replaced by Rosas, son of the educated elite in Buenos Aires although he was anything but that; by a false and cold-hearted Rosas, with a calculating spirit, who does evil without passion and slowly organizes despotism, with all the intelligence of a Machiavelli.[12]

As may be seen here, political and moral criticisms are entwined: Rosas's despotism is the result of an immoral character (a false, calculating spirit, "cold"). It may also be observed, however, that such moral criticism is not specified or leveled in the name of Catholic morals or in praise of the subordination of politics to religion.[13]

Alberdi also invoked Machiavelli when portraying Rosas's tyranny (or despotism – categories often used interchangeably). However, he did not base his criticism solely on moral aspects. Alberdi wrote of a Machiavellian Rosas because he applied the tactics taught by the Florentine author:

> Rosas's tactic is well known: it is very old, and Machiavelli formulated it in a code that is known to all tyrants. It consists, almost all of it, in smothering every idea, every system at its birth, which by its nature and means could become general. Divide and command: here, in two words, is the code of tyranny: this is the code that has governed Rosas's despotic march, and one by which there is not a single one of his acts that cannot be easily explained.[14]

In *Peregrinación de Luz del Día* (1871), Alberdi repeated that the concept of "divide and reign" was Machiavelli's principal advice to the tyrant, as it opened the doors to a state of internal conflict that enabled freedoms to be suspended or otherwise subjugated:

> If Machiavelli had had to encapsulate in one simple rule the entire art of making the establishment of internal freedom in South America impossible, it would have been sufficient to give governments this simple piece of advice: "Do not let the fires of civil war burn out for a single moment."

And also:

> the state of war is the state of siege [...]. In the name of public security, interpreted by individual health, the state of siege suspends freedom of the press, freedom of assembly, freedom of movement

or trade, electoral freedom, which stops being useful because public security requires the government to last indefinitely.[15]

This is an enduring theme in Alberdi's invocation of Machiavelli (as will be seen below): his conception of the author as the promotor of internal or external warfare, who is thus an enemy of freedom, since war is functional to arbitrariness. Furthermore, public security is used as a basis, in the words of this text, to justify the violation of civil and political liberties.

At the same time, the prevailing position of rejection or criticism of the Florentine author among leading Argentine scholars and intellectuals of the nineteenth century was frequently accompanied by a disdainful or derogatory opinion, whereby his relevance as an author was either overestimated or considered obsolete.

This is what Sarmiento wrote in the mid-1840s, in a letter to Juan María Gutiérrez, another member of the Generation of 1837. As we can see, once again, Machiavelli is synonymous with Machiavellianism. Rather than being a symbol of the incommensurability between politics and morals, his name is synonymous with immoral politics, and his amoral approach is taken as tantamount to condoning immoral behavior in politics in general: "Machiavelli, whose name has served in all languages to create a noun, Machiavellianism, to express the cold calculation involved in the crime by equation or the means to achieve a known end, power itself."

However, this type of politics belonged to barbarism and a bygone age. The modern invention involved a convergence of morals, politics, and justice. The condemnation of Machiavelli was, therefore, excessive. Rather than frightening, he was atavistic. Also, at the same time, he was over-estimated for another reason entirely: his maxims were nothing more than testimonies of his time. Based on an optimistic historicism and the decrease in stature of Machiavelli as author, Sarmiento dissociated him from modernity and ended his considerations with some empathy:

> Poor Machiavelli, who related in *The Prince* what the most justified people on earth at the time believed and practiced [. . .]. Morality and justice applied to politics are a purely modern invention, and we must enjoy this exceedingly, although there may still be, here and there, some who cling to the old ways, who refer to the prince of Machiavelli with a candor worthy of praise.[16]

Sarmiento repeated similar concepts throughout his work. Machiavelli "warned us about tyrants."[17] He was a "profound sage, inspired by the immorality reigning in his times," who had taught "for the use of princes and adventurers, the art of usurping authority and oppressing the people." And even if "Machiavelli has bequeathed us a noun: Machiavellianism," "many nations are nevertheless free."[18]

Bartolomé Mitre (1821–1906), another of the "founding fathers" of Argentina, left similar testimonies about the historical context and political meaning of Machiavelli's thought. Associated with the decline of medieval times, his work and his thought had come to represent some form of "relative progress, but this does not mean that he had had coined principles of 'progress.'" On the contrary, he condensed late fifteenth-century Europe as a political and moral disaster, whose supreme expression was a "reason of State" that pre-empted all "human rights":

> Before the end of the fifteenth century, Europe had lost its moral, political, and mechanical balance... The political morality of nations and their thinkers was based on Machiavelli's principles, placing the reason of State before all human rights, with the end justifying all the means, and this was seen as a relative advance. Any healthy evolution in the sense of progress was impossible within these outdated beliefs, and, thus, Europe was fatally headed for social dissolution because of a lack of a vital and regenerating principle.[19]

Alberdi also made similar, and even more emphatic, statements: "Machiavellianism is not a normal government; it is retrograde politics, at most, it is normal politics which date back to semi-barbaric times." This sentence implies a criticism of the Spanish legacy, especially the ideas of Philip II, the master of "duplicity, underhanded intentions, furtiveness." This is a suggestive judgement, particularly if we take into account the association prevalent at the time between the Habsburgs and the work of Machiavelli, and the criticism of absolutism contained in Iberian anti-Machiavellianism.[20]

In fact, Alberdi linked the Spanish absolutist monarchy to Juan Manuel de Rosas's "republican despotism" precisely because of another well-known tendency he displayed: a creole version of "bread and circuses."

> [R]epublican despotism has inherited Machiavelli's precept, which was so well understood by its contemporary Philip II, where you give people a hundred holidays in exchange for each freedom stripped. Nobody has lavished as many popular festivities on the people as Rosas because he was the one who stripped the people of most freedom during his rule. Every victory obtained in his

chronically systemic wars, every accident favorable to the cause of oppression, however insignificant, was a reason for a civic celebration to be enjoyed by the people, closing workshops and opening the pockets, only to be impoverished to the sound of music and the ringing of bells.[21]

This last statement poses a question: does the "republican despotism" attributed to Rosas and associated with "Machiavellianism" indicate that Alberdi noted a characteristic of the Rosas approach which has been proved by historiography, the republican foundations with which his leadership was presented before public opinion in the 1830s and 1840s?[22] Or is it a statement that merely projects, in republican times, a way of exercising power which is considered out of step and more typical of the times of absolute monarchy? The sense of the text seems to indicate the latter. But it should be noted that Alberdi observed that the relation between republic and freedom was neither necessary nor inevitable (as shown, for example, by his interest in the "liberal" phase of the French Second Empire in the 1860s), and he was also critical of the main principles identified with republicanism.[23]

In fact, it has already been said that Alberdi conceived of Machiavelli as synonymous with arbitrariness and immorality, as the author who provided tyrants with advice in *The Prince*. However, in another of his texts, *El crimen de la guerra*, Alberdi portrayed Machiavelli as an exegete in the Roman tradition:

> Machiavelli sought the revival of Roman and Greek values, and what is called Machiavellianism is nothing more than the restoration of Roman Common Law. It cannot be said that Machiavelli referred to another source of doctrine that was not Roman history, about which he had a profound knowledge. Fraud in politics, deceit in government, deception in the relations between states, this is no invention by the Florentine republican, who, on the contrary, loved freedom and worked for it under the rule of the Medici in Renaissance Italy. All the unhealthy doctrines attributed to Machiavelli's invention had been formerly practiced by the Romans.[24]

The tone is similar to Sarmiento's, and for Alberdi, Machiavelli was not an author of original ideas. And neither was he "modern," but rather "ancient."[25] But he not should be considered obsolete for that reason, or thus harmless, as emerged from the observations made by Sarmiento in his letter to Gutierrez (see above). On the contrary, for Alberdi, Machiavelli was responsible for projecting into modernity

Roman common law, a system whose distinctive traits were despotism and war, and pursuing a warmongering approach to international relations, as exemplified by Bismarck's Germany. As may be seen below, the link between Machiavelli and Bismarck was a common topic in the second half of the nineteenth century.[26]

However, as may be seen from the passage above, Alberdi also pointed out that Machiavelli "loved freedom," and called him the "republican of Florence." This suggests a rereading of *The Prince* or a veiled allusion to other works, especially the *Discourses*. Regardless of the reason, such a portrait did not make him praiseworthy. On the contrary, the republicanism of the Florentine author was an example of the passions of the "ancients" (militarism, patriotism, glory), revisited by the French Revolution and the Independence Revolutions, which Alberdi harshly criticized for their incompatibility and the danger this represented for modern liberties chiseled around the individual. He repeated this concept in several texts, particularly in *La omnipotencia del estado es la negación de la libertad individual*, whose arguments turned to the thought of Adam Smith or Herbert Spencer, picking up the distinction between the freedom of the ancients and the liberty of the moderns, made by Benjamin Constant, in Fustel de Coulanges: "One of the deepest roots of our modern tyrannies in South America is the Greco-Roman notion of patriotism and of Homeland, which we owe to the kind of classical education our universities have copied from France."[27] In conclusion, Machiavelli could variously strengthen arbitrariness or represent a threat to freedom, not only for his advice to the Prince, but also for being a republican.

In this sense, it could be said that, in Alberdi, it is possible to find all the topics related to nineteenth-century liberalism about Machiavelli (bearing in mind that one can only assume that his was a first-hand reading of the Florentine author, since there is no direct reference to his works). In his writing a critical portrait emerges, with words and expressions such as obsolete or ancient, unoriginal or overestimated, threatening, the enemy of freedom, synonymous with tyranny, the exponent of arbitrariness, for consecrating the "despotism of kings." He points to Machiavelli teaching the art of division, conflict, and war, and criticizes him for firing passions such as those underlying Roman republicanism, ill adjusted and a threat to modernity and freedom.

Furthermore, it could be said that nineteenth-century liberalism invoked Machiavelli as an excuse to call out the evils preventing the possibility of Argentina's political and constitutional organization as a modern nation: backwardness and barbarism, Hispanic legacies, revolutionary passions, civil wars, Rosas. From this point of view, Machiavelli was a label condensing a harsh judgement of the revolution and its legacies. As an enemy of freedom, he was deemed an appropriate figure to add elements and emphases to a gloomy diagnosis of post-revolutionary reality. This is probably why other conceptions already present in the nineteenth century, such as his association with freedom and national union, present also in influential tendencies among the "founding fathers" of Argentina (like Italian Romantic nationalism), did not have any relevance for the local representation of Machiavelli.[28]

Lastly, and as anticipated above, Argentine liberalism crafted a portrait of Machiavelli that, perhaps paradoxically, was not very different from the one offered by Spanish scholasticism. In both cases, criticism of Machiavellianism was the prevailing issue. This was certainly, in one case, to preserve modern freedom, and in the other, to reject atheism and the autonomy of politics from religion (a rejection that, in any case, had also nurtured anti-absolutist arguments). In fact, distinguished nineteenth-century Argentine Catholics issued pronouncements about Machiavelli which were every bit as disdainful and critical as those uttered by the Generation of 1837 (without, however, endorsing the absorption of politics by religion):

> I flee the atheist association between Machiavelli and Rousseau, but neither do I yearn for the theocracy that has confused the mission of the priest with the functions of the judge; such a system does not belong to the principles of Christianity.[29]

In other words, the way in which Machiavelli was invoked shows that the relationship between Hispanic legacies and the first manifestations of political thought in independent Argentina was, despite the desires and purposes of those involved, one of continuity rather than rupture, of similarity rather than discrepancy, when the matter at hand was how to judge the meaning of Machiavelli's work.

## Machiavelli's Reception at the Turn of the Century: A Theorist of Power Still in Vogue

Another period in the understanding of Machiavelli's work began in the 1880s. First of all, a change came about in Argentine intellectual life at the end of nineteenth century. The structural transformation taking place throughout the country at that time (economic growth, mass immigration, social mobility) demanded and sparked society's attention. This led to the creation of a "scientific culture," and the development of disciplines like sociology, social psychology, criminology, and psychiatry.[30]

Of course, this overview does not examine or contemplate the entire literary output or scope of intellectual concerns of the period. In fact, history and political studies had great relevance due to advances in the production of rigorous historical knowledge, the need to provide a "national tradition" for a new society affected by immigration, or the importance acquired by political reform in the public agenda, covering a broad diversity of themes from federalism to electoral rules. At all events, social sciences, and sociology in particular, not to mention the interest in reflecting on the degree of correspondence between society and politics, permeated the approach to the study of political phenomena, to such an extent that the outline of political science in more rigorous terms began to appear around the 1910s.[31]

In this scenario, then, references to Machiavelli were neither dominant nor usual, but when his ideas were invoked, there was a clear shift away from the attitudes described in the previous section. The most important point is that he was no longer associated merely with certain forms of the exercise of power or government (tyranny, despotism), or with the separation between politics and morals that legitimized immorality in politics. His reputation as an obsolete author, left behind by history, was similarly mitigated. Instead, he was associated with other political phenomena, whose assessment, unlike earlier movements, was positive rather than negative. In this area, we can identify at least two currents of reading.

First, the focus on Machiavelli's position regarding the importance of the State gained prominence. Second, it was held that he had proposed a series of government procedures as being required to deal with exceptional situations, with the intention of preserving order. From this point of view, the reason of State, or the concentration of power in the hands of the ruler, was not seen as synonymous with tyranny, but as a necessary resource to achieve a definite goal: the preservation of institutional and social order. Machiavelli and his political thought were thus seen ultimately as conservative (order being the goal of all his ideas), rather than him being considered as an author who had written in support of chaos or an institutional vacuum to legitimize tyranny or the personal power of the "prince."

Martín García Mérou (1862–1905), a member of the caste of intellectuals and politicians at the time of the consolidation of the Argentine state, commonly known as the Generation of 1880, assayed a theoretical description of these characteristics.[32] Machiavelli's work should not be analyzed in the light of moral criteria (the licenses of the Renaissance), but from a political perspective (the "anarchy" of the Italian peninsula). Thus, he could no longer be defined as an adviser of tyrants, but as a theorist of the reason of State, a principle which might be subject to censure, but one also historically justified and politically legitimate:

> *The Prince* is generally considered a textbook of tyranny, the result of a doctrine that teaches that the end justifies the means . . . Ultimately, this is profound error. Machiavelli exposes in his book a doctrine that highlights, above all, how low his country had fallen.

García Mérou, who defined the Florentine author as a "genius," concluded that:

> Political need is the supreme law, the salvation of the State is man's prime need, and the defender of the State may use everything within his reach to preserve it. As may be seen, Machiavelli's deepest belief is the supreme and absolute right of the State. If one reflects on the times of anarchy when this theory was developed, it is easy to find in it a bitter but frank and loyal lesson for his fellow citizens.[33]

Then, unlike the customary thinking of the Generation of 1837, in which tyranny and the reason of State seemed to be frequently referred to together in the same sentence, García Mérou, an intellectual from the Generation of 1880, pointed out the distinction between the two.[34] This was the starting point for a conception of Machiavelli as a theorist of the State. His work was no longer "a textbook of tyranny," and his "deepest belief" was "the supreme and absolute right of the State." Although freedom was not the main axis of his thought, he taught that the "salvation of the State," rather than being directed at the accumulation of power in the hands of the ruler, had as its purpose the "needs of the man"; furthermore, the State was "man's prime need."

Similarly, Belisario Montero (1857–1929), a contemporary of García Mérou, drew attention to the fact that Machiavelli was by no means obsolete and neither was he an apologist for tyranny. On the contrary, he had been a patriot committed to Italian political unification and an eminent expert in foreign policy.[35] Significantly, in Montero's opinion, Julio Roca, the main politician linked to the Generation of 1880 (and President of Argentina between 1880 and 1886), whose administration coincided with the consolidation of State authority, was a contemporary version of Machiavelli. In fact, according to Montero, Roca held the Florentine author in high esteem and also considered him to be a patriot.[36]

As just noted, it is important to take into account the fact that García Mérou and Montero were politically close to Roca or were part of his government teams (García Mérou, for example, was in charge of a ministry during Roca's second term of office between 1898 and 1904). We may also assume the existence of intellectual reasons for this shift in the reading of Machiavelli, such as better knowledge of (or easier access to) his texts.[37] And, of course, it is revealing to link the reading of Machiavelli as a writer concerned with the authority of the State with Argentina's political and institutional context at the time that these texts were written, taking into account the purpose and the actions of their authors, which had to do precisely with the consolidation of the national State. The truth is that, at the end of the century, Machiavelli was no longer the teacher of tyranny or an obsolete figure, but an authority on political thought, who had brought to the fore, in truly pioneering fashion, the vital role played by the State in achieving both political union and social order.

In 1916, one of the most important intellectual journals of Argentina at that time, *Nosotros*, published an article on Machiavelli by Miguel Ángel Rizzi, a doctor in social sciences from the University of Florence, who had taken classes there with Pasquale Villari, the author of one of the most important studies on Machiavelli at the end of the nineteenth century.[38] Rizzi's contribution deserves to be highlighted for two reasons: it condenses a series of interpretative shifts to which we have already alluded, and exposes another which is altogether more singular. This is a text with a marked academic tone and intent, far from the arena of political dispute, although not distanced from intellectual controversy.[39] In fact, Machiavelli's influence may be noticed in Rizzi's intellectual output: for example, in the volume dedicated to conflict as a fundamental dimension in the historical study of the relations between social groups.[40]

The text by Rizzi published in *Nosotros* addresses topics similar to those of García Mérou. The work of Machiavelli should not be judged according to moral criteria but studied in the context of the political circumstances of its times, the unsettled and fragmented Italy of the fifteenth and sixteenth centuries: "Some of the principles that seem absolute or intolerant to us are justified as measures of the moment to solve the serious problems of an anarchic social state."[41] It is from this premise that we should analyze his legacy ("the intimate thought of Machiavelli has not been properly understood"). Rizzi revealed a modern Machiavelli, a solid and original theorist, whose work centered on the problem of political union.

Regarding the first point, the modernity ascribed by Rizzi to Machiavelli was based on the former's conception of the Renaissance. Rather than being a moment of licentious behavior or a period which updated the ideas of classical antiquity, these times, according to Rizzi, fostered "spiritual union" and "ideological revolution," which Machiavelli tried to realize by advocating political union, a concept whose projections spread far ahead, right into the nineteenth century.[42] In this respect, he was a harbinger of the future, to the extent that "the genius of the action he foresaw for his times" appeared three centuries later with Napoleon.

Second, Rizzi held that the postulates about the concentration of power or the need for a "prince" – the "theory of a personal government," as he called it – had been overestimated and misinterpreted. In fact, they were merely the means proposed to achieve political union, the axis of his thought. In other words, Machiavelli, rather than being an apologist for disproportionate power, was a keen observer of the need for robust power to achieve certain (politically legitimate) goals.

Third – and this is where the singularity of the text becomes more apparent – the need for robust power, as expressed by Machiavelli, did not imply any praise for or recommendations in favor of tyranny. He mentioned, specifically, how to act in exceptional situations:

> If the capital defects of his work [...] had not ruined his political theory, undoubtedly it would be accepted today as a guiding principle for governments in abnormal cases, forming, rather than isolated norms, a body of external and internal doctrine of the States.

"Abnormal" is an imprecise or ambiguous expression in the text, which Rizzi attributes to the inconsistencies inherent to Machiavelli himself (a lack "of a methodology able to define and synthesize clearly the definite orientation of his thoughts"). If, then, he refers to times of "internal or external war," different situations are described below. So, on the one hand, "the abnormal cases" are associated with an institutional vacuum, anarchy: "if some of his principles seem absolute or intolerant to us, they are justified as measures of the moment to solve the serious problems of an anarchic social state and thus achieve permanent normality."

But, in other passages, "abnormality" alludes to the instability or crisis affecting the existing institutional order, not to a normative vacuum. This is not a semantic or minor difference. According to this second meaning, Machiavelli's "theory of personal government" was neither applied to anarchic situations nor set up by the will of the ruler to accumulate power for himself and break with order. Instead, it was applied to the necessary procedures to preserve institutional order.

Tellingly, Rizzi associates Machiavelli's thought with Lycurgus and Solon, two great legislators, and authors of political and institutional reforms, who were differentiated only by the situations that had challenged them. If the latter "established the legal norms for ordinary civil life," then Machiavelli,

> relying on history, tried to use the ideas making up his theory to build *a code of political procedures governing the acts of the ruler* with respect to his insubordinate subjects and regarding his relations with other States. *To implement different principles to subjugate individual will to collective will, delegated in the Head of the Nation* and thus channel those same phenomena related to individual activities *guaranteeing civil laws, and consequently political order.*[43]

In summary, and according to this last passage, it is not unreasonable to assert that, for Rizzi, Machiavelli was a writer who had detected a need to create emergency powers able to deal with extraordinary circumstances (it is worth noting that Rizzi does not allude to the notion of reason of State).[44] The "personal government" proposed by the Florentine author was not a tyranny in terms of either procedures or objectives. Neither was it a justification of force when dealing with factual situations, as was inferred, for example, when Alberdi condemned the "state of war."[45] Still, it was clear that his doctrine (a category employed by Rizzi himself) was at odds with individual liberties: "the individual, accessory to society, [must in exceptional circumstances] sacrifice his dearest beliefs for the sake of the safety of his associates."[46]

Some years before Rizzi's text, another leading Argentine intellectual of the turn of the century, Ernesto Quesada (1858–1934), had offered similar considerations, although with some key differences. Quesada appealed to Machiavelli to justify the discretionary exercise of power when the objective was the preservation of order. However, he developed this argument in a historical study, not in a text of political theory. Significantly, the central character of this study was the same target as had been invoked by the Generation of 1837: Juan Manuel de Rosas.

Machiavelli, for Quesada, was synonymous with "Machiavellianism." But, in some circumstances (when "necessity" prevailed), his procedures were legitimate rather than despicable. It was reasonable to reject "Machiavellianism" and keep a prudent distance from judging political action exclusively by its results, regardless of the means employed. But it should also be understood that circumstances might demand such behaviors. Thus, in these circumstances, political responsibility, not private morality, was what should guide the behavior of the ruler:

> [I]t is necessary to judge Rosas as a man of government, with the criteria of a statesman, and it would be to some extent hypocritical to want to measure him against standards of private morality. A ruler has, first of all, responsibility for the country he leads; he is obliged to act with forces, with situations, where not only is the morality of the individual irrelevant but ruling based exclusively on this would be perhaps the most unforgivable naïvety.[47]

In addition, it should be kept in mind that Rosas's actions had been a response to the equally "Machiavellian" conduct and tactics of his adversaries, consequences, both, of the scenario after the revolution:

> We repeat once more; it is not possible to endorse this doctrine from any point of view ["the doctrine of the illustrious Florentine," according to which "the reason of State" is the only benchmark for judging the actions and behavior of a statesman]. In this light, Rosas would simply be putting "Machiavellian" principles into practice. However, the fact is that, given *the state of decay in which he found the country*, the particular situation he faced in the international sphere, *the salvation of the nation*, its concentration, and overriding interest were the goals he constantly kept in mind. He tried to overcome existing setbacks, to do away with the obstacles arising before him, to tackle *the international dangers and difficulties that threatened the very existence of the country*, resorting to all possible means, without analyzing their greater or lesser morality, but with unshakeable firmness. *The amazing tenacity of his opponents left him, according to his criteria, with no choice but to resort to terror; and he used terror, without mercy, without hesitation, in full awareness of his responsibility.* Did he err in the means? Were these not indispensable? Could he perhaps

have governed in another way? These are questions that unfortunately *only the ruler himself can judge while he is governing.* In the life of nations, not all rulers hit the mark: this is undeniable; but *the results can be judged only by posterity.*[48]

The way in which Rosas's behaviors and procedures were portrayed – and even attributed to the context rather than to his personality traits – is not so different from what Sarmiento or Alberdi had written earlier. Both spoke of how revolution, anarchy, civil war, terror, and "Machiavellianism" are related. It is worth underlining this point, as Quesada did not praise Rosas simply because he observed qualities opposed to the traits emphasized by the members of the Generation of 1837. On the contrary, he took pains to praise the more controversial of his traits, the discretionary exercise of power, the terror, without appealing even to arguments such as that invoked by Rosism itself (the "restoration of the rule of law").[49] Thus, he placed terror in an institutional vacuum created by a revolutionary situation. The description, therefore, was similar, rather than antagonistic, to that penned by the intellectuals of 1837. The difference lay in the shifting viewpoint of evaluation. What was condemned then was now defended, invoking Machiavelli as an author who had written in support of power, even as a theorist of the reason of State.

However, in opposition to the anti-Machiavellianism espoused by the 1837 writers and expressed in their rejection of Rosas as a tyrant, Quesada presented an argument germane to political realism (or, at least, to some way of understanding it):[50] the separation between politics and morals may be reprehensible but it is unavoidable; thus, the moral condemnation of a politician is inappropriate. Machiavellianism as a negative label was a simplification and a mistake, since it prevented the recognition of the autonomy of politics. This view ignored the fact that the figure of Rosas as a Machiavellian tyrant was founded not only on the grounds of moral criticism, but also on the fact that he implemented the advice and tactics prescribed by Machiavelli.[51]

Certainly, Quesada's arguments are debatable because they justified Rosas in the name of the "salvation of the nation" or even of the "reason of State," assuming as realities circumstances that were far from being evident in Rosas's times (the very existence of the nation and the national State). But, without forgetting this, the point which needs highlighting here is a different one. Quesada recovered the distinction between politics and morals to portray

Rosas "as a man of government, with the criteria of a statesman," and not as a tyrant, and, with that, he justified a political experience at odds with freedom.[52]

It is worth saying that Quesada displayed similar considerations when drawing biographical sketches of other men in power. In them, Machiavelli was not always explicitly quoted, although the behaviors and procedures that Quesada highlighted, and the historical role and purpose he attributed to the personalities under study, are similar to those he attributed to Rosas. This is the case, for example, with his characterization of Bismarck, which was, in another sense, a clear indication of how close the Argentine writer felt to German culture throughout his academic and intellectual career.[53]

Bismarck was a "statesman," as he had achieved the "difficult unification of a nationality that, for centuries, had lived torn apart to the point of constituting merely 'a geographical expression.'" Quesada emphasized that "even if nobody can deny the evidence of the situation and these results, there are many that condemn the means he used to achieve them, and stigmatize the truly autocratic procedure he implemented."[54]

Bismarck had been the "founder and organizer of a nation,"[55] and his ideal was a "united, strong homeland, supported by a formidable military power."[56] In addition, he believed that "to achieve great ends, absolute unity of direction is necessary, and also at times to rid oneself of the irritating obstacles that usually arise from the texts themselves, when these are given a narrow and petty-minded interpretation."[57] He also "understood that providence would safeguard the actions enshrining high and elevated ideals, without nonetheless flagging in his efforts to raise the assistance in whose provenance he trusted."[58] In fact, Bismarck had put "the fickle Lady Fortune at his service."[59]

Years later, in another text, Quesada highlighted that

> politics, then, is not a logical system but part of the physiognomy of public life, as required by both situation and environment, without concerning oneself with what should or could be, but about what really is: the men of government are, then, those who see better how things are, what is possible, and they try to bring it about.[60]

Forms of government were thus irrelevant in comparison with the "methods of politics," for these "are the same in a monarchy or in a republic, in an autocracy or a democracy . . . Politics, then, is the art of commanding, in the government, and obeying, in the mass." Accordingly, "the statesman is, above all, an individual who rules without theories and doctrines, but who is a natural expert on men and things."[61] In addition, it should be added that (similarly to the assertion made in the study of Juan Manuel de Rosas), the statesman's "private beliefs should never hinder his freedom of action; as the politician can have no other conviction than a good sense of government."[62]

These texts by Quesada cannot be compared in a superficial manner. Besides their different nature and object (a study on Argentine history and the role of Juan Manuel de Rosas, a conference about Bismarck, and a theoretical text about Public Law), there are clearer intellectual references in some cases than in others. The 1924 text, as its title says, is based fundamentally on a reflection about the work of Oswald Spengler, whose associations with Machiavelli, as will be seen in the following chapters, occurred with some frequency in Argentine thought. Quesada´s texts have their origins in different historical contexts: the end of the century and the world that emerged after the First World War. In this last scenario, Quesada predicted that "Caesarism is the solution that seems to be emerging, the broom that will sweep away so much dirt."[63]

Without leaving aside such differences and nuances, Quesada alludes basically to Machiavelli to outline the procedures adopted by a man of government in exceptional situations. In fact, the chaos and conflict arising in the absence of political union were "the social condition that Machiavelli portrays so vividly in his famous book."[64] For Quesada (and for Rizzi, as well as for García Mérou), Machiavelli did not refer so much to tyranny as to the ways of exercising power demanded by special circumstances in specific times, and whose objective was, ultimately, the strengthening of power, political union, and the consolidation of the State.

At this point, it is important to underline that Quesada's interest in Bismarck regarding these topics, and the references to Machiavelli to encourage reflection or at least justify certain personal conceptions were not exclusive to him. In fact, the association between Machiavelli and Bismarck (already described by Alberdi), and consequently, the link between the former and nationalism and imperialism was a recurring topic of debate in other parts of the world and intellectual circles at the turn of the twentieth century. These controversies may explain or, at the least, provide a context for contributions such as Quesada's because he referred to or quoted authors with a prominent role in such thought. The differences consisted in the assessment of the individual and the phenomenon. That is, "Bismarckism" was understood as a contemporary form of "Machiavellianism," and thus imperialist nationalism was considered a genuine offshoot of Machiavelli's formulations. The main issue was to discern whether that assessment was worthy of rejection or approval.

## Nationalism, Imperialism, and Machiavellianism

In 1897, John Morley (1838–1923), the biographer of William Gladstone, and Chief Secretary for Ireland and Secretary of State for India, who was a prominent figure in British public life and politics in that time, published a text about Machiavelli. The text reproduces the talk Morley gave for the Romanes Lecture at the University of Oxford, the annual public conference hosted by this institution and an event inaugurated a few years earlier with the first lecture given by none other than Gladstone himself. Both speaker and place, consequently, constituted an important event in British cultural and academic life.

Interest increased as a result of the considerations articulated by Morley. According to him, the topics and ideas espoused by Machiavelli were germane to a fuller understanding of the main episodes and phenomena of European politics during the previous century:

> Revolutions in France, unification in Italy, unification in Germany, the disappearance of the temporal Power, the activity of the principle of Nationality, the realization of the idea of the Armed People, have all in turn and in different forms raised the questions to which Machiavelli gave such daring point.[65]

Morley shared several appreciations that revealed his reading of Machiavelli's work. For him, the Florentine author was neither an accomplice nor a supporter of tyrannies; his political sympathies were firmly republican. At all events, forms of government were not the central axis of his thought, but the consolidation of political power and the "preservation of the State":

> He has been charged with inconsistency because in the *Prince* he lays down the conditions on which an absolute ruler, rising to power by force of genius backed by circumstances, may maintain that power, with safety to himself and most advantage to

his subjects; while in the *Discourses* he examines the rules that enable a self-governing state to retain its freedom. The cardinal precepts are the same. In either case, the saving principle is one: self-sufficiency, military strength, force, flexibility, address, above all, no half-measures. In either case, the preservation of the state is equally the one end, reason of State equally the one adequate and sufficient test and justification of the means. *The Prince* deals with one problem, the *Discourses* with the other, but the spring of Machiavelli's political inspirations is the same, to whatever type of rule they apply – the secular state supreme.[66]

Machiavelli, then, was not a writer advocating tyranny, but neither was he in favor of freedom or the republic. Instead, he was an author who focused on how the consolidation and construction of power functioned in overcoming situations of conflict or an institutional vacuum. In fact, one of the reasons underlying his praise for the Roman republic, according to Morley, was that it saw dictatorship as a constitutional magistracy. According to the analysis made by the British author, as for Machiavelli, one of the virtues of Roman republicanism was that it envisaged an institutional mechanism able to deal with exceptional situations. Such magistracy, therefore, had nothing to do with the "revolutionary dictator" (whose highest example, according to Morley, was Caesar). Consequently, Machiavelli's writing had nothing to do with personal power, nor with the justification of the concentration of power for "good reasons," and much less with subverting or disrupting the political order.[67]

Morley also pointed out that the separation between politics and morals, which, in his opinion, was another central element of Machiavelli's work, implied that the behaviors displayed by the public persona (the ruler, the statesman) could not be judged by the same standards as those of a private individual. "If one were to try to put the case for the Machiavellian philosophy in a modern way, it would, I suppose, be something of this kind: – Nature does not work by moral rules"; "Why should the ruler of a State be bound by a moral code from which the soldier is free?"[68] From this, he derived that "such is the defense of reason of State [. . .] There are no crimes in politics, only blunders."[69]

Morley did not necessarily approve of these considerations. On the contrary, he pointed out that, since the sixteenth century, politics, the State, and diplomacy had made advances that allowed one to think that politics and morals should not be at odds or separated to the degree indicated by Machiavelli. The same could be said about the separation between politics and morals as a necessary condition to underpin political science as, according to Morley, such a statement lacked foundation.[70] But, even then, it was notorious that

> It is true to say that Machiavelli represents certain living forces in our actual world; that Science, with its survival of the fittest, unconsciously lends him illegitimate aid; that "he is not a vanishing type, but a constant and contemporary influence" (Acton). This is because energy, force, will, violence still keep alive in the world their resistance to the control of justice and conscience, humanity and right. In so far as he represents one side in that eternal struggle, and suggests one set of considerations about it, he retains a place in the literature of modern political systems and of European morals.[71]

Morley's diagnosis, in consequence, taken together with his personal reading of the doctrinal contents of Machiavelli's work, was that this clearly still applied to Western politics at the end of the nineteenth century and the beginning of the twentieth. Machiavelli had detected phenomena that, although dated by the historical times in which he lived, had proved to be reprehensible yet constant circumstances and behaviors at a universal level.

Morley's texts sent shockwaves through the intelligentsia of the times, according to subsequent reviews and the heated debates they raised. On the one hand, the reactivation of interest in Machiavelli's works could definitively be attributed to Morley's analysis and this, in the Anglo-Saxon sphere, took as its precedent the writings of Thomas Macaulay from the first half of the nineteenth century (a text certainly known in Argentina, as shown by references to it on the part of authors such as Montero).[72]

On the other hand, the reviews of Morley's work drew attention to the discussion about the relation between politics and morals. Above all, these texts comment on the association between Machiavelli and the phenomena guiding contemporary foreign policy: nationalism and imperialism. According to these evaluations, "the Machiavellian doctrine" has been "revived by the activity of the nationality principle, the greed for colonies [and] the competitions of imperialism."[73]

In this context, according to some analyses, Morley's text prompted a rereading of Machiavelli and shone a light on two different aspects of his proposals. In internal politics, violence, lying, and hypocrisy were indefensible, but in foreign relations – and all the more so in a context defined by imperialism – protecting the State from external threats or attacks was an unavoidable responsibility and all means to this end were legitimate, because war between nations (a statement that, retrospectively, seems prophetic) seemed an almost inescapable phenomenon.

According to other views (which have some points in common with Sarmiento's writing, for example), however, it was inappropriate to compare the Renaissance with the nineteenth century. This was because, since the sixteenth century, international legislation had been sanctioned which sought to bring about peace and even regulated war. From this point of view, the "salvation of the State" was an argument that could be invoked to preserve particular interests (especially those of the powerful), when faced with external threats or internal unrest, and, therefore, could not be considered a reliable principle of government in the context of preventing abuses or arbitrariness.

Consequently, the separation between morals and politics could not be justified, for reasons of either domestic politics or international relations, where good faith, justice, and peace should be not only non-negotiable principles or horizons, but also possible ones.[74] In other cases, otherwise, attention was drawn to how force or violence (perennial traits mentioned by Morley) had acquired a "quasi-ethical significance" due to the Theory of Evolution. That is, social Darwinism had proved, with scientific legitimacy, the truth of the theses Machiavelli had posited in his writing about politics in Renaissance times.[75]

Other analysts, however, reached less pessimistic conclusions. On the one hand, they agreed that, with Bismarck's Germany,

> one may fairly say that the morals of Machiavelli have become a more marked feature in Europe than a generation ago. Europe is today farther from realizing the ideal of politics transformed into morals than in the buoyant days of 1848. We all incline to hold now with the German doctrine that the world-movement is independent of morality.

But, additionally, in evoking a principle that could also be traced back to Machiavelli, they concluded that such a state of affairs did not have to be definitive, thanks to the ever-present nature of "the vivifying breath of civic Liberty."[76]

Machiavelli's association with nationalism and militarism, of course, was neither new nor the result of a reading which arose in the late nineteenth century.[77] The conception that the last chapter of *The Prince* revealed an intense patriotism in the search for political unification in the Italian peninsula had far-reaching roots and was reactivated in the nineteenth century, thanks to Italian Romanticism. The reading of Machiavelli's works as a key figure for nationalism and the construction of the State had also spread through Germany during the nineteenth century, mainly due to readings of Fichte and Hegel.[78]

However, the shift that took place at the turn of the twentieth century saw Machiavelli associated with an aggressive nationalism whose natural continuation was imperialism. Germany and Bismarck became, in this sense, proverbial examples of such tendencies, and, therefore, paradigmatic cases of what was seen as verification of the continuing relevance of Machiavelli, sparking a renewed interest in his work among both intellectuals and other public figures.

It is important to stress at least two aspects of these readings. On the one hand, Machiavelli's association with the construction of the nation and the State was not linked to a liberal repertoire. That is, if building the national State was a project, and frequently an achievement, of nineteenth-century liberalism, associating Machiavelli with nationalism at the end of that century and the beginning of the next was not focused on his relationship with liberalism but on phenomena seen as contrary to those of a liberal order: an aggressive and militarist politics of force.

On the other hand, the invocation of Machiavelli to understand or analyze imperialism must be highlighted for at least two reasons. First, and in relation to the understanding of his work, his link to imperialism implied a degree of tension with the republicanism often attributed to him. Historiography on Ancient Rome, featuring a number of famous exponents during the nineteenth century, such as Theodor Mommsen (also an opponent of Bismarck), routinely focused on the contrast between the republic and the empire. The empire involved the demise of the republic. The conception of Machiavelli as a republican who, at the same time, justified imperialism was, therefore, a controversial one as it proposed a connection between republicanism and imperialist expansionism, and in more general terms begged the question of whether republic and empire could, through Machiavelli, be thought of as converging rather than excluding phenomena.[79]

The second aspect to be highlighted concerning the invocation of Machiavelli to understand imperialism has less to do with the interpretation of his thought, and more to do with the way politics was analyzed and diagnosed by the end of nineteenth century:

that is, imperialism seen as proof of the relevance and *actualité* of Machiavelli's works (meaning the universal nature of his work, no longer a remnant of Renaissance times). This would seem to indicate that, during the "Age of Empire," the explanation of this phenomenon based on economic variables, like those initially raised by John Hobson and followed by Lenin afterwards, was not the only one. Machiavelli proffered a view of imperialism in strictly political terms, linked to the kind of nation state that had gained strength in different geographies throughout the nineteenth century.

Morley's contribution, in consequence, condensed several of these topics and there is evidence enough to suggest that it was a reading of Machiavelli that achieved such an impact and projection. In 1900, the North American political scientist and diplomat Paul Reinsch (1869–1923) published a major study on international politics. He quoted Greenwood and Harrison's comments on the studies written by Morley to propose Machiavelli as a reference that was central to a proper understanding of the dynamics of international policy guided by national competition and imperialism. Germany, once again, was the paradigmatic example. According to Reinsch,

> The treatment of Machiavelli at the hands of modern historians and literary critics fitly illustrates the political temper of the present era [. . .]. Within the past century, however, his character as the apostle of nationalism has won recognition; and especially in those countries that have been struggling for a realization of national existence, Germany and Italy – his fame has risen so high that, as a political philosopher, he ranks second only to Aristotle. His main doctrine – that in great historical developments, as at the birth of nations, ordinary rules of morality cannot be held binding upon a statesman, whose sole duty is to secure the existence of a state within which morality and civilization can thrive – has again become the guiding influence of politics.[80]

In other words, in "the birth struggle of national imperialism, just as centuries ago in the birth struggle of nationalism, Machiavellian thought and Machiavellian means are characteristic of political action."[81] Strictly speaking, Reinsch's argument was that this contemporary form of Machiavellianism had been reactivated by contributions made by authors such as Hegel and Heinrich von Treitschke (1834–96), and by the recovery of the "Greek" concept of the State as the "ultimate good" to which everything (and everybody) should be subordinated. He also referred, once again, to the Darwinian

Theory of Evolution. Force and violence, not reason, peace, and justice, guided the course of humanity, giving rise to an aggressive imperialist nationalism, opposed to liberalism.[82]

In the Spanish-speaking Atlantic world, Machiavelli as the reference point for an aggressive and hostile foreign policy was well known and often deployed. For example, in Hispanic America following the 1898 War, when the United States defeated Spain (which lost its last colonies, Cuba, Puerto Rico, and the Philippines), a period featuring North American expansionism in the region ensued; the Panamericanism proclaimed by United States foreign policy was seen as inherent to a power that had adopted the Machiavellian copybook as gospel.[83]

At the same time, the controversies surrounding German nationalism, due to its characterization as a contemporary version of Machiavellianism, were frequently the subject of discussion by Hispanic American intellectuals.[84] One strident voice to be heard rejecting German nationalism for this reason was that of Adolfo Posada (1860–1944), a key author in the field of Spanish political law between the end of the nineteenth century and the first half of the twentieth, whose interest in Machiavelli was long-lasting, as will be seen in more detail in Chapter 5. Posada was also an influential figure in Argentina, a country he visited during the 1910s and 1920s, and where he gave lectures that were published in Buenos Aires.[85]

At the beginning of the twentieth century, Posada posited a view of Bismarck as the new Machiavelli, nominating Treitschke as the key person responsible for continuing his ideas, all of which led inexorably to the repudiation of German imperialist nationalism:

> In spite of this being the time ... of the emancipatory Revolutions, of the swell of democracy, of optimistic radicalism, and the burgeoning awareness among nations of a scenario of great political movements, our lives are subject to the ideas and practices highlighted by the great Florentine, or better still, in the midst of the political landscape described in *The Prince*, reinforced by new philosophical bases and invigorated with the sap of broad sociological conceptions. These politics have been repurposed as a philosophy of history, becoming the art of success, for the purposes of national enhancement and international domination. Machiavellianism has become Bismarckian; nationalism has deployed to the maximum the political substance – full of vigor and passion – described in the Florentine's famous book. And now, this refined substance nourishes imperialist internationalism.[86]

Posada drew on the authors reviewed above – Reinsch, Harrison, and Greenwood – to develop these assertions. However, he specified that German imperialism was not a mere reversion of Machiavellianism because it had more elevated political and ethical horizons, a judgement he based, again, on a notion of history as progress, according to which the nineteenth century could not be compared with the sixteenth century:

> Undoubtedly, in the political philosophy of a State that is aggressive, imperialist towards the outside, and absolutist or dominating – ruling – in terms of its internal rule, there is more than the pure Machiavellianism of *The Prince*. Even in those manifestations that can be considered more typical, having a direct influence on the development of the catastrophic process of the State-Power, sometimes, the desire to rectify this concept of Machiavelli as something essential can be seen ... Those who now advocate the omnipotence of the State and prioritize the construction of a strong and dominant structure do not wish to dispense with ethics. Their point of view entails, undoubtedly, a broader and more mature conception of politics, and one with a more complex historical tradition than that of *The Prince*; there are other perspectives and views of universal history. At its heart – especially in Treitschke – beats a desire or longing for moral greatness.[87]

It is important to emphasize that, for Posada, as well as for Morley, Greenwood, Harrison, or Reinsch, Machiavelli had not been an author who wrote in favor of tyranny or personal power. He was instead a foundational theorist of the modern State. This reading was based on the purpose attributed to his intellectual (and political) work, which was the concretion of Italian national unification. However, due to his historical context, Machiavelli posited a form of the State – the State Force or "Power" – which was reactivated in the nineteenth century by nationalism and imperialism, as deserving of repudiation and criticism. This was even truer, considering that, when Posada published his text, the Great War had already begun.

The Argentine contributions relating to Machiavelli's work recounted on the previous pages drew on an intellectual context that went beyond national borders, which reflects the fact that their work was not fully original. However, at the same time, it indicates that Argentine perspectives were integral to an area of reflection making up political thought at the turn of the twentieth century, when the Florentine acquired the stature of a leading author for the study of contemporary politics.

The Argentine texts and authors discussed above pronounce judgements and impart diagnoses similar to those circulating in Anglo-Saxon and North American or Spanish debates. The point has been raised that, back in the 1870s, Alberdi connected Machiavelli with Roman republicanism, and in turn linked "Romanism" (as well as aggressive and imperialist foreign policy) to Bismarckian German militarism, all of which enabled this to be qualified as an expression of Machiavellianism. José Ingenieros (1877–1925), a well-known intellectual of these times, also drew associations between Bismarck and the Florentine author. The trait that defined both was the "fraudulent character," typical of "violent-type" civilizations, a suggestive statement in the nineteenth century, as civilization was linked to violence rather than peace or justice.[88] In these circumstances, the contribution of Ernesto Quesada is worthy of special attention because he did not repudiate Bismarck or German nationalism, instead writing complimentary portraits of them, one of his reasons being that he saw in them traits associated with the thinking developed by the author of *The Prince*.[89]

At the beginning of the twentieth century, in consequence, Machiavelli was no longer regarded as obsolete or as an author writing in support of tyranny, as claimed by the Generation of 1837 in the first half of the 1800s. On the contrary, 1880 saw the emergence and consolidation of a conception of his work as one of disturbing relevance, considering him a philosopher who advocated the necessity of the State, invoked nationalism, and proposed government procedures deemed necessary to maintain order. Still, none of this turned him, in general terms, into a writer who enjoyed a positive reception, or one close to liberal ideologies. He had written in support of power more than freedom.[90]

It is worth noting that such an interpretation was founded on the notion of State attributed to Machiavelli, as well as his identification with Roman republicanism, defined as aggressive and expansionist (and, therefore, close to rather than opposing imperialism) or based on principles antagonistic to modern freedom, as pointed out by Alberdi. The outbreak of the First World War prompted the spread of the belief that Machiavelli foreshadowed not only the specter of authoritarianism, but also, in more general terms, the decline of liberalism. From then on, he was associated not just with imperialism, but also with the violence that the Great War pushed to the surface, along with the emergence of Nazi Fascism.

Before moving in that direction, however, it is necessary to take stock of another aspect. Ideological or doctrinal readings were intertwined with the epistemological notions found in Machiavelli. The overriding topic in this field was political realism: that is, violence, war, and force were frequently understood to be the intrinsic consequences of the perspective he outlined when he defined politics as an autonomous dimension of human life, one with its own rules.

## Notes

1. See Leo Strauss, *Meditación sobre Maquiavelo*, Madrid, Instituto de Estudios Políticos, 1964. Also, on Machiavelli and the "fecundity of evil," see Pierre Manent, *Historia del pensamiento liberal*, Buenos Aires, Emecé, 1990, pp. 33–53.
2. Victoria Kahn, "Machiavelli's Afterlife and Reputation to the Eighteenth Century," in John N. Najemy (ed.), *The Cambridge Companion to Machiavelli*, Cambridge, Cambridge University Press, 2010, pp. 239–55; David C. Hendrickson, "Machiavelli and Machiavellianism," in Timothy Fuller (ed.), *Machiavelli's Legacy: The Prince After Five Hundred Years*, Philadelphia, University of Pennsylvania Press, 2015, pp. 105–26; Claude Lefort, *Maquiavelo: lecturas de lo político*, Madrid, Trotta, 2010, pp. 11–29; Yves-Charles Zarka, "Singularidad del antimaquiavelismo," in Yves-Charles Zarka, *Filosofía y política en la época moderna*, Madrid, Escolar y Mayo, 2008, pp. 145–52. See also the texts collected by Giorgio M. Scichilone in "Machiavellismo e anti-machiavellismo nel pensiero cristiano europeo dell' Ottocento e del Novecento," *Storia e Política: Rivista Quadrimestrale*, III, 1, 2011.
3. Giuliano Procacci, *Machiavelli nella cultura europea dell'età moderna*, Rome and Bari, Laterza, 1995; Filippo del Lucchese, *The Political Philosophy of Niccolò Machiavelli*, Edinburgh, Edinburgh University Press, 2015, pp. 120–55.
4. María Begoña Arbulu Barturen, "La fortuna de Maquiavelo en España: las primeras traducciones manuscritas y editadas de *Il principe*," *Ingenium: Revista de Historia del Pensamiento Moderno*, 7, 2013, pp. 3–28.
5. Outside Spain, a key author in this respect was Giovanni Botero. See Enzo Baldini (ed.), *Botero e la ragion di Stato*, Florence, Olschki, 1992; Rodolfo de Mattei, *Il problema della "Ragion di Stato" nell'età della Controriforma*, Milan, Ricciardi, 1979.
6. Howard, *The Reception of Machiavelli in Early Modern Spain*, pp. 83–95; José María Iñurritegui Rodríguez, *La gracia y la república: el lenguaje político de la teología católica y "El príncipe Cristiano" de Pedro de Ribadeneyra*, Madrid, UNED, 1998.
7. A name frequently associated with Machiavelli was that of Tacitus. Spanish "anti-Machiavellianism" was linked to the renewal of Thomism and natural law, especially through the School of Salamanca. See José Antonio Maravall, "Maquiavelo y maquiavelismo

en España," in José Antonio Maravall, *Estudios de historia del pensamiento español*, Madrid, Ediciones Cultura Hispánica, 1983, pp. 39–72; José Antonio Maravall, *La teoría española del Estado en el siglo XVII*, Madrid, Instituto de Estudios Políticos, 1944; Fernández-Santamaría, *Razón de estado y política en el pensamiento español del Barroco*; Puigdomenech, *Maquiavelo en España*; Forte and López Álvarez (eds), *Maquiavelismo y antimaquiavelismo en la cultura española de los siglos XVI y XVII*.

8. Paolo Carta and Xavier Tabet (eds), *Machiavelli nel XIX e nel XX secolo / Machiavel aux XIXe et XXe siècles*, Padua, Cedam, 2007; Nizar Ben Saad, *Machiavel en France: des lumières à la révolution*, Paris, L'Harmattan, 2007; Paul Rahe (ed.), *Machiavelli's Liberal Republican Legacy*, Cambridge, Cambridge University Press, 2006.

9. Vicente Quesada, *La vida intelectual en la América española durante los siglos XVI, XVII y XVIII*, Buenos Aires, La Cultura Argentina, 1917, pp. 238–40.

10. Tulio Halperín Donghi, *Proyecto y construcción de una nación (1846–1880)*, Buenos Aires, Ariel, 1995; Natalio Botana, *La tradición republicana: Alberdi, Sarmiento y las ideas políticas de su tiempo*, Buenos Aires, Sudamericana, 1997; Jorge Myers, "La revolución en las ideas: la generación de 1837 en la cultura y en la política argentinas," in Noemí Goldman (ed.), *Nueva historia argentina. Vol. III: Revolución, república, confederación (1806–1852)*, Buenos Aires, Sudamericana, 1998, pp. 381–445; Elías Palti, *El momento romántico: nación, historia y lenguajes políticos en la Argentina del siglo XIX*, Buenos Aires, Eudeba, 2009; Horacio Tarcus, *El socialismo romántico en el Río de la Plata (1837–1852)*, Buenos Aires, Fondo de Cultura Económica, 2016.

11. Tulio Halperin Donghi, *Revolución y guerra: Formación de una elite dirigente en la Argentina criolla*, Buenos Aires, Siglo XXI, 1972; Noemí Goldman and Ricardo Salvatore (eds), *Caudillos rioplatenses: nuevas miradas a un viejo problema*, Buenos Aires, Eudeba, 1998.

12. Domingo Faustino Sarmiento, *Facundo (1845)*, Buenos Aires, Emecé, 1999, pp. 25–6.

13. Since, as Sarmiento stated on another occasion, "I consider that morality when applied to the government of human societies does not belong to truths revealed, but to those conquered by civilization." Domingo Faustino Sarmiento to Juan María Gutiérrez, "Florencia, Venecia, Milán," Milan, 6 May 1847, in Domingo Faustino Sarmiento, *Viajes*, Barcelona, Editorial Universitaria, 1997, p. 259.

14. Juan Bautista Alberdi, "El color azul," in Juan Bautista Alberdi, *Escritos póstumos. Vol. XII: Miscelánea. Propaganda revolucionaria*, Buenos Aires, Imprenta Juan Bautista Alberdi, 1900, pp. 207–8.

15. Juan Bautista Alberdi, *Peregrinación de Luz del Día*, in Juan Bautista Alberdi, *Obras completas, Vol. VII*, Buenos Aires, Imprenta de La Tribuna Nacional, 1887, p. 369.

16. Sarmiento to Juan María Gutiérrez, "Florencia, Venecia, Milán," p. 259.
17. Domingo Faustino Sarmiento, "Los sanjuaninos: discurso en la inauguración de la casa de Gobierno (San Juan, 10 de mayo de 1884)," in Domingo Faustino Sarmiento. *Obras. Vol. XXII*, Buenos Aires, Imprenta Mariano Moreno, 1899, p. 255.
18. Domingo Faustino Sarmiento, "Darwin. Conferencia leída en el Teatro Nacional, después de la muerte de Darwin (30 de mayo de 1881)," in Domingo Faustino Sarmiento. *Obras. Vol. XXII*, p. 125.
19. Bartolomé Mitre, *Historia de San Martín y de la emancipación sudamericana. Vol. 1*, Buenos Aires, Imprenta La Nación, 1887, p. 14.
20. Juan Bautista Alberdi, *Sistema rentístico y económico de la Confederación Argentina* en *Organización de la Confederación Argentina. Vol. II*, Buenos Aires, Casa Editora de Pedro García, 1858, pp. 707–8. There are no details in the text of the sources giving rise to such comments. But it is worth pointing out that "furtiveness" was a quality of the Christian prince, differentiated from the "simulation" of Machiavelli by Spanish anti-Machiavellianism. Mario Prades Vilar, "La teoría de la simulación de Pedro de Ribadeneyra y el "maquiavelismo" de los antimaquiavélicos," *Ingenium: Revista de Historia del Pensamiento Moderno*, 5, 2011, pp. 133–65; Antonio Rivera García, "Maquiavelo en la España del siglo XVII: la razón de estado en Mártir Rizo," in Moisés González García and Rafael Herrera Guillén (eds), *Maquiavelo en España y Latinoamérica (siglos XVI a XXI)*, Madrid, Tecnos, 2014, pp. 177–204.
21. Alberdi, *Sistema rentístico y económico*, pp. 536–7.
22. Jorge Myers, *Orden y virtud: el discurso republicano en el régimen rosista*, Bernal, Universidad Nacional de Quilmes, 1995. It should be said that, in this study, Machiavelli is not referred to as one of the sources of Rosas's republicanism.
23. Oscar Terán, *Alberdi póstumo*, Buenos Aires, Puntosur, 1988; Jorge Dotti, *Las vetas del texto: una lectura filosófica de Alberdi, los positivistas, Juan B. Justo*, Buenos Aires, Puntosur, 1990, pp. 17–53.
24. Juan Bautista Alberdi, *El crimen de la guerra* (1870), in *Escritos póstumos de Juan Bautista Alberdi*, Bernal, Universidad Nacional de Quilmes, 1997, p. 14.
25. With one distinction: for Sarmiento, Machiavelli was not modern because he condensed the moral deficiencies of the Renaissance; for Alberdi, it was because he had reinstated Roman traditions. There are negative assessments of the Renaissance, differentiated from modernity by Sarmiento (not by Alberdi, who alludes to "modern Italy"), and about classical Rome in the work of Alberdi, who does not recognize any major differences between the republican and imperial periods, conquest and despotism being traits common to both, as the main Roman legacies.

26. International law during sixteenth- and seventeenth-century Europe has been defined, precisely, as one of the forms of anti-Machiavellianism. Hugo Castignani, "Guerra, Estado y derecho internacional en Maquiavelo, Vitoria y Suárez," in González García and Herrera Guillén (eds), *Maquiavelo en España*, pp. 49–92.
27. Juan Bautista Alberdi, "La omnipotencia del estado es la negación de la libertad individual" (1880), in Juan Bautista Alberdi, *Obras completas*, Vol. VIII, Buenos Aires, La Tribuna Nacional, 1887, pp. 157–82. In the *Bases* he included the consideration of poverty among those republican passions misaligned with modernity: "The poverty and sobriety of the republicans of Sparta were upheld as virtues worthy of imitation by our early republicans." Juan Bautista Alberdi, *Bases y puntos de partida para la organización política de la República Argentina*, in Juan Bautista Alberdi, *Obras completas*, Vol. III, Buenos Aires, La Tribuna Nacional, 1886, p. 409.
28. William Landon, *Politics, Patriotism and Language: Niccolò Machiavelli's "Secular Patria" and the Creation of an Italian National Identity*, New York and Berne, Peter Lang, 2005; Xavier Tabet, "Il 'mito risorgimentale' di Machiavelli," in Carta and Tabet (eds), *Machiavelli nel XIX e nel XX secolo*, pp. 67–85.
29. José Manuel Estrada, *El génesis de nuestra raza: refutación de una lección del Dr. D. Gustavo Minelli sobre la misma materia (1862)*, in José Manuel Estrada, *Obras completas. Vol. I*, Buenos Aires, Librería del Colegio, 1899, p. 93. On Estrada, Paula Bruno, *Pioneros culturales de la Argentina: biografías de una época, 1860–1910*, Buenos Aires, Siglo XXI, 2011, pp. 65–106.
30. On the transformation in Argentina during this period, Gino Germani, *Política y sociedad en una época de transición*, Buenos Aires, Paidós, 1962.
31. Eduardo Zimmermann, *Los liberales reformistas: la cuestión social en la Argentina, 1890–1916*, Buenos Aires, Sudamericana-Universidad de San Andrés, 1995; Natalio Botana and Ezequiel Gallo, *De la República posible a la República verdadera*, Buenos Aires, Ariel, 1997; Oscar Terán, *Vida intelectual en el Buenos Aires fin-de-siglo (1880–1910): derivas de la "cultura científica,"* Buenos Aires, Fondo de Cultura Económica, 2000; Carlos Altamirano, "Entre el naturalismo y la psicología: el comienzo de la 'ciencia social' en la Argentina," in Federico Neiburg and Mariano Plotkin (eds), *Intelectuales y expertos: la constitución del conocimiento social en la Argentina*, Buenos Aires, Paidós, 2004, pp. 31–65; Bruno, *Pioneros culturales de la Argentina*.
32. See Paula Bruno, *Martín García Mérou: vida intelectual y diplomática en las Américas*, Bernal, Universidad Nacional de Quilmes, 2019; Paula Bruno, "Un balance acerca del uso de la expresión generación del 80 entre 1920 y 2000," *Secuencia*, 68, 2007, pp. 117–61.

33. Martín García Mérou, *Libros y autores*, Buenos Aires, Lajouane, 1886, pp. 299–302.
34. Certainly, the problem as to whether the reason of State refers to the need of the State or that of the prince has been subject to extensive political reflection. Yves-Charles Zarka, "Arqueología y genealogía de la razón de Estado," in Zarka, *Filosofía y política*, pp. 135–43; Maurizio Viroli, *De la política a la razón de Estado: la adquisición y transformación del lenguaje político (1250–1600)*, Madrid, Akal, 2009, pp. 275–316.
35. Other specific considerations about Machiavelli and diplomacy, both negative and positive ones, respectively: Eduardo F. Sánchez Zinny, *Fe de América*, Buenos Aires, Ayacucho, 1946, p. 288; José León Suárez, *Diplomacia universitaria americana: Argentina en el Brasil*, Buenos Aires, Escoffier, Caracciolo, 1918, p. 451.
36. Belisario Montero, *Ensayos sobre filosofía y arte (de mi diario)*, Buenos Aires, Talleres Gráficos de Schenone Hnos y Linari, 1922, pp. 89, 172–80. The text is from 1888.
37. Montero indicated that both he and Roca discovered Machiavelli's work in 1888, when they traveled to Italy at the invitation of an aristocrat. Thus were they saved "from the sieve of Taine and the tyranny of other professors who are also very wise and have an identical professional deformation." Taine had endorsed the portrait of a "Machiavellian" Machiavelli, defined by perfidious immorality, an expression from the Italian Renaissance. It is worth recalling that the conception of Machiavelli as a patriot and champion of national union and State formation had gained popularity in nineteenth-century Italy, since Romanticism, and this was reinforced at the time of the Risorgimento. See Hippolyte Taine, *Historia de la literatura inglesa. Vol. II*, Madrid, La España Moderna, 1900, pp. 203–4; Hippolyte Taine, *Philosophie de l'art en Italie*, Paris, Germer Baillière, 1866, pp. 111–18; Paolo Carta, "Il Machiavelli di Angelo Ridolfi," in Angelo Ridolfi and Ugo Foscolo, *Scritti sul Principe di Niccolò Machiavelli: a cura di Paolo Carta, Christian Del Vento e Xavier Tabet*, Rovereto, Nicolodi, 2004, pp. vii–xxxiii.
38. Pasquale Villari, *Maquiavelo: su vida y su tiempo*, Mexico, Biografías Gandesa, 1953. The original edition was published in three volumes, between 1877 and 1882.
39. Miguel Ángel Rizzi, "Teoría política de El Príncipe," *Nosotros*, X, vol. 22, April 1916, pp. 153–8.
40. Miguel Ángel Rizzi, *La lucha entre los grupos sociales*, Buenos Aires, Imprenta French, 1913.
41. He added that Machiavelli "admitted to being moral when this is necessary for the union of the states."
42. As is known, the nineteenth century produced several works that are still read today as reference works on the Renaissance, among them

the classic tome by Jacob Burckhardt, *La cultura del Renacimiento en Italia* (1860). In the texts referred to in this chapter, there are no explicit mentions of these works, but their influence will be seen in later authors.
43. My emphasis. Taking into account the arguments displayed, his observation, also in the text, that Villari's classes had not been completely satisfactory is particularly worthy of note: the Italian author underlined Machiavelli's republicanism (and his work, as will be seen, influenced others who read him in this way in Argentina). Villari, *Maquiavelo*, pp. 214–43.
44. See José Antonio Aguilar Rivera, *En pos de la quimera: reflexiones sobre el experimento constitucional atlántico*, Mexico, Fondo de Cultura Económica, 2000. It will be seen in Chapter 3 that a projection of these arguments consisted in relating Machiavelli to Carl Schmitt.
45. It is worth remembering that, for Alberdi, war was the denial of law (as can be seen in his criticism not only of Machiavelli, but also of Grotius). *El crimen de la guerra*, pp. 19–24.
46. This was, at all events, carried out in a circumstantial rather than a definitive way. In other words, according to Rizzi, Machiavelli taught the need to suspend liberties, not suppress them.
47. Ernesto Quesada, *La época de Rosas*, Buenos Aires, Moen, 1898, p. 148.
48. Ibid. pp. 151–2; my emphasis. Instead of quoting Machiavelli, Quesada backed these arguments up by referring to John Morley, *Machiavelli in Modern Politics* (London, 1897). This British author will be discussed soon.
49. Myers, *Orden y virtud*.
50. In Chapter 2, the relation between Machiavelli and political realism will be discussed.
51. Rosism as tyranny was addressed from perspectives that were not Machiavellian, nor, in more general terms, were they a proper political study. This can be seen in another classic early twentieth-century text, by José María Ramos Mejía, who wrote from a perspective that combined social psychology and sociology with a biological and physiological imprint in tune with the trends current in the intellectual thinking of the time. Even emphasizing that Rosas had been "outrageously realistic," that he had not been "subject to anyone but his will," or highlighting his "rebellion against all moral principle," Ramos Mejía defined his biographical note by alluding to "Nietzschean Superman" (Nietzsche and Machiavelli, as will be seen in Chapter 2, were frequently linked together; but this was not the case with Ramos Mejía). José María Ramos Mejía, *Rosas y su tiempo (1907)*, Buenos Aires, Emecé, 2001, pp. 555, 642–76.
52. Mitre also had appealed to Machiavelli to highlight attributes rather than reporting vices. For example, regarding General José San Martín,

hero of the independence wars, he asserted that "like the General of Machiavelli, he had the strength of the lion and the astuteness of the fox." *Historia de San Martín*. Vol. 1, p. 269.

53. See Pablo Buchbinder, *Los Quesada: letras, ciencias y política en la Argentina: 1850–1934*, Buenos Aires, Edhasa, 2012.
54. Ernesto Quesada, *Bismarck y su época*, Buenos Aires, Peuser, 1898, p. 5.
55. Ibid. p. 6.
56. Ibid. p. 35.
57. Ibid. p. 42.
58. Ibid. p. 43.
59. Ibid. p. 45.
60. Ernesto Quesada, *La evolución del derecho público (política y económica) según la doctrina spengleriana,* Buenos Aires, Universidad de Buenos Aires, 1924, p. 100.
61. Ibid. pp. 102–3.
62. Ibid. p. 103.
63. Ibid. p. 116.
64. Ibid. p. 108.
65. John Morley, *Machiavelli: The Romanes Lecture delivered in the Sheldonian Theatre, 2 June 1897*, London, MacMillan, 1897, pp. 8–9.
66. Ibid. p. 26.
67. Ibid. p. 29.
68. Ibid. pp. 42–3.
69. Ibid. p. 44.
70. Ibid. pp. 46–7.
71. Ibid. pp. 49–50.
72. Thomas Macaulay, "Machiavelli" (1827), in Thomas Macaulay, *Historical Essays*, New York and Chicago, C. Scribner's Son, 1921, pp. 382–423. A short time before Morley's publication, Lord Acton's work is also worth mentioning (referred to by Morley, as seen above): John Dalberg Acton (Lord Acton), "Introduction to L. A. Burd's Edition of *Il Principe* by Machiavelli" (1891), in John Dalberg Acton (Lord Acton), *The History of Freedom and Other Essays*, London, MacMillan, 1907, pp. 212–31. See: Russell Price, "L. Arthur Burd, Lord Acton, and Machiavelli," in John E. Law and Lene Østermark-Johansen (eds), *Victorian and Edwardian Responses to the Italian Renaissance*, London, Routledge, 2005. Montero's reference to Macaulay, in *Ensayos sobre filosofía*, p. 182. Macaulay was a key reference in the writings of a relevant author concerning the reception of Machiavelli in Argentina, Mariano de Vedia y Mitre, to be covered in the following chapters.
73. Frederik Greenwood, "Machiavelli in Modern Politics," *The Living Edge*, vol. 214, 2777, 25 September 1897.
74. Greenwood, "Machiavelli"; Frederic Harrison, "The Modern Machiavelli," *The Eclectic Magazine of Foreign Literature*, vol. 66, 5, November 1897.

75. C. H. Hertford, "Mr. Morley and Machiavelli," *The Bookman*, July 1897, p. 92. See also: "Mr. Morley on Machiavelli," *Saturday Review of Politics, Literature, Science and Art*, vol. 83, 2171, pp. 619–20, 6 June 1897; "Mr. Morley on Machiavelli," *The Critic: A Weekly Review of Literature and the Arts*, vol. 28, 815, 2 October 1897, p. 185; Norman H. Smith "John Morley and Machiavelli," *Outlook*, vol. 56, 11, 10 July 1897, pp. 635–6.
76. William Clarke, "Bismarck," *The Contemporary Review*, 75, January 1899, pp. 1–17.
77. It is worth recalling that Machiavelli addressed this topic in *The Art of War*. This text is quoted by Morley, *Machiavelli*, p. 15.
78. del Lucchese, *The Political Philosophy of Niccolò Machiavelli*, pp. 156–60; Carta and Tabet, *Machiavelli nel XIX e nel XX secolo*; Lefort, *Maquiavelo: lecturas de lo político*, pp. 41–53.
79. See Mark Hulliung, *Citizen Machiavelli*, Princeton, Princeton University Press, 1983; Mikael Hornqvist, *Machiavelli and Empire*, New York, Cambridge University Press, 2004.
80. Paul Reinsch, *World Politics at The end of the Nineteenth Century, as Influenced by the Oriental Situation (1900)*, New York, Macmillan, 1916, pp. 14–15.
81. Ibid. p. 16.
82. Ibid. p. 17. Cf. also pp. 72–5.
83. Julio César Gandarilla, *Contra el yanqui*, Havana, Imprenta y papelería de Ramela, Bouza, 1913, pp. 9–27.
84. Orestes Ferrara, *La guerra europea: causas y pretextos*, New York, D. Appleton, 1915, pp. 151–8. Ferrara (1876–1972) was Italian but lived in Cuba most of his life (from 1897); he became the Cuban ambassador to the United States during the 1920s, Secretary of State in the 1930s, and delegate to UNESCO.
85. Adolfo Posada, *Teoría social y jurídica del Estado: el sindicalismo*, Buenos Aires, Librería de J. Menéndez, 1922.
86. Adolfo Posada, *La idea del Estado y la guerra europea*, Madrid, V. Suárez, 1915, p. 11.
87. Ibid. p. 13.
88. José Ingenieros, *La simulación en la lucha por la vida*, Buenos Aires, Talleres Gráficos Schenone Hnos, 1920, pp. 125–6.
89. It is nonetheless worth emphasizing a certain nuance: Quesada defined Napoleon III as "pseudo-Machiavelli" because he was an ambitious and immoral character, but also inept. Bismarck was Machiavelli inasmuch as he was the architect of national union, building the State, but, at the same time, Quesada appealed to "Machiavellianism" to denigrate a character he despised. Quesada, *Bismarck y su época*, p. 45.
90. The reactivation of interest in Machiavelli at the turn of the twentieth century was not limited to the discussion concerning his relationship with nationalism and imperialism, as it went beyond the academic

and political debate. A good example of this is the novel by H. G. Wells, *The New Machiavelli* (1911). See Mark Somos, "A Century of 'Hate and Coarse Thinking': Anti-Machiavellian Machiavellism in H. G. Wells' *The New Machiavelli* (1911)," *History of European Ideas*, vol. 37, 2, 2011, pp. 137–52.

Chapter 2

# Machiavelli and Political Realism

In Chapter 1, it was seen that the increasing interest in Machiavelli in Argentine political thought between 1880 and 1910 was the result of a shift in the appreciation or interpretation of his work. No longer considered an obsolete or old-fashioned author, an apologist of evil (who proposed an immoral politics and tyranny), he started to be read as an intellectual, a pioneer of the modern State, and (for good or for bad) a harbinger of the main political tendencies of the time, such as nationalism and imperialism. Machiavelli, no more the master of evil or advocate for arbitrariness, was invoked when giving name to phenomena and circumstances that challenged or contradicted the realities and promises of liberalism. The State that he had imagined, and which figures like Otto von Bismarck brought into reality, in the nineteenth century was, rather than a rule of law, an aggressive and militarist State-Power.

These considerations around the political meaning of his work were linked to the particular conception of politics attributed to his thinking. Here there was also a concurrence in interpretative nuances: Machiavelli had made "effectual truth" his object of study. This postulate contained two aspects: effectual truth implied a conception of politics as something in itself, something autonomous (that is, separated from morality or religion), and, at the same time, a study of politics without appealing to speculative abstractions and normative horizons. For this reason, Machiavelli was seen as an ineluctable author for "political realism."[1] The author of *The Prince* had proposed both an ontology (a way of understanding and defining what politics is) and an epistemology (a way of knowing or a field of knowledge).

However, connecting his name with militarist nationalism, imperialist expansion, or war was just one among many possible ways of understanding the political effects of his ontological and epistemological concepts. For this reason, the objective of this chapter is to identify the different interpretations circulating in Argentina in the first half of the twentieth century relating to the type of political knowledge proposed by Machiavelli, as well as to analyze which phenomena were distinctive of politics when studied from the "realistic" perspective he postulated. As will eventually be seen, the counterpoints concerning the doctrinal content of his work (what current of thought it belonged to and which were its defining substantial principles) were related to the ways in which his epistemology and his political ontology were understood.

Besides, the approach to Machiavelli taken by interests that went beyond controversy and the invocation of his name (generally) to repudiate phenomena and political figures was a manifestation of a qualitative change in the reception and reading of his work. This change was the result of a deep metamorphosis in the intellectual and academic environment of Argentina after the 1910s.

## A Qualitative Change

The period from 1910 to 1940 was very different to the years between 1880 and 1910. As stated earlier, instead of various allusions or mentions made in writings where the aim was not to analyze Machiavelli's thought, there was a plethora of essays, books, and articles on his person and his oeuvre. In addition, the contributions made during the later period did not revisit, whether to repeat or to criticize, the legacy of local political thought left by the previous period. This omission may well be seen as a confirmation of the particular traits of that legacy, a less than systematic and rigorous tradition of reading which swerved between disdain and repudiation, prompting neither review nor controversy.

One indicator of the greater attention paid to Machiavelli's ideas throughout the first decades of the twentieth century is that his books started to be published in Argentina, especially in the 1930s.[2] It could certainly be said that this was a relatively late date, and that would not be an unreasonable observation. In retrospect, this is an additional indication of the indifference to his work up to that moment, or even of the difficulty involved in accessing it. There were already editions in Spanish of his main texts in the nineteenth century, but it is uncertain whether former invocations and references to him were based on these or on editions in other languages, free translations or passing mentions, or simply on works by commentators and authors unconnected to Machiavelli. In fact, in the studies to be commented on in this chapter and the next, references to foreign-language editions (in Spanish or other languages) were quite frequent, in addition to the fact that their arguments were often supported by texts written by other authors, not merely by direct references to the writings of Machiavelli himself.

There are several reasons for the surge in interest in the Florentine and his works. One, which is circumstantial and perhaps more of a symptom than a reason, was the 400-year anniversary of his death, in 1927. In that year, several contributions were published, many directly at odds with each other. A second and more decisive aspect was the constitution of an academic and intellectual field that offered material and institutional conditions that were qualitatively superior to those prevailing until the last decades of the nineteenth century. The culminating point of this process was the so-called "University Reform" of 1918, which introduced, among other things, the appointment of teaching positions through open public contest, and prompted a considerable renewal and systematization of curricula and disciplinary knowledge, in a context of increasingly widespread access to university education.[3]

In fact, the advances in the publishing industry and in academia are crucial to understanding the prevailing characteristics of intellectual production between the 1920s and 1940, and how they differed from the kind of output common between 1880 and 1910. These differences include aspects such as greater rigor, academic tone, and the scope (and explicit mention) of quotations and bibliographic references. Unlike most of the writings seen in Chapter 1, the essays, books, and articles devoted to Machiavelli published from the 1920s on give the impression of a solid grasp of the reading traditions and interpretations available in other times and places, both past and contemporary. This does not mean that what was on offer was optimal, nor that local output was completely up to date or even solid, nor that Machiavelli's works could be found in all the most important libraries. But it is undeniable that, in general terms, critical output shows a better quality of consistency and erudition after 1920.[4]

In this general context, the qualitative leap in the reception of Machiavelli was largely supported by the specialization, expansion, and renewal of university studies of Law, mainly, although not exclusively, since the 1918 Reform. The most important change was the introduction of chairs of Political Law, first at the universities of Buenos Aires and La Plata in the 1920s, and later at the universities of the Litoral and Córdoba.[5]

The relevance of these chairs of Political Law for the development of a more rigorous and academic reception of Machiavelli stems from the fact that this university discipline, in Argentina, was a stimulus for the development of political philosophy, the history of political ideas, and political science.[6] It is worth mentioning, in relation to this, that interest in establishing and defining a "political science" in Argentina, unlike the social sciences that had gained prominence at the turn of the twentieth century, had grown during the early 1900s. This was exemplified by a number of key episodes in intellectual and academic life, such as the appearance of the *Revista Argentina de Ciencias Políticas*, edited by one of the leading intellectuals of the time, Rodolfo Rivarola.[7]

On the other hand, as outlined in Chapter 1, the conception of Machiavelli as a theorist of the modern State had spread in Western Public Law around the turn of the twentieth century. In the Spanish-speaking world, Adolfo Posada, an influential figure in Spanish Public Law (who, as has been mentioned, visited and gave lectures in Argentina), had made that interpretation his own. He also appropriated the identification of the link between Machiavelli and leading German political and intellectual figures at the turn of the twentieth century, such as Bismarck or Treitschke. The truth is that many of the authors quoted in these pages were jurists and professors of Public Law. In some cases, the interest in Machiavelli sprang from an obligation or a demand to do with university teaching. In others, it went beyond the requirements of the teaching discipline, and became an object of intellectual concern or interest in itself.

## Machiavelli and Political Epistemology

At the beginning of the chapter, it was pointed out that there was consensus around a general understanding of who Machiavelli was: a pioneer in the study of politics as an autonomous sphere of human affairs. Politics as something different from morality or religion was one of his main themes, and therefore, his political, historical, and doctrinal considerations should be understood in this light.

The autonomy of politics as a statement was one of the seminal elements of his work due to its historical implications. It condensed and reflected how the Christianity of Renaissance Italy had been superseded, as it implied questioning the role of a transcendent authority in the affairs of "this world." After Machiavelli, politics became immanent, purely human, and worldly. Most of the Argentine authors who studied him during the first half of the twentieth century saw things that way. In this argument, therefore, there is a point that deserves to be highlighted: Machiavelli's epistemology and political ontology made him a pioneer of modernity, decisively responsible for the closure of the Christian and feudal Middle Ages.

However, his status as a turning point in Western history, as a hinge between the Middle Ages and modernity, and the (positive or negative) judgement concerning the meaning and consequences of this historical role influenced the ways in which the type of political knowledge that could be found in his work was weighed up and valued. The assessment of his historical role in Western political thought affected considerations of his epistemological legacy. What type of political knowledge did Machiavelli bequeath to us? Science? Art? Theory? History? Technique?

In this area, the first corpus of readings to be considered was made by intellectuals and scholars linked to Catholicism. Chapter 3 discusses in detail the context for the renewal of Catholic thought in Argentina at the beginning of the twentieth century. For the purposes of this chapter, however, it is enough to highlight that it was one of the clearest, most lucid, and influential expressions of the crisis of liberalism which picked up speed in the first few decades of the 1900s (and which accelerated after the 1930s). This phenomenon can be understood only partially through local circumstances because it was influenced by the reactivation of Thomism throughout the Western world following the First World War: for example, through the work of Jacques Maritain, whose influence (and presence) in Argentina were relevant.[8]

Catholic intellectuals, perhaps unsurprisingly, repudiated Machiavelli, rejecting his conception of politics and the body of knowledge and thought he left behind. From this point of view, this was yet another expression of the anti-Machiavellian tradition prevalent in Catholic thought in general, and in the Spanish and Hispanic American brand of Catholicism in particular, as seen in Chapter 1. The singularity of the Catholic authors of this period, a result of their historical context, lies in the political phenomena that they associated with Machiavellian "political science" and realism.

Catholic opinion of Machiavelli may be exemplified in three leading figures of Argentine Catholicism during the first half of the twentieth century: Tomás Casares, Faustino Legón, and Arturo Sampay. Casares (1895–1976) was a professor at the universities of La Plata and Buenos Aires, Director of the Catholic Culture Courses (a decisive area for the introduction of Thomism in Argentina), and President of the Argentine Supreme Court of Justice between 1947 and 1949. Legón (1897–1959) was another founder of the Catholic Culture Courses, the first tenured Professor of Political Law at the Universidad Nacional de la Plata during the 1920s (he also served in that chair at the Universidad de Buenos Aires), the first Dean of the Faculty of Law and Political Sciences at the Universidad Católica Argentina, and a member of the Board of Directors of another Catholic university, the Universidad del Salvador, in the 1950s. Sampay (1911–77), Legón's disciple, was an eminent jurist who was closely involved in the constitutional reform that took place during the first administration of Juan Domingo Perón, in 1949.[9]

The basic premise of Catholic criticism was the separation between politics and Christian morality. This separation, as will be seen in Chapter 3, supported an ideological and doctrinal interpretation (and repudiation) of Machiavelli. After him, politics as immanence had entered the realm of moral relativism. This was the intrinsic consequence of conceiving it as exclusively human. In addition, the separation between morals and politics cast Machiavelli in the role of a foundational figure of modernity and a key author in the genealogy of liberalism. In strict reference to the kind of knowledge that could be constructed based on these postulates, Casares and Sampay underlined how Machiavelli's realism was nothing more than historicist empiricism devoid of scientific character. Thus, the conception of politics driven by this "realism" as separate from morality, the foundations of the matrix of modern political thought, was unsustainable; it lacked rigor and consistency.

In an article published in 1927 on the occasion of the 400-year anniversary of Machiavelli's death, Casares held that "there is no doubt that, in Machiavelli, there is more political art and government art than political science, strictly speaking." According to him,

> Machiavelli has been able to teach in *The Prince* and the *Discorsi* everything taught there about political art because he begins by stating with apparent force of absolute truth that politics is independent of morality, and even more, that it is absolutely autonomous. Hence, all the force of conviction, all the normative authority that could be derived from *The Prince* and the *Discorsi*, relies on the scientific value of the thesis we just pointed out as the backbone of the Machiavellian system.

This scientific value, in Casares's opinion, was non-existent, something that was not the result of any eventual incompatibility between principles of universality and historicism, between speculative abstraction and historical study, or the irrevocable differences between contexts that prevented any regulatory exercise. The lack of scientific value was due to the fact that Machiavelli's theses were the result of "the simple generalization of externally similar experiences," ignoring the fact that "universality is not given by the number of experiences, but by the intellectual abstraction of the intimate nucleus or Aristotelian form." In Machiavelli, if there was "a brilliant finesse in grasping individualizing traits," there was "not even the attempt to unravel the remotely universal in every fact observed." His work had, at most, a "longing for realism." It was not science, but neither was it art or history. His was an "individual fantasy with no doctrinal value."[10]

Arturo Sampay developed similar arguments. In his opinion, Machiavelli shared with "Aristotelian–Thomistic Political Science" an interest in knowing the "facts." But that was where all similarities ended. If "both Aristotle and scholasticism, on one side, and Machiavelli, on the other, start from political facts, without whose first moments of empirical observation a Political Science cannot be achieved," the first ones, "in the light of that empirical reality, understand the essence of the State in the social nature of man." Machiavelli was instead concerned about "the *political situation* of his country, and then, about offering a *solution* to that critical historical reality." Therefore, his statements, besides being dangerous and despicable (since they were "regulatory politics which were confessedly amoral, which for that reason, taken to an extreme, implied the annihilation of man himself"), were the result of study or reflection conditioned by the circumstances he had himself fostered. Machiavelli had thus not overcome "the experience of political reality."[11]

For these reasons, for Sampay (who quotes Casares), Machiavelli did not belong to the world of political science. Neither was he a key author writing about an "art" or a "fantasy." He had been the "founder of the Theory of the State, or political Sociology."[12] Such a statement, however, did not make him a major author since, according to Sampay, the theory of the State was a minor field, subordinate to political science. If the latter was dedicated to analyzing "the essence and the universal properties of the State," the former addressed "the concrete-historical reality that concerns us and, for that reason, is singular and unique in the irreversible flow of history."[13]

For both Sampay and Casares, in sum, Machiavelli exposed a form of understanding politics, and hence a conception of politics, that were both wrong and limited, with a regulatory aspiration implicit in the name of the search for realism (based on the knowledge of "effectual truth"). However, this was merely vulgar empiricism, a reflection that depended on a particular and contingent situation, the prevailing scenario on the Italian peninsula at the end of the fifteenth century and beginning of the sixteenth. Therefore, the separation between politics and morals, his negative anthropology, or his "misguided political philosophy" were, in Sampay's words, entirely unfounded.

The third of the afore-mentioned Catholic scholars, Faustino Legón, also expressed a disdainful view of Machiavelli's scientific status. In his opinion, another main axis or topic of his work, fortune, was what distanced him from any scientific claim. Alluding to Ernst Cassirer, Legón reasoned that "talking about a 'science of fortune' would be a contradiction in terms."[14] For that reason, Machiavelli's work should be included among those who conceived of politics as art.

Such a characterization did not, however, allude to an aesthetic and sophisticated conception of politics; it meant (once again) a brutish empiricism, a "service aimed at achieving success and personal aggrandizement."[15] All of this, ultimately, led to a degraded version of politics as mere technique.

> Considering this as a simple empirical technique, with which the ruler "gets by" with public business, by no means exhausts the real scope of political art [. . .] [;] the deepest meaning of political art [is]: the skillful execution of certain objectives according to plans illuminated by intellectual and moral principles.[16]

For Legón, Machiavelli's teachings were based on a "false realism": that is, on an unsustainable distinction between politics and morals, since politics was not possible without an ethical dimension.[17] Turning to Jacques Maritain, Legón pointed out that "Machiavelli, like other pessimists, had a fairly summary and simple idea of moral science, ignoring its realistic, existential character."[18]

However, disdain for Machiavelli's conceptions of politics, or for the knowledge that could be gathered from his work, was not exclusive to Catholic authors. A second corpus of voices may be found in another area of academic and intellectual life in Argentina, one involving figures linked to the University Reform of 1918. This was when criticism of positivism and materialism (roughly speaking, the currents of thought prevailing in academia at the turn of the twentieth century) combined in different ways with a leftist political–ideological position. One of the leading exponents of this current of thought in the 1920s was Carlos Astrada (1894–1970).[19]

In a text published during that decade, which includes a diagnosis of a "crisis of civilization" as a consequence of the First World War, Astrada understood that the "effectual truth" postulated by Machiavelli meant the association of politics with power. From this point of view, the Florentine author was connected to Oswald Spengler and a "biological" conception of politics (as favored by Ernesto Quesada, explained in Chapter 1), in addition to the "apparent decline of the ideals we witness in these times. Perhaps, it is the result of the disillusionment and weariness that have taken hold of humanity after the war."[20] According to Astrada, to postulate that politics fundamentally consisted of actions performed in the interests of acquiring power could be a plausible conception in troubled times, but not one that could last. The reason was that the evolution of processes and intellectual formulations "since Machiavelli wrote *The Prince*," like the French Revolution or a conception of the State that tasked politics with an ethical purpose (the product of German idealism, with Hegel as its maximum exponent), made "the radical establishment of political realism [. . .] an evident impossibility. We cannot eschew the victories achieved by mankind in its march through history."[21]

Astrada added that politics understood as a quest for power only could be conceived of as art:

> Realistic politics, according to Machiavelli's definition in *The Prince*, is an art translated by an action indifferent to any universal principle, which does not easily respond to a conceptual pattern; an activity that does not ask history for guidance because it does not conceive of any purpose for this. Understood in this way, politics is confined to an isolated sphere, lacking contact with ethical values, alien to what we consider today to be the peremptory demands of mankind.[22]

The definition of politics as art, then, implied a pejorative judgement. The other aspect of the autonomy proclaimed by Machiavelli's realism was, according to Astrada, a self-absorbed politics, severed from any type of regulatory horizon, whether scientific or ethical, or derived from a philosophy of history.

Finally, the critical appreciation of realistic politics as art was linked to inconsistencies between realism and political theory.

These inconsistencies sprang from a point that has already been brought up: the fact that Machiavelli's work was subordinate to political motives. He had subordinated "the events observed [...] to his intentions as an activist." This meant that he had failed to exercise the objectivity demanded by all realism, as its effectiveness depends on fidelity to the events observed: "Realistic politics, as was formulated in *The Prince* [...,] pursues, above all, objectivity, and its dictates, to achieve effectiveness, must stick entirely to reality." Thus, in order to draw up general formulations (to elaborate a "political code") on the basis of observations which have been historically situated and politically biased, implied a betrayal of the very premises of realism: "*The Prince*, exceeding the limits of strict observation and thus betraying the realistic criteria of the author, aspires to become a Political Code, the Statesman's Bible."

Astrada did not, however, conclude that Machiavelli's "political biology" lacked theoretical stature, since, despite its epistemological and methodological inconsistencies, its postulates had "achieved universality":

> It has been said that Machiavellianism was not a theory of politics, but a biology of political phenomena. We believe that one does not exclude the other, since the case is, as we have seen, that realism in politics is mainly, in its origins, the conceptualization of a certain historical reality [that of the Italian Renaissance]. However, as this insinuates itself into his writings as a tendency, it becomes gradually, with the passage of time, a systematic attitude.[23]

A third and last objection comes from those who held that Machiavelli's realism was obsolete (and, therefore, devoid of "realism") with regard to the circumstances prevailing in the twentieth century. That is, Machiavelli had formulated a notion of politics and a way of studying it based on principles and notions that no longer corresponded to the present. Although there are certain similarities in this sense with the arguments pronounced by nineteenth-century liberalism, it is also worth remembering that, for individuals like Juan Bautista Alberdi or Domingo Faustino Sarmiento, Machiavelli was not synonymous with realism, but with despicable forms of politics. He was associated with a conception of the human condition which belonged to a past historical period, one alien to modernity. However, this line of questioning may also be read in works by critics of classical liberalism, such as Carlos Sánchez Viamonte (1892–1972), another intellectual who owed his public visibility to the 1918 University Reform, and a leading figure in Argentine socialism during the first half of the twentieth century.

In his reading, registered in a volume titled *Derecho Político*, Machiavelli was synonymous with an obsolete way of defining politics, precisely because he had conceived of it as an "art," instead of something both necessary and appropriate at the beginning of the twentieth century: to wit, a "technique." He had turned "politics into the art of obtaining and conserving power."[24] This was dangerous, not only for the aims he espoused, but also for the conception of politics itself. Machiavelli, who "has become fashionable," condensed a broader phenomenon, the rejection of thinking of politics as a technique:

> All progress may be resolved in a technicality with a single and surprising exception: politics. Thanks to an inexplicable psychological flaw, men have resisted political technicality, after having understood and enjoyed all other forms of technicality with which human ingenuity enhances mankind's collective experience.

Machiavelli was an obstacle when it came to consolidating politics as a science, such as the kind of knowledge that could sustain the techniques for a political organization of society, consistent with current trends. In Sánchez Viamonte's opinion, it was necessary to abandon the idea of politics as an art, along with principles like the reason of State (also associated with him), sovereignty, or liberal "subjective law." All this should be replaced by concepts such as public service, social function, cooperativism, and the representation of interests (arguments that Sánchez Viamonte supports with reference to the work of León Duguit).[25]

As may be seen in these pages, the criticisms of realism attributed to Machiavelli were leveled at many different targets, the result of different ways of understanding his definition of politics and the type of knowledge he had built. He was thus associated with an arguable, if not openly inconsistent, way of studying politics, which spawned unacceptable as well as unfounded arguments. These ranged from a "biological" characterization that reduced politics to a question of survival, to a crafted conception of political knowledge, or a historically contextual or crudely pragmatic concept, which simplified the meaning and the purposes of politics in human affairs, and were simply inadequate for the societies of present times.

All these criticisms were based on different and even opposing intellectual, philosophical, and political currents of thought. In fact, Astrada recognized, among the implications of Machiavelli's realism, the reason for the condemnation of his work by the Catholics. This was based on his "denial of medieval transcendentalism," a symbol of the "humanist awakening" and, thus, the "transformation of politics as an independent discipline, capable of being tuned and improved thanks to man's intelligence," and even "the delirious exaltation of vital forces."[26] Similarly, there were notorious clashes between the postulation of perennial truths (a stance typical of the Catholics) and the assertion, made by Astrada, based on a notion of history as progress or, alternatively, as a process punctuated by cyclical oscillations. At all events, in both cases, he saw this as being driven by humanity, due to its material actions, formulations of ideas, or the interaction between them (a different approach to the conception of this process as a decline, a topic present in Astrada's discussion with Spengler). Finally, there was also dissent concerning the conception of politics as technique (Sánchez Viamonte hailed it, Legón criticized it).

None of the above prevents us, however, from seeing that, beyond these differences and contrasts and despite singular perspectives and languages, there are topics which criticism of the realism attributed to Machiavelli has in common, even though its characterization as such has differed. The topics found in common include: first, its definition as a false or imperfect realism, in the best case, more as phenomenology than a correct ontology of politics (because of the exclusion of fields of knowledge, for being intrinsically linked to specific contexts, and thus devoid of universality; for considering as political reality phenomena that were genuine and recurrent but circumstantial); second, the argument that realism as a form of knowledge can achieve theoretical or regulatory status only by betraying itself; and third, the understanding that it is harmful to strip politics of regulatory horizons (whether these are provided by science, history, philosophy, or religion).

In an opposite sense to what has been seen hitherto, for other thinkers, Machiavelli had fathered a coherent understanding of politics and, furthermore, founded an entire field of knowledge in the study of political affairs.

An example of this type of argument is offered by José Luis Romero (1909–77), one of the most famous Argentine historians of the twentieth century. In 1943, Romero published his book *Maquiavelo historiador,* a detailed exposition of the political realism described by the Florentine author. According to Romero, there were two distinctive traits, profanity and empiricism, both of which were the expression of a broader movement: the assertion of "man eminently installed in a reality of the senses."[27] Romero positively evaluated the implications of Machiavelli's realism so deplored by Casares, Legón, or Sampay.

According to the historian, realism meant calling "things by their name precisely at the moment when the commitment to omit this was at its zenith." Machiavelli was not synonymous with simulation and lies, deception and hypocrisy, concepts that Romero himself defined as "the curious fate of his thought, stamped with the label of Machiavellianism." The Florentine's realism was an operation designed to unmask impostors and tear down the veils of deceit:

> He has challenged the politics of hiding behind a mask, revealing all the possibilities of a bourgeois mind [. . .]. With a clear head, he stripped away the dense network of conventions, and took to an extreme the basic bourgeois attitude underpinning a direct understanding of reality.[28]

In second place, realism as a form of knowledge was a "radical empiricism." That was the meaning of the invocation of the "*verità effetuale.*"[29] In Romero's opinion, such criteria had framed a significant and positive change because they averted biases and prejudices, although there were also controversial aspects. On the one hand, in connection with the postulation of the "complete autonomy" of "political action," this became an "overestimation of the political phenomenon," a "subordination of all other levels [of social life] to the political one."[30] The autonomy of politics was questioned, but for reasons different than those posted by Catholic authors: it was not its immanent and earthly character that was called into question, but the possible overestimation of its importance in the study of social life (an objection that can certainly be connected to the type of historiography cultivated by Romero: social history).

On the other hand, according to Romero, Machiavelli had not applied what he proposed throughout his work, since, even if his attention to "*verità effetuale*" was visible in his political writings, this was not the case with his historical texts. Such was the result of putting his work as a historian in the service of a political endeavor, the unification of the Italian peninsula. These biases also colored his studies on Ancient Rome, where he was "guided not by the desire to achieve a faithful image [of the past], but by the *a priori* political ideal subordinate to its sources."[31] This political ideal was the republic, compared to which the empire was seen as a "decadent aftermath."[32] In summary, according to Romero, Machiavelli was troubled by an "immanent contradiction" between the "two poles of his spirit: the historical and the systematic"; the consequences of this were "a frustrated historian," who was also a triumphant "theorist of the modern State."[33]

These statements emphasize critical judgements about Machiavelli's "realism" which have already been dealt with. Astrada had pointed to the problems of a realism that sought general regularities in politics. In turn, for Sampay or for Casares, historical empiricism excluded Machiavelli from political science. For Romero, however, the normative thinker had triumphed over the historian, precisely because his empiricist rigor was subordinate to a political objective. This last point had also been picked up by Astrada, who had conceived of Machiavelli as a "militant," and by Sampay, for whom the subordination of his reflection to a political endeavor was another reason why he was alienated from political science.

At all events, the criticism made by Romero of Machiavelli's application of realism is not mixed with a more frontal criticism of realism itself, as it is in the other authors mentioned here. The balance is generally positive because of its historical and epistemological significance. Behind realism, Romero (like the Catholic intellectuals and Astrada) saw how bourgeois mentality outgrew the Christian-feudal mentality. Machiavelli was not an "ancient," for he expressed the configuration of "modern man," and this shift, which included the denial of medieval transcendentalism and the confirmation of a profane view of a reality of the senses, was far from being considered a problem.[34]

Similarly, the empirical rigor proposed by Machiavelli, regardless of its imperfect execution, had been a relevant change for an understanding of the "historical individual." Moreover, Machiavelli, a frustrated historian, was the object of study thanks to another offshoot of his approach to realism: the assertion that human beings are the architects of their destiny and, therefore, of historical consciousness: "Historical knowledge is, then [for Machiavelli], first of all, vital, essential and inalienable knowledge, inherent to man and inextricably linked to his most specific activity, which is the fulfilment of his will to dominate, manifested in his political actions."[35]

Perhaps the most enthusiastic appreciation of Machiavelli's contributions to the study of politics in Argentina during the first half of the twentieth century came from Mariano de Vedia y Mitre. Mayor of the city of Buenos Aires between 1932 and 1938, de Vedia y Mitre was a leading intellectual and scholar (a facet which has received little attention in Argentine historiography). Professor of Argentine History at the Faculty of Philosophy and Literature of the Universidad de Buenos Aires, he was the first tenured Professor of Political Law there, between 1924 and 1946.

De Vedia put forward an explicit epistemological recognition of Machiavelli's work. De Vedia believed that the Florentine had been both the founder of modern political thought, thanks to the distinction he made between politics and morals, and the father of political science, for proposing a realistic approach based on historical evidence rather than speculation. According to him, this approach did not undermine but rather strengthened the scientific nature of his postulates, and he was a true master of the art of government.

In De Vedia's words, Machiavelli "as a political writer is the founder of political science based on history and on the experience of peoples."[36] He had elaborated "a science of the State, separated, independent from any moral concept. In this separation, he saw that the only way to conceive clearly of the true art of government was to found it anew."[37] It was both an art and a science strengthened by realism, not aimed at "achieving the 'Supreme Good'" or "moved by some metaphysical abstraction," but devoted to examining "the reality of life."[38]

For Romero or De Vedia, then, Machiavelli's definition of politics as an autonomous, immanent, and human sphere, based on the separation between politics and morals, had laid the foundations for a new form of scientific knowledge, in both political and historical studies.[39]

It is worth adding that this consideration of the political knowledge proposed by Machiavelli was well known in the Spanish-speaking Atlantic world, as observed from a range of different political and ideological positions. For example, Orestes Ferrara (1876–1972), a Cuban intellectual, politician, and diplomat of Italian origin (quoted in Chapter 1), like Romero or de Vedia y Mitre, recognized Machiavelli as the author who broke with feudal Christianity, and saw, in his epistemology, one of the main manifestations of this rupture. Machiavelli had designed and applied an inflexible "experimental method," a "method that was practical, historical and realistic." He "was a man of his times, because he was the direct result of the Renaissance in the sense that this word is synonymous with Truth."⁴⁰

At the same time, Spanish anti-liberal intellectuals and scholars recognized the contributions he had made to the study of politics. Francisco Javier Conde (1908–74), one of the most important intellectuals of Francoist Spain (and Director of its main academic institution, the Instituto de Estudios Políticos), held that Machiavelli had left a

> political knowledge [that] is "positive," "technical," and "pragmatic." The politician is a *technites* [sic], whose function is to know political reality as it always is, to pre-dict [sic] the necessary course of political affairs and to know how to manage them in the simplest way possible.⁴¹

Technique was not, for Conde, a lesser type of knowledge and, at the same time, the separation between morals and politics had meant, strictly speaking, neutrality in terms of values: "The words *good* and *bad* lose their autonomous and moral content of substance to become neutral terms belonging to a mathematical function."⁴²

Then there is Luis Legaz y Lacambra (1906–80), a renowned jurist whose legal thought and public trajectory career have been a matter of some debate. Many scholars have pointed to his republican sympathies in his youth and later links with the Falangists and Franco's regime; his interest in Carl Schmitt and Hans Kelsen – who was introduced to Spain by Legaz; his anti-liberalism, his enthusiasm for Fascism, and his stature as theorist of the Syndicalist National State; his Catholicism and praise for classical iusnaturalism – in a critical dialogue, however, with scholasticism; and his Christian humanism with differing diagnoses on liberalism. Legaz y Lacambra maintained that Machiavelli had been "the great theorist of new politics" and, rather than representing "an expression of radical political immorality," had created "the purely theoretical–technical way of treating science, without any assessment."⁴³ In any case, the objectionable conception of politics as an autonomous dimension of human life should not be confused with the characterization of politics as a space of specific knowledge and understanding.⁴⁴

As can be seen, then, these testimonies reveal possible concurrences in the epistemological assessment of Machiavelli among those figures anchored in opposing political and ideological positions.

However, they also reveal something else: there were differences in the assessment of Machiavelli within the same political and ideological field. This is exemplified in the arguments made by Spanish anti-liberals compared with those of the Argentine Catholic writers mentioned above. In other words, the different receptions of Machiavelli are an enlightening avenue of analysis which enables tensions and differences within the same political and doctrinal groups to be identified, be these anti-liberal or liberal.[45]

For the moment, and as a synthesis of what has been described in this section, it is worth emphasizing two points. On the one hand, the discussion about Machiavelli's realism did not materialize as a confrontation between realism and normativism, but was permeated by controversy over what type of knowledge about politics was promoted by such a supposedly "realistic" perspective (in terms attributed to Machiavelli). On the other hand, the evaluations of his epistemology were linked to an interpretation of his political ontology: that is, to the distinctive phenomenon of a politics understood as an autonomous sphere of human life, separated from Christian morality and religion. In this sense, it is worth saying that the concurrences in the answer to what he had defined as "effectual truth" can be explained only partially by political or ideological affinities.

## Machiavelli and Political Ontology

There was also praise and criticism which did not stem from the kind of knowledge Machiavelli had enabled, but from the phenomena he highlighted as constitutive or distinctive of politics. It is worth recalling that this was exactly the kind of controversy that arose when the issue of his contemporaneity came up at the end of the nineteenth century. In those debates, the discussion centered not on his methods or proposals for political study, but on the behaviors and actions that his political realism and the separation between politics and morals legitimized, such as militarist nationalism or imperialism.

With the outbreak of the First World War and the crisis of liberal democracy that followed, due to the appearance of Nazi Fascism and Bolshevik communism, such opinions acquired widespread popularity, this time because they connected Machiavelli's realism with war (or, in a broader sense, with politics seen as an agonal conflict) or with the exercise of limitless power. This did not mean dusting off the conception of Machiavelli as the master of tyranny, understanding him as an author who justified political forms that were arbitrary and obsolete (or ill adjusted to the present), as had been the case in nineteenth-century liberalism, as shown in Chapter 1.

In fact, the collapse of certainties about progress, civilization, and reason, and the rise of totalitarian forms of government shone a light on Machiavelli as a writer whose thinking was relevant to the times, enabling a reading of his political realism as an explanation of irrationality and authoritarianism. As will be seen in Chapter 3, this way of conceiving what was "effectual truth" for him was projected onto an anti-liberal reading of his doctrinal and political postulates.

The association of Machiavelli with irrationalism, war, and Nazi Fascism was quite common in the intellectual reflection of the Spanish-speaking Atlantic world. His link to Nietzsche was exemplary in this sense, as proposed by a previously mentioned figure, Adolfo Posada (Spanish Professor of Political Law), who maintained that (mainly German) militarist nationalism was a construction based on the ideas of Machiavelli, Hegel, Treitschke, and Nietzsche.[46]

In Argentina, in reference to a previously mentioned author, it is worth remembering Ernesto Quesada's statement in 1924 that "Caesarism is the next solution, it is the broom that will sweep away so much dirt." In those years, one of the intellectuals who read, and celebrated, Machiavelli's realism in a similar key was Leopoldo Lugones (1874–1938). Lugones was one of the most influential Argentine writers of the first half of the twentieth century, and one of the intellectuals who showed the most enthusiasm and support for anti-liberal authoritarianism, and Fascism in particular, after spending his youth displaying markedly anarchist leanings.[47]

Lugones held that the essential legacy of Machiavelli had been to dismantle metaphysical absolutes and principles, showing politics for what it really was: a brutal struggle for power in which the strongest prevailed. Realism ratified the prevalence of violence and inequality in human affairs, contrary to the preachings of Christianity and liberalism, and Fascism exemplified this in all its forcefulness.[48]

One important point is that, for Lugones, politics in Machiavelli was an art, considered as an elevated, rather than disdainful or impoverished, conception as it referred to a creative and vital activity. The author of the *Discourses* was a symbol of the Renaissance in a very precise sense, due to his opposition to medieval transcendentalism and its "morality of absolute renunciation," and to being an exponent of the "sublime man." With him, "the value of life itself reacquired its capital importance." In addition to being a "political writer," he was also a "poet, novelist, and artist," a "genius."[49] According to Lugones, Machiavelli's political realism was at odds with Christianity, liberalism, and democracy because its biological component refuted absolutes, and because its aesthetic and vitalistic dimension implied a celebration of mundane and anthropocentric politics, not subordinate to the transcendent, but also hierarchical and inegalitarian, since it hailed men of genius and strength. The vitalistic reading of realism, for the rest, also kept its distance from a decadent conception of "biological politics." Action was "doing'" and not just about survival.

A reading in line with that of Lugones, but whose evaluation is critical rather than exultant, came from an author also mentioned previously in these pages, Carlos Astrada. He also considered that the conception of Machiavellian realism referred to "biological politics," an approach developed by other intellectuals who were generationally close to Astrada, such as Enrique Martínez Paz (1882–1952), Professor of Philosophy of Law and Comparative Civil Law and Vice Chancellor of the Universidad de Córdoba.

According to Martínez Paz, Machiavelli was synonymous with a "Real Politik [. . .] [which] is the mastery of biological laws, [. . .] the spirit of self-preservation."[50] The objection to realism in this sense was not, however, a denouncement of its falsehood. Martínez Paz recognized that the "crude and disturbing realism" of Machiavelli rang true: "It cannot be denied [. . .] that, in Machiavelli's politics, there are elements of universal and permanent truth that make his glory an enduring one." Biological politics was realistic because it was portrayed as it happened, during

> historical periods of revolution when the indispensable social order in collective life is preserved by an authority that represents the simple wielding of force; then Machiavellianism returns to flourish again, with ephemeral vigor, but revealing elements of his eternal substance.[51]

That is, the dismissal of realism understood in this way lay in the fact that it presented as permanent some traits that were circumstantial. Similarly, the key role great figures could play, such as Machiavelli's prince, should not overlook the fact that "the politics that created by heroes and princes has a deceptive appearance; the creative power of the individual is insignificant if it is compared with the work of the community of which the individual is merely one of its creations."[52]

It was shown above that one of the reasons for Lugones's enthusiasm for Machiavelli was not only that he saw him as laying bare the impostures of Christianity and liberalism. The other element of the "effectual truth" postulated by the Florentine author was how he shone a light on inequality as a constituent element of politics (and society). Politics, as an art (rather than a technique), was the purview of a chosen few. Another famous Argentine anti-liberal intellectual of the 1940s, Marcelo Sánchez Sorondo (1912–2012), also a Professor of Constitutional Law at the Universidad de Buenos Aires, expressed a similar point of view. In his words, "not being either something technical or vulgar, and inasmuch as it always implies doing, politics should be defined as an artistic feat." And, since "political doing as an art is not suitable for anything else other than what is bestowed upon it by its own operation," from this, "it follows that politics is the purview of the few."[53] Machiavelli's realism (also connected to Fascism) was, above all, elitism.

In texts of another tone, it was also noted that the truth uncovered by Machiavelli was the presence of inequality. That is, to construe politics after him implied recognizing hierarchy as a constituent phenomenon. This was the case with Ernesto Palacio (1900–79), a key figure of one of the most influential variants of Argentine anti-liberalism, so-called nationalism, as may be seen in detail in Chapter 3. In one of his best-known books, *Teoría del Estado*, published in 1949, Palacio held that Machiavelli's realism provided elements for a theory of politics because, by showing the constants behind changing circumstances, it enabled the postulation of regularities for any time and place. These constants were inequality and the existence of elites, whatever the political and institutional order. It is important to notice that Palacio's considerations were not based exclusively on Machiavelli. In fact, he connected inequality with a "natural political order," a concept hardly linked to the Florentine's thinking, and his references include a vast variety of authors, like Gaetano Mosca, Vilfredo Pareto, Robert Michels, Edmund Burke, Montesquieu and, tellingly, Thomas Aquinas, among others.[54] At all events, the point to highlight here is that Palacio conceived of Machiavelli's realism as knowledge enabling a particular understanding of a theory of politics (neither "art" nor technique), which also supported an elitist form of politics that eschewed institutional agreements and ideological elaborations, as well as democratic egalitarianism.

Finally, another way of considering the realistic conception of Machiavelli was to attribute to him an essential role in incorporating a historical perspective into the study of politics. It has been noted that this was the main argument espoused by José Luis Romero. Machiavelli may have been a "frustrated" (or imperfect) historian, but he deserved only praise for his decisive role in building a "historical consciousness."

In this sense, Machiavelli's realism seen as historicism was ennobled by another type of reading. According to this perspective, the immanent conception of politics combined with attention to the effects of time on political vicissitudes meant an uncertain present and an open future. He taught that there were no end stations, whether for good (a perfect regime), or for bad (terminal and definitive crises). Conceiving politics as a purely human activity implied that there were no overdeterminations. And on this basis, history was neither decadence nor progress, simply an open course of events that could lead to happy or dark moments, but never definitive ones. Machiavelli's approach was, from this point of view, key in its support of an attenuation of optimism, but also the avoidance of nihilism and fatalism. In sum, as a realist, he was an author who understood uncertainty and freedom, in the previously mentioned sense of absence of supra- or extra-human dimensions that conditioned sensory or earthly life.

It is portentous that this style of appreciation gained strength after the mid-1910s, when certainties, both in the Western world and in Argentina, were on the wane. For some, Machiavelli's realism was a sign of the times in its ability to express "biological politics" and the "denial of all systems," or because it supported a form of authoritarianism designed to eradicate liberal democracy, or because it condensed the aporias of modernity. For others, it was a compendium of those turning points in history because such a realism revealed instability and transience to be intrinsic elements of human life. This approach to Machiavelli's work was an intellectual gesture which went in entirely the opposite direction to that identified as a way of understanding the popularity achieved by Thomism during these same years: to seize upon ultimate and perennial truths in the face of the collapse of all certainties.[55]

It is revealing that such a perspective may also be observed in individuals who, for generational or even social reasons, differed from those covered hitherto: men who hailed from the Argentine political and social elites, born in the last third of the nineteenth century. They were therefore already at a mature or even advanced age, occupying influential positions in public and academic life, when they had to face the profound changes which took place after the 1910s. For these figures, survivors of a waning liberal Argentina, Machiavelli's realism justified disillusionment, but at the same time offered up elements which fostered hope.

This may be read, for example, in a short text by Juan Agustín García (1862–1923), one of the leading Argentine intellectuals at the turn of the twentieth century; the piece is dated 1917 and titled "La actualidad de Maquiavelo."[56] The author of *La ciudad indiana* (1900), a seminal work that established him as a key figure in the nascent field of Argentine sociology, García was a professor at the universities of La Plata and Buenos Aires (teaching at both the Faculty of Law and that of Philosophy and Literature, respectively). He was also in charge of the Faculty of Philosophy and Literature at the University of Buenos Aires at the time of the 1918 University Reform. In his text, García vindicated the continued relevance or the return of Machiavelli.[57]

In his opinion, Machiavelli's timeliness stemmed from the verification that the "universe seems more difficult and complicated." He had reread *The Prince* "to understand better the events of these times of sadness and anguish, which have banished so many cherished illusions of culture, intelligence, justice, and moderation." "The old moral concepts [of *The Prince*], unpleasant and distressful," seemed to be revived; the belief in solid ethical foundations, such as those promoted by "Kant's imperative," had "vanished in the smoke of battle." Such appreciations were reminiscent of those seen in Enrique Martínez Paz or in Carlos Astrada, who had foretold the "return" of Machiavelli due to a "crisis of civilization."

Nevertheless, García's emphasis was different. In the first place, he defined *The Prince* as a "masterpiece," "from the technical point of view," due to its empirical soundness: "each of its maxims is based on a series of facts." But, especially, García rescued from the book the call to action, the trust in human qualities to influence the course of events, the importance of addressing the problems rather than leaving them to chance, the warning about the uncertainty of the results without giving up the vocation to deal with vicissitudes. Machiavelli had underlined how

> Romans did not accept that principle of "*savi de nostri tempi*", of trusting the action of time, as they rather [trusted] in their courage and prudence (*virtù*) because *time sweeps everything away and can lead us to good or evil* [. . .] a policy followed for centuries, of not avoiding problems, of addressing them immediately.[58]

The premise that politics must be based on existing conditions and that it was, therefore, illusory, if not irresponsible, to embark upon any radical kind of transformation, accompanied by consideration of the fact that there were no perfect regimes, may be seen underpinning other contributions. Without undue enthusiasm for democracy or universal suffrage, even in the acknowledgement of disillusionment, neither did they find (at least from a doctrinal point of view) reasons to call for it to be replaced by other alternatives.

One example of a proponent of this stance is Norberto Piñero (1858–1939), Dean of the Faculty of Philosophy and Literature of the Universidad de Buenos Aires during the first decade of the twentieth century; he abandoned academic life in opposition to the Reform of 1918.[59] He wrote a book that was published in 1929 and quoted Machiavelli as an authority in the prologue, in a political climate marked both in Argentina and in much of the West, by a growing mistrust of, and even opposition to, liberal democracy. He pointed out that "a swift glance at the systems devised and the reforms suggested reveals that political woes and difficulties cannot be cured or solved by a change of regime, with the modification of institutions." It should not be forgotten that "a political form is neither superior nor inferior to another, because its merit lies in its practical effectiveness."[60]

Finally, the afore-mentioned Mariano de Vedia y Mitre put forward a similar appreciation. In the mid-1940s, when drawing up a balance of Argentine political and institutional history during the nineteenth century, he noted that,

> in fact, there is nothing definitive in the life of the peoples. If history teaches us something, it is that everything is movement and renewal [. . .] the relative meaning that all social and political things have [must always be borne in mind].[61]

This was as much an expression of a waning enthusiasm as one of skepticism in the face of the possibility of radical and definitive solutions (no matter their ingredients). Such "realistic" diagnoses, then, expressed disillusionment and even a certain politically conservative tone, but it was for this reason that they were not doomed to end in either blatant anti-liberalism or the outright repudiation of democracy.

## Machiavelli as a Founding Father of Modernity

A first conclusion that could be drawn from this chapter is that there were clearly very different ways, which were sometimes in frank opposition to each other, of defining the tenets underlying Machiavelli's conception of politics as an autonomous activity in the sphere of human affairs, and political realism (the interest in the "*verità effetuale*") as the best way to study it.

However, this first conclusion requires a degree of refinement. In the first place, it is worth highlighting the recognition of the fact that Machiavelli's work exhibited a decisive ontological and epistemological dimension, and not only a theoretical or doctrinal one. This means that he was not seen merely as the promoter of a determined form of government or a theorist of the State. Additionally, focusing on the interpretation made of this aspect of his tenets, it is worth stressing that this form of understanding Machiavellian ontology and epistemology did not mean sharing a particular judgement or evaluation of these. For example, associating his arguments with "biological politics," founded on the fight for power and force, could lead to laudatory as well as disapproving judgements.

Second, the similarity between the opinions circulating about Machiavelli's political realism cannot be limited to a certain political or ideological stance. On the contrary, writers who held major differences in this respect shared similar assessments of Machiavellian proposals. For this reason, such concurrences should not hide the fact that the criticisms were based on dissimilar arguments and perspectives.

Writers such as Astrada or Martínez Paz joined Catholic authors in conceiving of Machiavellian realism and politics in a similar way (empiricist, historically and politically biased, aimed at the acquisition and preservation of power). However, their criticism was rooted in major differences (the eternal truths of Christianity or the need for a philosophy of history that vested in politics an ethical purpose). Similarly, José Luis Romero, Mariano de Vedia y Mitre, Juan Agustín García, Leopoldo Lugones, and Ernesto Palacio wrote in praise of Machiavellian realism, but they each identified very different things within it: aspects ranging from profanity and historical consciousness; a guide to a view of history without overdetermination; a rigorous and rational method of studying politics; or the recognition of inequalities, hierarchy, genius, and authoritarianism as intrinsic traits of politics.

Third, it should be emphasized that these controversies share similarities with those occurring in other intellectual geographies, where Machiavelli's work had been the object of debate for centuries, almost since the 1500s. Perhaps the most illustrative example in this sense concerns the references made to the author of *The Prince* by both Benito Mussolini and Antonio Gramsci during the interwar years in Italy.[62] From this point of view, the issues analyzed in this chapter show that the controversies around the meaning and sense of politics in Machiavelli had many themes and topics in common in an intellectual sphere such as that of Argentina, where historical roots were shorter and there was less familiarity with the work of the Florentine author. If we expand the scale of observation (Chapter 5 will address this issue again), these controversies are clearly visible in the Spanish-speaking Atlantic world – that is, beyond Argentina – as may be seen in the previously quoted texts by writers such as Francisco Javier Conde, Orestes Ferrara, Nicolás Rodríguez Aniceto, and Luis Legaz y Lacambra. In other words, the differences in the backgrounds and reading traditions of Machiavelli (it has already been pointed out that anti-Machiavellianism or, more generally, a critical and condemnatory opinion had been a distinctive trait of his reception in the Spanish and Hispanic American world since the sixteenth century) were not reflected in superficial or hasty readings. The themes and issues that Machiavelli's work brought to light were similar to those being examined in intellectual milieus where he occupied a consolidated place as a key author or as an object of interest in a more lasting way than in the Spanish-speaking Atlantic world.

From what has been discussed in previous pages, two other conclusions may be drawn that go beyond identification of the diverse and controversial opinions of Machiavellian epistemology and ontology. To start with, and unlike what might be construed at first sight, the connection between realism and authoritarianism (which, between 1880 and 1910, had had a singular precedent in Ernesto Quesada) was neither obvious nor necessary. The link between realism and political "ills" (that is, ills whose nature was understood as strictly political, not as politically legitimate immoralities, such as imperialism, violence, militarism, war, or arbitrariness) was one among many other possibilities. The relationship between realism and authoritarianism was a broad one, but so was the link between realism and liberalism (or, at least, freedom and human agency).

The reason for this lies in a second aspect which must be highlighted. The controversy around the notion of politics in Machiavelli and the type of knowledge he had built was rooted in the relationship between politics and morals, one of the axes of his work that sparked the most debate. The ontological and epistemic possibility of conceiving of politics as "a thing in itself" had required such a relationship to be broken. This was a point in common among all the readings discussed in this chapter, regardless of any subsequent evaluation.

The point to be highlighted is that the separation between politics and morals was also related to the place occupied by the Florentine in history. This was a watershed moment between medieval times and modernity, between a Christian feudal view of society and a bourgeois, secular one. Machiavelli's modernity (notwithstanding certain nuances coloring his relationship with classical and Roman influences and different ways of understanding the historical period in which he lived, the Renaissance) was another point of consensus among all the intellectuals mentioned so far. This, in turn, implied a break with the majority of the ways in which his works had been read until the nineteenth century.

Throughout the twentieth century, Machiavelli was no longer seen as an outdated writer and was portrayed instead as contemporary because he gave name to or legitimized phenomena relevant to the present – phenomena which, before the First World War, with society's confidence in progress and civilization, were considered to have been definitively overcome. However, he was also defined as modern in the sense of being the writer who had pioneered the course of modern political thought in the West.[63]

The conception of Machiavelli as a founding author of modernity was, then, a point in common underlying the many different political readings of his work. The connections of realism to both liberal and anti-liberal politics were concerns based mainly on consideration of him as a modern author, rather than as the architect of the reactivation or recovery of old principles. Taking this into account, it is now appropriate to examine how he was read and understood from both liberal and anti-liberal perspectives. This means analyzing how a modern Machiavelli could be the object of diametrically opposing political appropriations and, thus, be understood as a key figure in authoritarianism or, in the other case, as an author of freedom.

## Notes

1. See Pier Paolo Portinaro, *El realismo político*, Buenos Aires, Nueva Visión, 2007; Michael Jackson and Thomas Moore, "Machiavelli's Walls: The Legacy of Realism in International Relations Theory," *International Politics*, vol. 53, 4, 2016, pp. 447–65.

2. In 1937 and 1939, the Anaconda and Espasa Calpe publishing houses published *The Prince*. In 1946, Hachette did the same (including texts by Francesco de Sanctis, Ugo Foscolo, Giuseppe Ferrari, and Alfredo Oriani), and in 1943 Editorial Poseidón published a selection with the title *Obras históricas de Nicolás Maquiavelo*. See Alejandro Patat, *Un destino sudamericano: la letteratura italiana in Argentina (1910–1970)*, Perugia, Guerra, 2005.
3. Pablo Buchbinder, *¿Revolución en los claustros? La reforma universitaria de 1918*, Buenos Aires, Sudamericana, 2012; Ana Clarisa Agüero and Alejandro Eujanián (eds), *Variaciones del reformismo: tiempos y experiencias*, Rosario, Universidad Nacional de Rosario, 2018.
4. In the Library of the Ministry of Foreign Relations and Worship, for example, at the beginning of the twentieth century, there were no books by Machiavelli. *The Prince* was also not found in the National Library in 1925: *Catálogo de la Biblioteca, Mapoteca y Archivo del Ministerio de Relaciones Exteriores y Culto*, Buenos Aires, Taller Tipográfico de la Penitenciaría Nacional, 1902; *Catálogo metódico de la Biblioteca Nacional. Vol. VI. Historia y geografía*, Buenos Aires, Biblioteca Nacional, 1925.
5. Horacio Sanguinetti, "La verdad acerca de la creación del Instituto de Enseñanza Práctica," *Academia: Revista sobre Enseñanza del Derecho*, 21, 2013, pp. 91–8; Raúl Arlotti, "Las primeras lecciones de Derecho Político en la Facultad de Derecho y Ciencias Sociales de la UBA," in Tulio Ortiz (ed.), *Nuevos aportes a la historia de la Facultad de Derecho de la Universidad de Buenos Aires*, Buenos Aires, Facultad de Derecho, UBA, 2014, pp. 47–82; Raúl Arlotti, "Faustino J. Legón: la primera comunidad epistémica del Derecho Político en Argentina y la introducción del Derecho Político en la Universidad Nacional de La Plata," *Revista Anales de la Facultad de Ciencias Jurídicas y Sociales*, 47, 2017, pp. 653–68; Ramón Yanzi Ferreira, "La enseñanza de Derecho Político en la Facultad de Derecho y Ciencias Sociales de la Universidad Nacional de Córdoba," *Revista de la Facultad*, vol. III, 2, new series II, 2012, pp. 177–98. More generally, Víctor Tau Anzoátegui, *Las ideas jurídicas en la Argentina (siglos XIX–XX)*, Buenos Aires, Perrot, 1977.
6. Arlotti, "Faustino J. Legón: la primera comunidad epistémica del Derecho Político en Argentina y la introducción del Derecho Político en la Universidad Nacional de La Plata."
7. Jorge Myers, "La ciencia política argentina y la cuestión de los partidos políticos: discusiones en la *Revista Argentina de Ciencias Políticas* (1904–1916)," in Darío Roldán (ed.), *Crear la democracia: Revista Argentina de Ciencias Políticas y el debate en torno de la República Verdadera*, Buenos Aires, Fondo de Cultura Económica, 2006, pp. 103–35; Natacha Bacolla, "A propósito de Rafael Bielsa. Semblanza para una historia de la ciencia política en Argentina en los inicios del siglo XX," *Araucaria*, 38, 2017, pp. 545–73.

8. Olivier Compagnon, *Jacques Maritain et l'Amérique du Sud: le modèle malgré lui*, Villeneuve-d'Ascq, Presses Universitaires du Septentrion, 2003; José Zanca, *Cristianos antifascistas: conflictos en la cultura católica argentina, 1936–1959*, Buenos Aires, Siglo XXI, 2013.
9. See Juan Fernando Segovia, "Faustino Legón: del derecho natural al derecho constitucional," *Anales de la Fundación Francisco Elías de Tejada*, 17, 2011, pp. 83–136; Arlotti, "Las primeras lecciones de Derecho Político del profesor titular Faustino J. Legón en la Facultad de Derecho y Ciencias Sociales de la UBA"; Jorge Dotti, *Carl Schmitt en Argentina*, Rosario, Homo Sapiens, 2000, pp. 171–84.
10. Tomás Casares, "La política y la moral: a propósito de Maquiavelo (1927)," in Tomás Casares, *Conocimiento, política y moral: jerarquías espirituales*, Buenos Aires, Docencia, 1981, pp. 53–5.
11. Arturo Sampay, *Introducción a la teoría del Estado*, Buenos Aires, Politeia, 1951, pp. 27–30; emphasis in original.
12. Ibid. p. 30. This was a stronger judgement than the one formulated on previous occasions because, even in the context of objections, he was associated with a "substantial political science, with specific and unique ends in itself, amoral in its essence, since it is radically severed from any ethical system of universal validity." Arturo Sampay, *La crisis del Estado de derecho liberal-burgués*, Buenos Aires, Losada, 1942, p. 132.
13. Sampay, *Introducción*, p. 370.
14. Faustino Legón, *Tratado de derecho político general*, Buenos Aires, Ediar, 1959, vol. I, p. 50.
15. Ibid. p. 60.
16. Ibid. p. 64.
17. In some passages, Legón moderates the categorical separation attributed to Machiavelli between politics and morals, when he evokes his considerations about the relation between good laws and good manners. The target of his attack frequently seems to be Machiavellianism rather than Machiavelli himself. Ibid. pp. 71–2; Ibid. vol. II, p. 323, footnote.
18. Ibid. vol. I, p. 80. In these pages, Legón criticizes both realism and idealism: that is, "an ideological politics that only knows pure simplified essences" because "it suffers from a Platonism that will make it non-existent," p. 79.
19. See Natalia Bustelo and Lucas Domínguez Rubio, "Vitalismo libertario y Reforma Universitaria en el joven Carlos Astrada," *Políticas de la Memoria*, 16, 2015, pp. 295–310.
20. Carlos Astrada, *La Real Politik: de Maquiavelo a Spengler*, Córdoba, Estudio Gráfico Biffignandi, 1924, p. 22. See Guillermo David, *Carlos Astrada: la filosofía argentina*, Buenos Aires, El Cielo por Asalto, 2004, pp. 31–2.

21. Astrada, *La Real Politik*, pp. 23–5. In any case, he celebrated the "realistic demand," which asked for a correction of the "abstract formulism where sometimes the democratic ideal vanishes."
22. Ibid. p. 18.
23. Ibid. pp. 13–15.
24. Carlos Sánchez Viamonte, *Derecho político (ensayos)*, Buenos Aires, Sagitario, 1925, p. 195.
25. Ibid. pp. 141–52. On the influence of Duguit in Argentina (he visited the country in 1911), Carlos Herrera, "Jean Jaures y León Duguit en Buenos Aires: el político, el científico, lo social," in Paula Bruno (ed.), *Visitas culturales en la Argentina, 1898–1936*, Buenos Aires, Biblos, 2014, pp. 97–119.
26. Astrada, *La Real Politik*, pp. 11–12, 17.
27. José Luis Romero, *Maquiavelo historiador (1943)*, Buenos Aires, Signos, 1970, p. 14.
28. Ibid. p. 18.
29. Ibid. p. 112.
30. Ibid. pp. 74–5.
31. Ibid. p. 104.
32. Ibid. p. 107. It is worth highlighting a point implicit in these statements: the link between Machiavelli and republicanism (not tyranny or, more generally, personal and arbitrary power), and a republicanism detached from imperialism. In Chapters 3 and 4, this subject will be discussed further.
33. Romero, *Maquiavelo*, pp. 125–7.
34. Ibid. p. 115.
35. Ibid. p. 118. See Omar Acha, *La trama profunda: historia y vida en José Luis Romero*, Buenos Aires, El Cielo por Asalto, 2005, pp. 24–7; Julián Gallego, "De Heródoto a Romero: la función social del historiador," in José Emilio Burucúa, Fernando Devoto, and Adrián Gorelik (eds), *José Luis Romero: vida histórica, ciudad y cultura*, San Martín, UNSAM, 2013, pp. 165–84.
36. Mariano de Vedia y Mitre (ed.), *Maquiavelo*, Buenos Aires, Facultad de Derecho y Ciencias Sociales, Universidad de Buenos Aires, 1927, p. XLVII.
37. Mariano de Vedia y Mitre, *Historia general de las ideas políticas*, Buenos Aires, Kraft, 1946, vol. V, p. 285.
38. De Vedia y Mitre, *Maquiavelo*, pp. xxiii–xxiv.
39. It is important to point out a nuance: Romero saw in empirical rigor a valid form of knowing the "historical individual" (betrayed by Machiavelli himself); De Vedia, instead, attributed scientific status to his work because the historical study, instead of singularities, provided evidence of constant behaviors, which were replicated beyond the particularity of contexts. History, for De Vedia, played the role of an auxiliary discipline in the true objective of Machiavelli: to create a political science.

40. Orestes Ferrara, *Maquiavelo*, Havana, Imprenta el Siglo XX, 1928, pp. 204–5, 217.
41. Francisco Javier Conde, "La sabiduría maquiavélica: política y retórica (1947)," in Francisco Javier Conde, *Escritos y fragmentos politicos, Vol. I*, Madrid, Instituto de Estudios Políticos, 1974, p. 131. See José Antonio López García, *Estado y Derecho en el Franquismo: el nacionalsindicalismo: F. J. Conde y Luis Legaz Lacambra*, Madrid, Centro de Estudios Constitucionales, 1996, pp. 79–126.
42. Francisco Javier Conde, *El saber político de Maquiavelo*, Madrid, Instituto Nacional de Estudios Jurídicos, Ministerio de Justicia y Consejo Superior de Investigaciones Científicas, 1948, p. 171.
43. Luis Legaz y Lacambra, *Estudios de doctrina jurídica y social*, Barcelona, Bosch, 1940, pp. 49–50. See López García, *Estado y Derecho en el Franquismo*, pp. 127–71; Ricardo García Manrique, *La filosofía de los derechos humanos durante el franquismo*, Madrid, Centro de Estudios Políticos y Constitucionales, 1996, pp. 179–85, 223–36; Jesús P. Rodríguez, *Filosofía Política de Luis Legaz y Lacambra*, Madrid, Marcial Pons, 1997, pp. 85–141, 203–40; Benjamín Rivaya, *Filosofía del Derecho y primer franquismo (1937–1945)*, Madrid, Centro de Estudios Políticos y Constitucionales, 1998, pp. 34–8, 50–75, 95–108, 200–4, 209–11, 230–4, 336–45, 386–95, 446–9; Benjamín Rivaya, *Una historia de la filosofía del derecho española del siglo XX*, Madrid, Biblioteca Jurídica Básica, 2010, pp. 87–9, 114–29, 153–9; Nicolás Sesma Landrin, "'La dialéctica de los puños y de las pistolas': una aproximación a la formación de la idea de Estado en el fascismo español (1931–1945)," *Historia y Política*, 27, 2012, pp. 51–82, particularly pp. 69–70.
44. It is worth pointing out that, in alluding to politics as an autonomous sphere of human life according to Machiavelli, Legaz y Lecambra established a relation with Carl Schmitt's notion of "the political." Luis Legaz y Lacambra, *Introducción a la Ciencia del Derecho*, Barcelona, Bosch Casa Editorial, 1943, pp. 241–8.
45. The separation between morals and politics as amorality, rather than immorality, was also an argument developed with ambiguities. Chapter 4 will discuss this topic in detail with an examination of the interpretation of De Vedia y Mitre.
46. Posada, *La idea del Estado y la guerra europea*, p. 14; more generally, pp. 11–22. See also Nicolás Rodríguez Aniceto, *Maquiavelo y Nietzsche*, Madrid, Imprenta de Fontanet, 1919.
47. About Lugones, see, among others, Enrique Zuleta Álvarez, *El nacionalismo argentino*, 2 vols, Buenos Aires, La Bastilla, 1976, vol. 1, pp. 102–64; Fernando Devoto, *Nacionalismo, fascismo y tradicionalismo en la Argentina moderna*, Buenos Aires, Siglo XXI, 2002, pp. 87–119; Tulio Halperín Donghi, *Las tormentas del mundo en el Río de la Plata: cómo pensaron su época los intelectuales del siglo XX*, Buenos Aires, Siglo XXI, 2015, pp. 19–65.

48. See Asli Calkivik, "Revisiting the Violence of Machiavelli," *International Politics* vol. 53, 4, 2016, pp. 505–18.
49. Leopoldo Lugones, "Elogio de Maquiavelo," *Repertorio Americano*, vol. XV, 19, 19 Nov. 1927, pp. 300–1. Originally published in *La Nación*, 19 June 1927.
50. Enrique Martínez Paz, *Sistema de filosofía del derecho* [1932], Buenos Aires, El Ateneo, 1940, p. 288.
51. Ibid. p. 226.
52. Ibid. p. 226
53. Marcelo Sánchez Sorondo, *La clase dirigente y la crisis del régimen*, Buenos Aires, Adsum, 1941, pp. 17–19.
54. Ernesto Palacio, *Teoría del Estado* [1949], Buenos Aires, Eudeba, 1973, pp. 13–19, 47–59, 71–82, 103–18. Chapter 3 revisits Palacio's counterpoints with Machiavelli.
55. Tulio Halperín Donghi, *Vida y muerte de la República Verdadera (1910–1930)*, Buenos Aires, Ariel, 1999, pp. 218–34.
56. Juan Agustín García, "La actualidad de Maquiavelo," *Anales de la Facultad de Derecho y Ciencias Sociales*, vol. 3, series 3, Buenos Aires, 1917, pp. 99–102.
57. See Juan Agustín García, *La ciudad indiana, sobre nuestra incultura y otros ensayos*. Preliminary study by Fernando Devoto, Bernal, Universidad Nacional de Quilmes, 2006; Botana and Gallo, *De la República posible a la República verdadera*; Terán, *Vida intelectual en el Buenos Aires fin-de-siglo (1880–1910)*, 2000.
58. My emphasis (except in the Italian expression).
59. Pablo Buchbinder, "De la impugnación al profesionalismo a la crítica de la Reforma: perspectivas de la universidad," in Darío Roldán (ed.), *Crear la democracia:* Revista Argentina de Ciencias Políticas y el debate en torno de la República Verdadera, Buenos Aires, Fondo de Cultura Económica, 2006, pp. 260–1.
60. Norberto Piñero, *Política. El momento presente. Problemas sociales y políticos. Estabilidad de la constitución*, Buenos Aires, Menéndez, 1929, pp. 58–9, 68.
61. De Vedia y Mitre, *Historia general de las ideas políticas*, vol. XI, p. 169.
62. Benito Mussolini, "Preludio al Machiavelli," in Benito Mussolini, *Scritti e Discorsi*, I/1, Milán, Ulrico Hoepli, 1924 (the text was originally published in *Gerarchia* magazine); Antonio Gramsci, *Notas sobre Maquiavelo, sobre la política y sobre el Estado moderno* [1949], Madrid, Nueva Visión, 1980.
63. This precision refers to the fact that Machiavelli could be understood to be contemporary and, at the same time, as an ancient: in other words, as a current expression of phenomena that could not last because they were either extemporaneous or accidental, or because his influence, even when recognized in both ideas and politics, was inadequate or even harmful, precisely because it was unsuited to present times. This is how it was presented by the intellectuals of the Generation of 1837.

Chapter 3

# Machiavelli and Anti-Liberalism

The decades between 1920 and 1940 saw the emergence of an unprecedented amount of attention to Machiavelli in Argentine political thought. His works and legacy were the object of controversy and debate, and his "revival" often came up in texts and writings devoted to the study and analysis of his ideas. In Chapter 2, it was seen that some controversies revolved around the nature of politics, the ways of addressing and studying it, its place and meaning in human affairs, and its defining and decisive phenomena. Another aspect of the discussion was related to doctrinal and ideological definitions. What was the tradition or current of thought in which Machiavelli should be inscribed? Was he a key figure for liberalism or anti-liberalism? Is it possible to define him as a republican? If the answer is affirmative, what relation was there between his republicanism, liberalism, and democracy? Was Machiavelli's authoritarianism based on his praise of the prince? Or was it also an aspect of his republican convictions? Argentine intellectual output analyzed all these questions.

It is revealing to link the degree of attention paid to Machiavelli with political developments in Argentina between 1910 and 1945, approximately. During these years, the consensus that had been formed about the liberal project of the Nation, enshrined in the 1853–60 Constitution, fell apart, and consequently, a current of anti-liberalism (in a range of different expressions, to be explored in this chapter) gained importance in political thought. In the realm of political life, the crisis of liberal Argentina followed a tortuous path. In 1912, secret, mandatory, universal (male) suffrage was established; in 1930, the democratic experience was upended by a coup (the first of five in Argentina during the twentieth century), but efforts to install an authoritarian regime failed. This led to constitutional restoration in 1932, marked by institutional and electoral distortion (electoral fraud being the order of the day). The period wound up with a fresh coup attempt in 1943, whose outcome was the return to an electoral system in 1946, when Juan Domingo Perón was elected president.[1] It has been pointed out that the crisis and instability that were features of public life during this period could well be conceived of as a "Machiavellian moment," given the reflection and political and ideological debates they sparked in the context of a global scenario defined as "the storm of the world."[2]

In any case, the political context, although a necessary variable to understand the interest in Machiavelli, is not in itself enough. As was seen in Chapter 2, the qualitative and quantitative leap in academic intellectual output on Machiavelli stemmed largely from the consolidation and renewal taking place in the academic and university field in general, and within that scenario, from the appearance of Public Law as a discipline and field of knowledge.

In addition, the attention to Machiavelli in Argentina may, and should, be understood as a particular chapter within a broader global movement. Two exemplary cases illustrate this point. As was seen in Chapter 1, both local and foreign writers recognized the attention paid to Machiavelli and his influence on German politics and culture throughout the nineteenth century and the turn of the twentieth, due to the work of key figures such as George Wilhelm Friedrich Hegel, Leopold von Ranke, Jacob Burckhardt, and Heinrich von Treitschke. In the years following the Great War, in Weimar Germany, the current of Machiavellian influences was evident in the political theory of Carl Schmitt and the sociology of Max Weber, to mention the two best-known cases. It is also worth recalling that the 1920s saw the publication of the first studies by Hans Baron, which broke new ground in their research into Florentine civic humanism. It was also at this time that the classic work by Friedrich Meinecke on the reason of State was published. The texts of all these authors were, as will be seen, reference material in Argentina.[3] Additionally, there was more obvious attention paid to Machiavelli in Italy, a current which was reactivated at the beginning of the nineteenth century by Romanticism and deepened during the Risorgimento (thanks also to writers who were well known in Argentina, such as Pasquale Villari, Francesco de Sanctis, and Orestes Tomassini). The movement gained new strength between 1920 and 1940, particularly given the way in which Machiavellian ideas were invoked by Mussolini, studied by Antonio Gramsci, and bore an influence on the thought of the sociologist and economist Vilfredo Pareto and the political scientist Gaetano Mosca.[4]

In the Spanish-speaking Atlantic world, Machiavelli also received greater attention than in the past, due to circumstances that shared certain features with developments in Argentina: that is, the reception given to the Florentine author in the field of Law and the interest in his work, in parallel with the growth in anti-liberal and authoritarian political ideas and projects. As has been mentioned in previous chapters, to be analyzed more systematically in Chapter 5, these parallelisms in readings throughout the Spanish-speaking Atlantic world are important and it is even possible to identify borrowings and references which echo those in Argentina.

In consequence, the interest in Machiavelli during this era of Fascism, as well as the crisis in the Weimar Republic, the collapse of the Spanish Second Republic, and the 1936–9 Civil War followed by consolidation of Francisco Franco's rule, points to the fact that attention to his work was an extremely widespread phenomenon. It coincided with a crisis in liberal democracy during the interwar period, and the appearance and rise of totalitarian movements. However, this does not mean to say that one should ignore, as has already been highlighted, how the debates around Machiavelli were also spurred by less passionate and more specific academic and scholarly motives, which may, at first sight, have been less directly connected to circumstantial situations. The truth is that Machiavelli was seen throughout these years either as the main factor responsible for inspiring the crises in liberalism and democracy, or, conversely, as one of the writers to be consulted when seeking to overcome or reverse them.

With certain differences in nuance, these diagnoses and concerns underpinned Argentine approaches to Machiavelli between the 1920s and the 1940s. Indeed, certain singularities of the crisis of liberalism in Argentina should be underlined in order to understand such nuances. In this context, such a crisis was not surprising if seen within the international context. In turn, however, it would be an oversimplification to characterize it as a particular variant of a widespread phenomenon. Its singularity is visible in the light of a series of events mentioned previously: the crisis in liberal and democratic institutions (exemplified by the 1930 coup, which overthrew a constitutional government) did not continue with the installation of an authoritarian regime. This means that the appearance of anti-liberalism in political ideas and thought did not imply its immediate political success. All this led to a growing sense of repudiation of liberalism (because of its ability to survive), but, even so, at the same time its opponents were obliged to recognize the depth of its roots in Argentina. In these circumstances, confrontation and controversy were variously entwined in their coexistence and both liberal and anti-liberal fields even exchanged reciprocal influences.[5]

In this context, then, for the critics of liberal democracy in Argentina, Machiavelli was a recurring, long-lasting reference: a name to use when justifying the repudiation of liberalism and democracy, not only for his arguments, but as a figure exalted by the authoritarian and anti-liberal political experiences between the wars, such as Italian Fascism. From a broader perspective, to summarize what was seen in Chapter 1, this reading could be understood as a posthumous foundation for the rejection suffered by Machiavelli from within nineteenth-century liberalism.

However, the appeal to Machiavelli in an authoritarian and anti-liberal key was not unequivocal. Some believed he was the precursor of Fascism, while others saw him as the inspiration for a republicanism opposed to liberal democracy. These nuances are important because they reveal the disagreement behind the points that seemed to be in common: that is, the doctrinal differences and variety of political projects pursued by those fighting against liberal democracy in Argentina between the 1920s and the 1940s.

Indeed, such differences may be seen in the fact that there were more than just dissimilar, although positive, appropriations of Machiavelli. The anti-liberal reception of his work was not unequivocal because the interest in it was not always synonymous with praise and esteem. There were ambiguities and changing opinions regarding his ideas, which prompted a swing in the tone of such manifestations ranging from exaltation to criticism or, in some versions, even explicit rejection and absolute condemnation. Machiavelli was both a source and a problem for the criticism of liberalism and democracy, as well as for the justification of authoritarian proposals.

## Machiavelli as a Harbinger of Fascism

In the 1920s, the association of Machiavelli with Fascism, and more generally with the crisis affecting liberal democracy and the expansion of authoritarianism in post-war Western Europe, was eloquently expounded by figures who were themselves an expression of the political and intellectual – even generational – changes taking place in Argentina at the time.

This is the case with the three authors introduced in Chapter 2: Enrique Martínez Paz, Carlos Astrada, and Carlos Sánchez Viamonte. All had biographical and intellectual traits common to the 1920s (to be followed by divergences and separation in later years): their participation in, or at least their support of, the 1918 University Reform; their criticism of positivism as intellectual posturing; sympathies or affiliations with the left; and their experience in the field of Law and its teaching. Another point in common was, specifically, their interest in Machiavelli.

Carlos Astrada, as seen in Chapter 2, referred to Machiavelli when writing about the troubled times following the First World War and the violence and excesses of power, even the disenchantment coupled with "the confusion reigning in contemporary life." In other words, he was used to putting a label on the "crisis of civilization."[6]

Martínez Paz, Professor of Philosophy of Law at the Universidad de Córdoba (also Vice Chancellor of this university), as described in Chapter 2, was critical of Machiavelli's brand of realism because he saw it as a "biological" notion of politics, subject to struggle and the use of force, violence, rivalry, survival, and preservation. These were considerations which revealed allusions to Oswald Spengler (as in Astrada).[7] This reading of Machiavellian ontology was projected through the identification of his ideas with Fascism.

In 1924, Martínez Paz published an article announcing "the return of Machiavelli."[8] What scenario could justify such an assertion? In his view, it was the "crisis of liberal democracy" and the consolidation of "an authority without principles," the dissolution of "the ideals condensed in constitutionalism," the affirmation of governments that "are, mostly, above and beyond the Constitutions; [and that] have arrived in power through acts of violence and violation, which protect it through a program of effectual action, thus ignoring the constitutional foundations of the State."[9]

These tendencies, according to the author, were expressed in exemplary fashion by Italian Fascism, although he pointed out that the exercise of power "without another faith or illusion other than force" was visible also in the "pacifists" and the "Bolsheviks," as well as in "imperialist England." The central point, however, was that Machiavelli gave a name to the period. According to the professor from Cordoba, the Florentine was the intellectual author responsible for contemporaneous phenomena because he had considered "power for power's sake."

For Martínez Paz, on the one hand there were constitutionalism and liberal democracy, and, on the other, violence and authority bereft of principle. Machiavelli was a key figure for the latter and a sign of the times. For all these reasons, Machiavelli was "Machiavellianism" incarnate, which, "elevated to a political doctrine, is, in addition to repulsive, absurd, because Machiavelli is the negation of all systems." This was the state of affairs in the world at that time, for Martínez Paz, a situation in which the "supreme principle of necessity [prevailed]. And once again, the reign of Machiavelli comes about, he who lives and rules with 'immortal youth.'"[10]

The afore-mentioned connection between authoritarianism, as a distinctive trait of Machiavelli's ideas, and realism should be specified, or highlighted, as a key part of this rationale. Machiavellianism, according to Martínez Paz or Astrada, did not exalt tyranny: that is, a corrupt form of exercising power. Machiavellianism, in fact, consisted of revealing power as it was. The works of the Florentine author "do not even deal with the praise of tyranny; the thing is that Machiavelli presents a simply natural authority, based on force, cunning and sagacity."[11] Fascism, seen from this point of view as a contemporary version of Machiavellianism, was thus singularly disturbing, inasmuch as it was a political experience revealing the true nature of politics: limitless power.

In this sense, unlike in customary nineteenth-century liberal criticism (such as that formulated by Domingo Faustino Sarmiento), the meaning (and danger) represented by Machiavellian thought was not how he transformed morally despicable practices, from deception to crime, into politically legitimate ones. For Martínez Paz or Astrada, the "evil" attributed to the author of *The Prince* had no moral connotations. He was not an author who preached "evil" because of the separation between morals and politics that led to immoral politics. Neither did they believe that the separation between politics and morals took shape as a form of amorality that made the very notion of "evil" an inappropriate category in politics. Machiavelli's evil ideas about power and its excesses, as the expression of the nature of politics revealed by his "realism," were about an evil that was truly political in nature.[12]

This is why Martínez Paz ended his article "El retorno de Maquiavelo" by pointing out that contemporary politics, with Fascism as its main expression, had its own "laws," which were not comparable with those of other spheres, whether human or transcendent.

> Cardinal Pole said once, when judging "The Prince" of Machiavelli: this book has been written by the hand of the devil himself.

> If we were able to set the kingdom of nature in opposition to the kingdom of God, the Cardinal's judgement would be correct. A natural, biological politics must be founded in the laws of fatal necessity, it cannot seek its roots in the realm of the spirit, and since we are in the process of restarting, let us read Machiavelli once again, free of all prudishness, because he embodies, in the philosophy of the Devil, the most perfect image of the politics of today.[13]

Carlos Sánchez Viamonte, who is also mentioned in Chapter 2 and was a professor at the Faculty of Law and Legal and Social Sciences at the universities of Buenos Aires and La Plata, observed the relevance Machiavelli had acquired in the 1920s with the comment "invoking the precepts of *The Prince* is frequent, and has also become fashionable."[14]

For Sánchez Viamonte, who decried the epistemic implications of Machiavelli's work which prevented turning politics into a technique, the Florentine author was the mentor of Fascism. He said as much in an essay that took as a starting point the praise proffered by Mussolini himself in 1924. The "explanations made by Machiavelli and Mussolini, whether theoretical or dramatic, about the art of government, and remaining in it, are alien to political law." This was because "the mere ability to sway a crowd and even beat it up does not teach us anything that can be considered a matter of political law, other than the conviction that everything we call law constitutes a vain illusion that conceals the triumph of the use of force."[15]

Fascism vindicated what, according to Sánchez Viamonte, was the central point of Machiavelli's work, the reason of State, understood from a very different perspective than that insinuated by García Mérou or Rizzi between 1880 and 1910. For Sánchez Viamonte, unlike these two authors, the reason of State was not a principle to be invoked for the purposes of ensuring public order in exceptional circumstances:

> The State, when, by a miracle of its functional organization, it genuinely represents society, will be its political and legal will at the same time, and public order will have definitively displaced the reason of State, a phrase made up by Machiavelli which turned politics into the art of acquiring power and maintaining it.

Instead of acting as a valid legal category, the reason of State had become the "doctrinal justification of the arbitrariness of despots," a way of "smoothing over with the appearance of necessity the abuses of power, when these affect individual rights."[16]

Finally, Saúl Taborda (1885–1944), another intellectual who was generationally close to Martínez Paz, Astrada, and Sánchez Viamonte, alluded to "Machiavelli's school of thought" in a text he published as a young man. In his opinion, Machiavelli was synonymous with realism, understanding this to be a politics marked by a fierce struggle for power, exercised in turn also to favor the powerful. This realism was proof that Machiavelli had been "logical and sincere" by revealing the distinctive traits of politics, hitherto either stylized or downright avoided. In Machiavelli, Taborda saw a thinker who understood conflict. But he also posited that the conflictive nature of politics was precisely the aspect making arbitrariness its inexorable outcome. Machiavelli taught about the intimate connection between conflict and oppression: "the war of man against man leads directly to the formation of a public power of coercion and conquest." For this reason, for Taborda, invoking Machiavelli and seeing politics from the Florentine's perspective was a passage to submission, not freedom: "We have summoned Rousseau to declare ourselves free yet submitted ourselves voluntarily and deliberately to Machiavelli."[17]

Later, in the 1930s, Taborda linked Machiavelli to Fascism, seeing him as a distant but contemporary reference for critics of liberalism. From this point of view, Taborda held that Machiavelli's words resonated in the work of Carl Schmitt.[18] As Sánchez Viamonte had posited before, Machiavelli was to be situated in the "age-old dispute between force and law," similar, in his words, to the conflict between absolutism and liberal constitutionalism. In this struggle, the Florentine author was on the side of force and absolutism (as well as an amorality that, in fact, justified immorality). All of this, thus, was the result of realism. The reason of State had justified force and violence, and this had only been possible thanks to a view of politics based on "reality."

In his terms, "absolutism," from Machiavelli to his contemporary descendant Mussolini,

> has found it sufficient to adhere to *immediate reality* in order to justify an amoral conception of the State, to impose its will without considering itself responsible before anyone or anything, except for the success of its endeavors, to surrender to crime and exaction, turning religion and ethics into instruments subject to the "reason of State."[19]

Amorality, the result of realism, rather than immorality, had cast legitimacy on a notion of politics that hailed power as its main principle, in the name of success or efficacy. Realism and authoritarianism were intimately connected, and that made Machiavelli the forerunner of Fascism.

The link to Carl Schmitt arose from criticism leveled by the German jurist against parliamentarism. Taborda mentioned the distinction made by Schmitt between democracy and liberalism in his arguments pointing out the compatibility between "dictatorship" and democracy. Schmitt's crisis of parliamentarism justified doubts about "the possibilities that the Legislative Power be the custodian of truth," which, in turn, allowed him to suggest that it was "the privilege of just one man, whether tyrant or dictator, and that democracy lives and acts through his decisions and mandates."[20]

Machiavelli was, from this point of view, a distant predecessor, as the main axis of his work had been the irreducible unity of power, whose necessary political translation was the concentration of its attributes, preferably in only one person. *The Prince* had been, at the same time, a paean of praise for personal power and the theory of the State, for despotism and absolutism. In contemporary times, both Schmitt in his works and Mussolini in his actions revived similar concepts to show that they might be incompatible with liberalism, but not with democracy:

> For Machiavelli, the essence of the State relies on a particular form of government, and the conclusion to which Schmitt has come today does not refute this: far from it, his inferences merely reaffirm it by holding that the suppression of the division of powers is compatible with democracy. For Machiavelli, the Prince is the State itself, and Carl Schmitt, who is nostalgic about the lack of this "point of union" essential to the concept of State power in the modern world, reaffirms such a need, at a time when Mussolini is proclaiming the identity of the Nation-State-Party-Mussolini and trampling the ruins of the deliberative body, turning the interpreters of the laws into his lackeys.[21]

As may be observed, the relation between Machiavelli and Fascism here acquired meanings which were somewhat different to those postulated by Martínez Paz, Astrada, or Sánchez Viamonte. Machiavelli was the symptom not only of a crisis of civilization, or the triumph of force over law, but also of plausible authoritarianism in a democratic society.

Without leaving aside these crucial distinctions, derived in part from different intellectual references and singular perspectives (from philosophy to law), these diagnoses presented a portrait of Machiavelli as an enemy of freedom, as an author whose work showed a manifest incompatibility with liberalism. Such disagreement came, not from his role as an apologist for tyranny (as maintained by nineteenth-century liberalism), but from the issues commented on in Chapter 2: a particular reading of his "political realism," whose main feature was to reveal power in its all its brutality. That was what made him a forerunner, a distant source of inspiration for Fascism. If this position found an eloquent defense in the appeal made by Mussolini himself to the Florentine author, it is worth remembering and repeating that the connection between Fascism and realism, the conception of Machiavelli as the "intellectual father" of Fascism (or, more generally, of authoritarianism) was entirely due to a version – neither obvious nor evident – of political realism.

However, Machiavelli's connection with Fascism, through a relation between realism and authoritarianism, was also postulated by other voices, but this time with words of praise. This relates those who were enthusiastic, rather than concerned, about the crisis affecting liberal democracy and, particularly, about the rise of Fascism. This was the case, for example, with Leopoldo Lugones, who has been mentioned earlier in this book. In the text he published on the occasion of the 400th anniversary of the death of Machiavelli in 1927, tellingly entitled "Elogio de Maquiavelo," he develops two main arguments. The first one is the assertion that "any diatribe against Machiavelli is [...] a distortion of his philosophy, or, if you want, a persistent misunderstanding."[22] The second point is the definition of the author of *The Prince* as a "contemporary of Mussolini's."[23]

Lugones's contribution is important, and not only for his influence on Argentine culture at the time. Its relevance lies in the fact that it shows the persistence of a reading or way of understanding Machiavelli: that is, as an adversary of freedom in support of the use of force and violence through *The Prince*. This reading, as was seen in the first two chapters, was common among writers with varying political and intellectual perspectives, and also during different historical periods. The differences were to be found in the way they judged Machiavelli.

Lugones is relevant because he praised Machiavelli explicitly because of the anti-liberal and anti-democratic character he attributed to the Florentine's thinking. Such praise cannot be compared with the view of those who had also identified Machiavelli as an author writing about power more than freedom, who had even reaffirmed the most controversial concepts associated with him, such as the reason of State. Such favorable judgements were used to justify specific experiences or individuals (the portrayal of Juan Manuel de Rosas by Ernesto Quesada, for example), or procedures designed to tackle specific political circumstances ("anarchy"), in the belief that tyranny and reason of State should not be confused. Or even that, between the reason of State and individual freedom, there might exist tensions of a temporary nature, but no major incompatibility (according to Rizzi or García Mérou). Lugones, instead, saw in Machiavelli a doctrinal justification for doing away with liberalism and its inherent continuation, which, from his perspective, was democracy. In fact, the topics Lugones found worthy of praise in Machiavelli were the same that Alberdi had condemned in his time: patriotism, militarism, a classical (especially Roman) legacy, the subordination of individual freedoms to the "greatness of the nation."

As was the case for the writers referred to in earlier paragraphs, for Lugones, Machiavelli was also a key figure for a "biological politics" that revealed the "truth," and was therefore "realistic."[24] If, for some, the appearance of that truth in contemporary politics framed a crisis of civilization, for Lugones, this was something to be embraced and even celebrated, since it meant the collapse of legal and ethical fiction, of principles and ideologies opposed to the "laws of life" which Machiavelli had identified:

> The law of life is the law of force. The systems devised by the generous illusion of eluding it, subordinating it to a criterion of equality before theological or legal entities, are merely verbal creations. They provide comfort through hope, and that is a merit, verily, but they offer no help. Their negative action always consists of preventing the strong from what they can achieve on their own in favor of ensuring the weak have a right to live that life itself denies them.[25]

The political translation of this "law of life," both among nations and within societies, was the prevalence of the strong. The nation was itself "a phenomenon of natural history, concerning the biological process of the installation of species. Alien, thus, to any moral notion, it pre-exists, subsists, and prevails over the entire ethical, rational, or political system."[26] From this, it may be deduced that there was no contradiction between force and law. Positive legislation was the legal manifestation of force. "Power" was the "dynamic expression of sovereignty": "The country reserves the right to modify and suspend personal guarantees for its benefit [. . .]. The power of the country to impose its will on whomsoever and wherever it wants has no limit other than its force to do so."[27]

Machiavelli was thus the harbinger and key author for all these arguments. The main principle underlying his thought had been the greatness of the homeland. His work had "an exclusive purpose: the prosperity and force of the nation." Due to the "law of life," the army and war played a crucial role in achieving that objective. In addition, Machiavelli's praise for a "national army," instead of mercenary troops, meant that war ceased "to be a profession in order to assume its noble and tragic character of human function, inherent to the nature of man, as is taught by history."[28]

However, to conceive of Machiavelli as a writer focused purely on the greatness of the homeland did not mean he was an apologist for immorality or tyranny (a possibility that, according to the same arguments posited by Lugones, was nonsense, since, if the person who has the power makes the law, then tyranny, by definition, does not exist):

> What Machiavellianism asserts is that politics and morals are different things and do not determine each other. However, he does not deny that the coincidence of both, when possible, is preferable and indeed better. When this is not [possible], politics must fulfil its objective, that is, the prosperity of the nation. But this must be done, *to the exclusion of personal benefit for the statesman who executes it.*[29]

The greatest emphasis of his arguments, nevertheless, was that the core of Machiavelli's thought was anti-liberal and also anti-Christian: "Putting the country before the individual is an anti-Christian and anti-liberal concept, because it denies the absolute." For Lugones, Christianity, liberalism, and democracy were intimately entwined. They shared an "ecumenical" conception of the human condition and a conviction of the perfectibility of the human being; they agreed in the initiative to "consider humanity as an ethical–legal unit, when it is no more than a zoological species," whose projections were democracy and pacifism. According to Lugones, "a liberal ideology, including socialism, is connected with Christian ethics."[30]

Machiavelli was thus a response to a Christian, liberal, and democratic heritage. His was an intellectual and also historical refutation, as the appearance of his work in the sixteenth century put an end to the "wooden medieval synthesis" (of Thomas Aquinas), as well as to the "anarchic barbarism of the Middle Ages."[31] For this reason, even if his work was inspired by a desire to recover the Roman tradition, he was by no means an "ancient":

> A love for one's country, exempt, in its intangible purification, from any other purpose than the nation itself, inspired the work and the life of Machiavelli. This is why I once said that he was the last great pagan of Rome and the first great modern citizen.[32]

This last description, certainly, could well be the expression of a "reactionary modernism."[33]

In another text written at this time, Lugones pointed out that "the philosophical tyranny that reached its peak during the French Revolution" had had an anticipated refutation in Machiavelli, confirmed by the events of the Great War. "The critical anticipation of such a fallacy corresponded to Machiavelli's genius; but its positive confirmation through a historical expression of general nature, and the concurrent scientific information, was lacking. The past World War was the first."[34] Another argument should also be added, as referred to in Chapter 2: politics for Machiavelli, according to Lugones, was a response to egalitarianism because it was an art and, therefore, a vital activity, about "doing" (rather than a mere fight for survival), whose main actors were the intelligent and the strong.[35]

It is worth remembering, in addition, that Lugones was not alone in this reading of Machiavelli. A leading scholar and university professor, the architect and protagonist of different expressions of Argentine anti-liberalism throughout his extensive career, Marcelo Sánchez Sorondo (1912–2012), drew a semblance of the Florentine author that shared many similarities with that developed by Lugones. Sánchez Sorondo linked Machiavelli to Fascism through his connection with a "Roman" conception of politics – that is, a politics based on facts and unconcerned with intellectual elaborations: "In Europe, Fascist politics preside over the revenge taken by events against ideologies, retribution of the positive order over the disorder of anti-historical constructions. Politics has turned back to deal with things anew, returning to its classical, Roman status."[36]

In addition, he underlined that Machiavelli was the key figure for a "politics of the few" because of a political realism that is based on action and not ideas, and contains, in turn, an aesthetic notion:

To anticipate events is tantamount to containing them or even precipitating them [...] to manage events in the interests of the good of the nation, that is what doing politics is. Politics can go only so far, and within this, Machiavelli is allowed everything [...] political aptitude lies in the suitability of the subject.

Politics is an art, an "artistic doing" (the essence of political virtue). It is thus the task of the "best."[37] As he asserted elsewhere: "A creative politics understands that the agility of its art obliges it to take its distance from any other concern that could hinder, falsify, or distort its fight. This is the truth and the deep honesty declared by Machiavelli."[38] In sum, politics is action and decision, underscored by need and "facts," not by principles or ideas. And, at the same time, it is an "artistic doing"; therefore, it is elitist. Machiavelli, from these appropriations, writes in favor of power and force, as well as of an aristocratic form of politics.[39]

As a summary of what has been seen so far, it is worth bearing two points in mind. First, Lugones and Sánchez Sorondo are clear exponents of the link between realism and authoritarianism (which they evaluated as something positive, unlike the view taken by Martínez Paz, Astrada, Sánchez Viamonte, or Taborda). This permitted a conception of contemporary authoritarianism, and especially Fascism, as a genuine expression of the nature of politics, not as a degraded or corrupted version. Lugones's contribution in this area, in the Argentina of the first half of the twentieth century, is perhaps the clearest account of a reading of Machiavelli that identified the Florentine with Fascism, finding in him a full repertoire for the development of a manifest criticism of democracy and liberalism. Sánchez Sorondo's reading, in turn, reveals a conception of Machiavelli that was widespread among the exponents of Argentine anti-liberalism for another reason: its relationship with Roman history.

The second point to be emphasized is that Lugones's reading, just as it displays the impact and the attraction exercised by Machiavelli for local critics of liberal democracy, also offers clues to the ambivalence, and even the rejection, he provoked in some of them. If Machiavelli's work was founded on the greatness of the homeland, turning the army and war into the pillars of that greatness, he nonetheless recognized the intrinsic inequality and hierarchy of human beings, with his celebration of the "strong" and his own stature as a "genius," consolidating an elitist view of politics; in sum, even if he had refuted the fictions on which liberal democracy was founded, he was also a pagan and a critic of Christianity, and had founded a politics centered on the human being and far from any form of transcendence.

## Machiavelli and Nationalism

Julio Irazusta (1899–1982) and Ernesto Palacio (1900–79) were also exponents of the process of generational renewal, as well as the political and ideological twists and turns typical of the Argentina of the 1920s and 1930s, particularly so-called nationalism. This label embraces an eclectic variety of political voices and positions which nonetheless designated themselves in much the same way. There were nationalist variants that considered themselves as belonging to the left (mainly since the 1960s), and others that referred to themselves as right-wing, but it is important not to forget that they disagreed on their position concerning the most important political phenomenon of the twentieth century: Peronism. In fact, the influence and transverse nature of nationalism have prompted much questioning of the relevance of the left/right distinction in Argentine politics and ideas. However, and beyond all this, a common basis for all the variants was anti-liberalism. Irazusta and Palacio shared oscillating and winding itineraries, their ubiquitous nature itself a reflection of the problems faced by nationalism as it struggled to find a long-lasting role in Argentine politics. They were also pioneering figures of this intellectual and political current of thought that was in vogue in Argentina during the 1920s and 1930s.[40] For the purposes of this book, they are of interest as they paid significant attention to Machiavelli, through an output that included texts of political intervention, historical essays, and writings of a more doctrinal hue.

Their attention lasted for a long time but was not immutable, since it shifted from referentiality to objection. One key element which remained constant despite these changes is that their interest in Machiavelli was based on conceptions which were different to those seen in Lugones, or in Martínez Paz, Sánchez Viamonte, Astrada, and Taborda. Palacio and Irazusta did not invoke Machiavelli because they saw in him a harbinger of the more contemporary or novel versions of anti-liberalism, or a writer whose work had as its central pillar the greatness of the homeland or the nation (which was perhaps a curious, even paradoxical omission for authors that defined themselves as nationalist). Instead, they saw him as a reference of republicanism.

This approach can be read in some of their texts, especially Irazusta's, which was published in *La Nueva República*, a pioneering journal of Argentine nationalism (launched in 1927) that counted these two intellectuals among its driving forces. In its pages, one of the usual ways of criticizing democracy was to contrast it with the republic, although these invocations tended to be couched in different terms. To begin with, a distinction was made between republic and democracy based on the assertion that the 1853–60 Argentine Constitution enshrined the former, but not the latter.[41] That is, democracy was opposed to a liberal republic. Liberalism and democracy could be differentiated through a rereading, rather than an open criticism, of nineteenth-century liberalism (a connotation that has underpinned observations about the faint anti-liberalism slant of this publication in its early years).[42]

However, on the other hand, the republic was opposed to democracy based on a set of ideas that was very distant from liberalism. Irazusta underlined that the republic implied the admission of "the differences established by nature." Liberalism and democracy were a continuum of each other, since liberal individualism had its inexorable derivation in universal suffrage. Thus, it was necessary to warn the "unwary" who believed that "any republic should tend to democracy."[43]

In another text, Irazusta associated the republic with a "mixed government," understood as a political form (a combination of institutions with monarchic, aristocratic, and democratic traits) that was, in turn, a translation of the "natural order of things": that is, a hierarchic rather than an egalitarian society. The republic understood in this way allowed for a reconciliation of "the desire for freedom with the demands of authority."[44] Machiavelli was, along with many other authors and historical references, including the Roman republic and French monarchy, as well as Plato, Aristotle, and Thomas Aquinas, one of the authorities used as a reference basis for these assertions. He was held to be synonymous with a hierarchical or even corporate republic, which upheld the principles of authority and an anti-liberal and anti-democratic republicanism.

Over time, Irazusta's opinion of Machiavelli underwent a transformation. Although he continued to consider him a republican author, his republicanism was close to liberalism, which meant that he was an author to be criticized rather than praised. This was seen in his book about Titus Livy and the history of republican Rome, published in 1951. The essay is underpinned by his questioning of the prestige of the Roman republic in "the Western spirit," "construed by him [Livy] as a way of showing that everything was fine in the destroyed republic, and everything wrong in the empire built on its ruins."[45]

According to Irazusta, Livy had commended the republic for two attributes that, in his opinion, lacked foundation: the excellence of its constitution and its association with freedom. For Irazusta, the republic was an undertaking to do with conquest, whose guiding principle had been, not freedom, but the desire to achieve greatness. From this it may be seen that, contrary to what was emphasized by republican authors, there were no meaningful contradictions between republic and imperialism (as, in Irazusta's opinion, was proved by the United States of the time).[46] Besides, this expansion had demanded "the need to suspend the regular functioning of the political regime at the urgent behest of national security": that is, it had required "systematic violations of the constitution."[47] For that reason, "the Roman constitution was the result of Roman politics, rather than the latter being the result of that constitution."[48] In sum, the Roman republic was not "an ideal of perfect government," but a conquering endeavor even more brutal for those peoples it subjugated than the empire of the Caesars.

To all this should be added the fact that the other major driving force of the republic had been the achievements of its aristocracy: first, because it was "open to merit"; and second, because it took into account the importance of harmony. Both aspects had won over the deferential obedience of the people, which endured even when the equality of political rights had been declared (meaning that natural hierarchies were preserved despite political equality).[49] This was the reason for the consolidation of "the time of great virtue, natural among the patricians thanks to a more developed understanding of the indissoluble solidarity with lower orders, and acquired by the plebeians in their zest to rise to nobility, without suppressing it."[50] In other words, the splendor of the republic was due less to its institutional architecture than to the virtue and harmony achieved between the aristocracy and the people.

The discussion about freedom and the excellence of the constitution as distinctive traits of the Roman republic was mainly directed at Titus Livy, as well as his disciples, who were held responsible for his unjustified and long-lasting glorification in the "Western spirit." One of these was Machiavelli. Irazusta criticized many of his considerations, such as the relationship between the crisis of the republic and the extension of military command as posited in the *Discourses*.[51] On the other hand, as pointed out earlier, Irazusta's arguments about the splendor of the republic emphasized the desire for greatness, aristocracy, and harmony. Such assertions also appear in the text by Marcelo Sánchez Sorondo quoted in the previous section, or in Ernesto Palacio.[52] In Irazusta's opinion, traits of the republic such as aristocracy, harmony, greatness, and conquest (mainly the last two) were in disparity with those he attributed to Livy. But they were similarly in disparity with the Machiavelli of the *Discourses* and his comments about a free republic as a product of conflict and the involvement of democratic elements.[53] Irazusta recognized and listed the conflicts of republican Rome, but also saw in them a symptom of the imperfection of constitutional design rather than a cause of "free government."[54]

Similarly, his observations on the relation between republic, war, and conquest can be read as an exchange with Machiavelli. This is because, although it has been shown that, in his work, he recognized the role played by war in ensuring or extending the external and internal freedoms of the city (by arousing the *vivere politico* through the arming of its people), he also criticized war when this was guided by a desire for conquest, and he saw greatness as opposed to freedom.[55]

In this sense, Irazusta endowed the Roman republic with many of the efforts and passions that Alberdi had identified in his time. The main difference lay in the association between these and Machiavelli. For Alberdi, Machiavelli had been a staunch defender of Roman militarism (understood as common ground between the republic and the empire), and for that reason he was an enemy of modern freedom. However, as far as Irazusta was concerned, Machiavelli had attempted to allay those passions, or, at least, he belonged to a tradition that connected the Roman republic with freedom rather than imperialistic impulses, greatness, and conquest. Ultimately, the author of the *Discourses* had drawn a portrait of the Roman republic that built a bridge between the republican tradition and liberalism. In fact, if Irazusta described Titus Livy (and Sallust and Tacitus) as "liberal conservatives,"[56] other authors discussed throughout this book, with whom Machiavelli is associated rather than differentiated, were linked to liberalism, from Montesquieu to Mommsen or Fustel de Coulanges.[57]

In this vein, it is important to underline the counterpoints that Irazusta's reading had with the interpretations of Machiavelli and his relation with imperialism which prevailed at the turn of the twentieth century, as was seen in Chapter 1. Similar to the formulations developed by Alberdi in Argentina, the connection between Machiavelli, aggressive militarism, and imperialist expansionism (exemplified by Bismarck's Germany or the triumphant United States in the 1898 war against Spain) was a common topic used to illustrate the alienation or opposition between Machiavelli and liberalism.

Irazusta's intervention is, in fact, an account of a point of view which is opposed to the former. It recounts the close association between Machiavelli (and the republican tradition) and liberalism. This is the reason for the emphatic tone of denunciation and unmasking with regard to what, at the turn of the century, was seen as a certainty: the connection between (Roman) republicanism and imperialism. The main difference was that, at the turn of the twentieth century, Machiavelli was regarded as a writer who had connected both aspects, while, according to Irazusta's text (because he was a "liberal"), he was one of the architects responsible for concealing the relationship between imperialist military expansionism and the republic in the history of Rome. In addition, it would be forcing the issue to attribute a literally anti-imperialist perspective to Irazusta's text (as there was in other texts[58]), precisely because he gives the empire a more positive role than the republic in Roman history. His criticism is directed, strictly speaking, to the imperialism of republican Rome, pointing out, in the context of this argument, that Machiavelli had deliberately sought to conceal this aspect, instead of validating it.[59]

Parallel to all this, it is telling that Irazusta admitted to a "delay" in discovering Titus Livy and, by extension, republican historiography, specifying that he read him for the first time in the summer of 1932–3. This was after he had written the articles for *La Nueva República*, as noted above.[60] In other words, between the 1920s and 1940s, Irazusta went from conceiving of Machiavelli as the key figure for an anti-liberal and anti-democratic republicanism, to regarding him as the exponent of a republicanism of a liberal hue, or at least projection (to the extent of attempting to ignore any imperialist impulses).

Such shifts cannot be taken separately from those which took place in the very notion of republicanism as seen by these authors. From an understanding of republicanism as an alternative or opposition to liberal democracy, republicanism became the object of criticism. In Irazusta's case, this happened, first, because he believed that republicanism, as a political and historiographic tradition, had left as its legacy an unfounded consideration for its main historical reference, the Roman republic. Second, it occurred because all this revealed that this was a political tradition that converged with rather than confronted liberalism.

Ernesto Palacio proffered another type of criticism. From his perspective, republicanism was a misrepresentation, since republican institutions had been characterized by protecting and strengthening the interests of the powerful, of the "oligarchies." He said as much in a reference book on the subject, *Catilina contra la oligarquía*, published in 1935. In his text, instead of contrasting republicanism with liberalism and democracy, he placed liberal and oligarchic republicanism in opposition to a "democratic dictatorship," disparaging the former and praising the latter. In his words: "The anti-oligarchic dictatorship: the dictatorship of the *caudillo* of the people against their exploiters, imbued with legal means; a democratic dictatorship."[61]

These political and interpretative shifts could be attributed to the changing diagnoses and positions of these individuals regarding local politics. The consideration of a republican crisis as the result of the corruption of an aristocracy mutating into an oligarchy, and the emergence of "personal regimes" as the only possible solution in this scenario have a connection with the political disillusionment suffered by Irazusta and Palacio following the failure of the authoritarian project that arose in the wake of the 1930 coup they had supported. The constitutional restoration following this episode prompted in these intellectuals a repudiation of the ruling classes of the time, who were accused of being accomplices or arch-supporters of liberalism. Such a portrait, certainly, omitted the not particularly liberal behaviors of those ruling sectors, if we take into account the fact that institutional distortion and electoral fraud were distinctive traits of Argentine political life in the 1930s. A tone of anti-elitism became typical of the nationalist discourse in its criticism of the "oligarchy," visible in the aforementioned text by Palacio, as well as in that published by Irazusta with his brother Rodolfo in 1934, *La Argentina y el imperialismo británico*.[62]

More generally, such a review of republicanism is linked to the shift in forms of government as a subject of interest among those authors, in favor of a political reflection that prioritized a connection with social and economic dimensions – as exemplified by the topic of oligarchic domination – or concerns such as imperialism or the State, rather than political regimes.[63] These perspectives, which run through the *Tito Livio* of Irazusta (and other writings of his, such as those in *La Nueva República*, mentioned above), may also be seen in another text of Palacio's where he alludes to Machiavelli and even praises him: *Teoría del Estado*, published in 1949.[64]

Previously referred to in Chapter 2, this book mentions Machiavelli in relation to its central objective: the study of "political realities," and the subject of the separation between morals and politics. According to Palacio, "political reality par excellence" is a mixed government, since, in any political society, monarchical ("chiefs" or personal leaderships), aristocratic, and democratic traits coexist.[65] This is why he points out the irrelevance of the distinction between different forms of government based on their legal or institutional designs, or on their ideological principles, which he describes as "myths."[66] The "reality" of politics lies in the "real distribution of power" between the three factual powers, and in the fact that, however this distribution takes place, whether in favor of the aristocracies, the people, or the prince, any political regime must always be the government of "ruling classes."[67]

Palacio's "realism," then, revealed an elitist conception of politics. As we saw above in connection with Lugones and Sánchez Sorondo, and in Chapter 2, it was not unusual to turn to Machiavelli to support such views, although it is worth saying that realism as elitism was based on different perspectives. In Sánchez Sorondo (who criticized Palacio's book), this arose from a conception of politics as "art"; in Palacio, however, it was rooted in a closer approach to political sociology. For that reason, Palacio's realism is associated less with praise for power in itself and more with the postulation of a "natural political order" (an expression which is, in fact, difficult to attribute to a reading of Machiavelli), where the "relations of command and obedience" are constitutive phenomena. Taking all of this into account, it is perhaps not surprising that the influences of Aristotle or Polybius prevail in Palacio's reflection on mixed government, or that there is a greater incidence of the elites theory espoused by Italian "neo-Machiavellians" such as Gaetano Mosca or Vilfredo Pareto, than that of Machiavelli.[68]

In fact, Palacio raised objections and explicit criticisms to *The Prince*. There is a revealing passage in *Catilina*. In his opinion, "the politician moves within full moral order. His specific purpose is the common good"; "the conquest of power will mean, for the politician, the condition of fulfilling a moral duty."[69] For that reason,

> "The Prince" is wrong when, in deliberate ignorance of moral laws, he only thinks of the mere conquest or maintenance of power, which is not an end in itself, and does not justify the means employed to obtain it, since its possession has to be justified through a beneficial exercise.

This did not imply that political ambition should be sacrificed for the sake of morals. According to Palacio, "this dilemma simply does not exist. A means necessary to obtain a beneficial end cannot be bad."[70] For Palacio, the separation between politics and morals wielded by Machiavelli was a "false problem" that undermined – or at least did not strengthen – political action.

Palacio emerged here, then, as a critic of "Machiavellianism." But this is for reasons that differ from those of the nineteenth-century liberals, or authors such as Martínez Paz, Astrada, or Sánchez Viamonte. Like these writers, his considerations revolve around the Machiavelli of *The Prince*. He also saw in that text an author interested in power and ambition. But, unlike the writers mentioned, he neither objects to nor censors these interests; instead, he questions the arguments raised to justify it. That is, Machiavelli's problem, for Palacio, is not that he is an eventual apologist of a liberticidal power. The issue is that it does not offer an unequivocal legitimation of political action and, thus, of the figure of an ambitious "prince" (or "*caudillo*," as he portrays the character in his text), when he holds that the prince's motive is the mere quest for power. Machiavelli alone is insufficient as a justification for political action and ambition, for the same reasons as the other writers, including Lugones, understood these to be strengthening factors by granting them autonomy and stripping them of any moral foundation. According to Palacio, the justification of the means by the end ("a means necessary to obtain a beneficial end cannot be bad") gains strength if, in addition to being political, it is also moral (if goodness, and not only efficacy, is attributed). In sum, even recognizing the autonomy of politics, for Palacio, there could not be a complete divorce severing politics and morals. Irazusta also maintained that "politics is not independent of morality." He stated that this relationship should be conceived of from "the concrete particular" and not from "the abstract universal," but at all events, he underlined that "Rome in its best epoch could not have a higher virtue than the Christian medieval one."[71]

If we look at the texts from 1920 to 1940 as a whole, a change of appreciation of Machiavelli and his work may be recognized in both Julio Irazusta and Ernesto Palacio, at two levels. First, and in parallel to the revision of Roman republicanism, Machiavelli went from being associated with a classical republicanism enshrining order and virtue, authority and hierarchy, conceived of as an antidote to liberal democracy (which is where Machiavelli coexisted with Thomas Aquinas and Aristotle), to a form of republicanism that converged with liberalism.

Second, Machiavelli was objected to because of the way in which he dissociated politics from morals. These arguments are connected to a doctrinal trait of local anti-liberalism (which took on differing amounts of relative importance according to different authors and currents), Thomism. In fact, concerning Palacio's *Catilina*, it was pointed out that he belonged to the "Thomist school" and that his arguments were "a thousand leagues from the clumsy amorality of Machiavelli."[72] Irazusta himself held, in another of his texts, that Machiavelli (like Plato or Rousseau) was an author who astonished the reader for his "brilliant paradoxes," but not for "finding the truth," as did Aquinas.[73]

In fact, the scope of the authors alluded to by Irazusta and Palacio in the texts referred to here is broad and eclectic[74]; they were even accused of Machiavellianism from within the anti-liberalism school of thought for their praise of political action, while other more radical opinions objected to the desire for power and opportunism. These views reveal just how broad the disqualification of Machiavelli was in its scope (accusations which ran parallel to other objections leveled at their "Maurrasisme").[75] Still, Machiavelli was not included as one of their main or more enduring references. On the contrary, he was criticized and challenged, on the basis of concepts and notions familiar to Thomism.

## Machiavelli in Catholic Thought

The influence of Thomism in the culture and political ideas of Argentina in the 1920s and 1930s, and the appearance of an "integralist Catholicism" were other manifestations of the political and ideological tensions of the period. Certainly, the political projections of the time were not unequivocal. Neo-Thomism (which was far from being a local phenomenon and had key international figures such as Jacques Maritain) could drift into positions that accepted liberal democracy in parallel with others that openly rejected it, to the extent that, according to certain perspectives, Thomistic Catholicism was the key expression of local anti-liberalism, from which other variants (also heterogeneous in themselves), like nationalism, should be put in context and understood.[76]

Machiavelli could not be revalidated by Thomistic thought, regardless of the degree of doctrinal orthodoxy or even political sympathies (at both local and international levels) of its exponents. As was seen in Chapter 2 regarding the epistemological and ontological proposals attributed to him, Catholics generally tended to repudiate Machiavelli and were even dismissive of his intellectual stature. He was associated, at the least, with the separation between politics and Christianity, even between the State and the Church, and (according to Lugones) with a denial of the absolute in favor of history and human action. That is, he was associated with maxims opposed to the conviction that politics was subordinate to a transcendent dimension or eternal truths. That is the reason why, beyond the degrees of intransigence and orthodoxy – meaning whether a new "Middle Age" or a Christian State was being postulated, or whether natural law was claimed as a limit to state sovereignty or political decision – Machiavelli was on the receiving end of an open and explicit rejection from the most outspoken exponents of Thomism in Argentina, from the 1920s to the 1940s.

However, although such condemnation should not be surprising, it is relevant to present the arguments, as they are revealing in themselves, and because they also show the different, even opposing, evaluations of Machiavelli prevalent among the figures sharing a common repudiation of liberal democracy during this period. The conclusions about Machiavelli reached by Catholics were not the same as those assumed by the writers that saw him as a key figure for an anti-liberal republicanism or the harbinger of Fascism. From a neo-Thomistic perspective, Machiavelli condensed, at the same time, liberalism and totalitarianism.

From the perspective of the Catholic reading, Machiavelli represented the foundation of contemporary totalitarianism, not because his thought was a response to liberalism, but because it contained all the elements that had made liberalism possible, and whose inconsistencies could be resolved only through totalitarianism. Machiavelli was a "modern" and represented a totalitarian threat as a result of the separation he wrought between religion and politics, for having founded a purely human politics that oscillated between contrived, relative principles, whose conflict could be solved only by the use of force.

Unlike the tenets sustained by liberalism, Machiavelli's beliefs were despotic, but precisely because he was modern and a liberal, not ancient. His praise of the State, his position as the author who wrote about power, including the reason of State, was not a genuine opposition to liberalism, but part of a reasoning that, having configured politics on the basis of immanent principles, was intrinsically linked with liberalism. Thus, unlike other critics of liberal democracy such as Lugones, Machiavelli did not offer arguments for the eradication of democracy or the restoration of order. He was not a symbol of force and action against ideas and principles but rather responsible for the consolidation of (false) principles that required force in order to be imposed. He was, in sum, part of the problem, an ineluctable figure for the apostasy that was a feature of the Western world since modernity, and responsible for the turbulence typical of the times. Machiavelli and liberalism were part of the same sequence.

In the early 1930s, Julio Meinvielle (1905–73), one of the most intransigent voices of Catholicism at that time, referred to Machiavelli in a gloomy diagnosis of modernity. According to Meinvielle, modernity implied abandoning the principles and forms designed to ensure a perfect political society. That is, modernity had caused the disappearance of a political society "demanded by the nature of man"; oriented towards material, intellectual, and moral perfection; hierarchical and corporate; directed by an earthly power leading to the temporary common good, with its own sphere of action, but subordinate to a transcendent dimension: "the political society is a natural product, that is, vindicated by the social impulses lying within every man. Then God, the author of human nature, is also the author of political society."[77] Reimplanting this type of society required nothing less than a new Middle Ages: "Christianity produced the ideal type of political society, where the rights of God and of the Caesar, those of the State and the nation, those of freedom and authority, were in harmony, the political society of medieval times."[78]

Machiavelli was integral to the sequence that had buried that perfect political society, in a foundational way. Since then, politics had turned on "false absolutes": the State, class, the individual, the nation. In this sense, he was both a key figure for and harbinger of tendencies such as those condensed in the work of Charles Maurras or in Fascism (particularly the latter). These were, however, different from each other (the first one was "amoral"; the second, "immoral because it establishes the reason of State as norm of morality"), but they shared common ground: "to exalt the notion of State, reviving pagan statism." In opposition to these were the tendencies feeding on the ideas of Rousseau or Kant, such as individualism, liberalism, democracy, and socialism.

Nonetheless, all these trends, beyond their oppositions ("all modern systems, apparently antagonistic"), had a key principle in common: "the adoration of man."[79] And this was dangerous, since, if human nature called, "imperiously, [for] the existence of an absolute," modernity offered only imperfect imitations.

> Any doctrine, ignorant of the First Principle, which departs from an idea or a fact, call it individual freedom or nation, State, community, working class or race, will simulate an Absolute, and for that reason cannot be limited by anybody or anything.[80]

A purely human politics, as had emerged with modernity, thus supposed a dispute between false absolutes, a relativism and an artificialism that could end only in anarchy or despotism. For that reason, "only the devil could hypnotize Christian nations with this spawn of imbecility, convincing them that there are sectors of human activity that are self-sufficient [. . .] that do not have to yield either to the Church or to God."[81]

In Meinvielle's view, to sum up, Machiavelli was responsible for an anti-Christian, even diabolic, form of politics (the echoes of Pole's opinion, as referred to by Martínez Paz, may be heard here). He was the architect of one of the false absolutes of modernity, the "statolatry" (derived from his "Greco-Roman conception of life"[82]), a precept worshipped at the time mainly by Fascism, but separated from liberalism by a difference of degree, not of nature. If Machiavelli could be considered an adversary of liberalism, he also shared with it, ultimately, the affirmation of the radical autonomy of politics.[83]

Similar judgements may be found in the writings of the professors of Law and jurists affiliated to Thomism, discussed in Chapter 2: Faustino Legón and Arturo Sampay. For these authors, as was seen, the autonomy of politics had provided grounds for an imperfect and limited type of knowledge. That same ontological principle applied to politics had, of necessity, realized itself in the autonomy of the State, and this inexorably led to totalitarianism. There was, in consequence, a far-reaching relation between the liberal State and the Fascist State.

According to Legón,

> the mind-set that leads to a conception of the State or political body as free of ethical obstacles, naturally leads to what has been labelled "statolatry", that is an overvaluation of the State as an end in itself. Hegel and, before him, Machiavelli contributed to this.[84]

From his perspective, "Machiavellian tendencies" led to a "tyranny without claim," inasmuch as they were inherent to a view of politics where "the first absolute is suppressed or forgotten, [and] it stands on secondary political absolutisms, which are intolerable, as it is not because they are second-hand absolutes that they cease to be overbearing."[85]

Sampay, in turn, alluded to the "morally unconditioned politicism of the *ragioni di stato*" when he referred to Machiavelli and his key role in the "secularization of the State" during the "passage from the Middle Ages to modernity" and during the "immanentization of culture," to all of which "the vigorous resurgence of scholasticism in the sixteenth century" was opposed.[86] With the Florentine author, "who takes the principles of the Renaissance to the limit," an immanent and amoral conception of the State had taken "definitive hold," something which the "Spanish theologians of the sixteenth century" had attempted to ward off, with no success, in order "to save Europe from its imminent Machiavellianization." From this point of view, Machiavelli was part of the genealogy driving the "liberal-bourgeois rule of law." At the same time, the "real-historical formulation" of the "brilliant prefiguration of the Prince" had arrived four centuries later, with the dawn of Fascism, and, once again, Mussolini's appeal to Machiavelli was strong evidence of that fact.[87]

As was held in a later text,

> all those who possess, not a true concept of divinity but at least a belief in a rational and natural law that ensures the moral values of the human person, will perceive the monstrosity implied by the absolute autonomy of the State.[88]

The negative anthropology of Machiavelli, in this sense, made the State necessary, but it did so in order to curtail and put down man's vices, not to strengthen human perfection. "The greatness of the State" was the "greatest good of the man," but its ends made it potentially despotic:

> Machiavelli infers that the State is necessary and that man is usually perfidious in the field of political action. But [...] he was unable to see that the State is necessary because it is a natural community springing from the social essence of the individual, whose intrinsic purpose is to achieve his own peak of perfection. Because he did not understand the latter, he was unable to grasp that this purpose of achieving perfection is the yardstick with which one may evaluate political actions. From this, one may conclude that what is useful for the State cannot be the eminent good of human political action, if this is not subordinate to the supreme end of human perfection.

Therefore, Machiavelli "progressed into a confessedly amoral normative politics that, for the same reason, if taken to an extreme, implied the annihilation of the human person."[89]

Sampay, certainly, also left passages where he criticized Machiavelli's patriotism for its intrinsic paganism, since he replaced "the *caritas Dei* with the *carità della patria*," implying the "supremacy of the Homeland over God." This, as was seen, connected the Florentine author with Fascism and, at the same time, enshrines a judgement that suggests Sampay's distance from a version of the anti-liberalism proclaiming itself to be nationalist. In fact, he emphasized the visible nature of the "rebirth of Machiavelli's pessimistic ideas in the schools of idolatrous nationalisms, in the manner of Maurras, Spengler, Carl Schmitt, or in the sociology of Pareto, so influential in contemporary totalitarianism."[90]

Whether from a theological conception of politics or from a revalidation of natural law, Machiavelli condensed principles antagonistic to the postulates of neo-Thomism: an immanent and autonomous politics, sovereignty and legal positivism, "statolatry," and pagan values like patriotism, whose contemporary projections were relativism, a denial of the absolutes, and totalitarianism. In other words, what Lugones had praised about Machiavelli (it is worth remembering that, for Lugones, there was also an intimate connection between Christianity and liberalism, and for that reason Machiavelli was anti-liberal and, at the same time, anti-Christian) was repudiated by the authors inspired by Thomism (who, certainly, recognized Machiavelli's echoes in Lugones).[91]

However, Tomás Casares was perhaps the figure who presented the most forceful judgement on Machiavelli from a Catholic perspective, also at an earlier date than the afore-mentioned contributions. In the text published on the occasion of the 400th anniversary of the death of the Florentine, in 1927 (at the same time as Lugones's text), Casares portrayed Machiavelli as the crucial architect of modernity, defending the historical substitution of Christian politics, but also, explicitly, painting him as the author of a work whose matrix was a doctrinal precedent of liberalism.[92]

For both reasons, Machiavelli's thought had a disturbing validity. It was the symbol of a battle that had been waged since the sixteenth century:

> [E]verything is vigorously disposed for a battle against the supremacy of the Church and against its doctrine of the subordination of man to a transcendent good and truth, a terrible battle in favor of the rights of the State which would win the supreme scepter if the battle were won. Posterity has understood this so, the battle has been under way since the Renaissance and the Reformation, and

the weapons provided by the Florentine are seen everywhere for their changing reflections.[93]

These considerations were based on arguments that have already been described: the rupture with the Christian and medieval tradition brought about by Machiavelli's thought, the separation between politics and morals, the consequent autonomy and absolutization of politics (that is, as a sphere justified in itself), the affirmation of its immanent character, and the praise of State omnipotence as the result of all this. However, Casares's particular point was that the postulation of an omnipotent State did not make Machiavelli an upholder of tyranny or an enemy of freedom. On the contrary, he was the unavoidable figure to turn to when endeavoring to understand the appearance of the substantial principles of liberalism (as well as its inconsistencies and aporias). Machiavelli had invoked, "frequently, freedom as a political ideal." And that freedom was the "freedom of the State," but also "individual freedom."[94]

According to Casares, affirmation of the radical autonomy of politics and State was a necessary condition for conceiving of freedom as understood by modernity. This would be an individual and exclusively earthly freedom, unencumbered by duty, something purely concrete and sensible, alien to any notion of moral improvement and transcendent projection:

> We are facing an individual end, as in the case of the scholastic response, but one with a very serious difference. In the latter, the individual end is condensed in *duty*, an absolute duty that transcends time, space, and any contingent circumstances. In Machiavelli's stance, which at this point keenly expresses the Renaissance view of life, the end is expressed in a *right*, the individual right to live life with a maximum of concrete happiness.[95]

In Casares's opinion, the absolutization of politics promoted by Machiavelli did not signify either the politicization of all the spheres of human activity, or the absorption of earthly life by politics. He meant that political power was not incumbent upon individuals in any other dimensions than politics.

> The State that has been erected as an end and has subordinated individual personality unconditionally in everything related to political activity, does not have any other reason for its omnipotence and absorbent force than the need to offer its subjects an environment favorable to the unconditional exaltation of individual personality.[96]

Machiavelli taught that "the end of the State can be an amoral one, without compromising the fate of its subjects, because the individual end is not only one of morality." For Casares, the problem was not "Machiavellian immorality," but the disengagement that encouraged amorality arising from the separation of politics and morals: "The starting point is the total and fundamental independence of the man with respect to everything that is not himself."[97]

Machiavelli had opened the faucet, releasing a stream of thought which was followed by liberalism. From this point of view, the Renaissance was connected to the Reformation (and Machiavelli with Luther), and both to "current political realism," understood not as a politics of force or "biological" politics, but as the consolidation of politics independent and autonomous from morality, associated with the exaltation of the life of the senses. "The only possible relation of the State with the fate of the subject in the logic of Machiavelli, the Renaissance and current political realism," was that

> life has value in itself, it is an absolute value: living to the full in freedom as long as the freedom of the other is not violated, is man's fate. And if the State is to cooperate in the same way with that fate, it will be offering its subjects an environment favorable to their full expansion.[98]

However, the aporia consisted in the fact that there was a

> violent and unavoidable contradiction between the State's omnipotence and the individual exaltation promoted by the example of the State and its lack of concern regarding the discipline governing moral behavior. It is the intrinsic weakness of all greatness that desires to stand against God.

The only way of overcoming such a contradiction was, precisely, to understand "individual freedom as the freedom to achieve the expansion of the senses and happiness," since "any other form of personal expansion – free and intelligent self-affirmation, for example – would mean erecting an individual end against the State."[99]

Such modern relativism, announced by Machiavelli and condensed by liberalism, could be solved only by force:

> The definitive purpose of the exaltation of the State is the release of the individual from his subjection to God, creating an order of subjection of which he himself is the omnipotent creator [. . .] The

affirmation of that absolute autonomy fosters a permanent danger in the political order – a danger that beats at the very heart of the system – of a new and infinitely worse subjection because it would come from the hand of man himself. It would be arbitrary since the regulatory value of transcendent law, which offers, in its transcendence, the guarantee of its unyielding and steadfast nature, its universality and its permanence, has been denied.[100]

Therefore, it was wrong to look at Machiavelli as a guarantor of order. The ontological and epistemological rupture he had promoted – as seen in Chapter 2, the decisive element of his thought from a Catholic perspective – turned him into an adversary of a genuine affirmation of authority. The forms of government (principality or republic, for which Machiavelli – Casares underlined – had had manifest sympathies) were a false problem: "any form of government that rests on the principle of the State's omnipotence" was equally unacceptable:

Whether such omnipotence is recognized and attributed by chance to a dictator, due to a display of force, or is enshrined legally in a permanent constitution, the danger to man's individual dignity is always the same. This is even more serious in the last case, because the State will add to its material force the formal entitlement that its people have themselves granted.[101]

In sum, for Casares, Machiavelli was more than a modern, responsible for the relativism of a politics without God, which led to the ruin of men by lowering their horizons to the world of the senses and the concrete, or which led to a form of unavoidable immanent authoritarianisms. Unlike Meinvielle, who conceived of him in similar fashion, but highlighted his doctrinal resonances in one of the "false absolutes" of these times (Fascism), Casares believed that Machiavelli was essentially the author of the matrix that had promoted liberalism. He had had "liberal aspirations" and "republican inspirations."[102] In Casares's opinion, anybody eager to criticize liberalism should read Machiavelli – not because he offered an anti-liberal political conception (as posited by Lugones), but because he was the compendium, the foundations on which liberal thought was based.

This way of understanding Machiavelli certainly found an echo, as it may be observed in the texts by Legón or Sampay (who quoted Casares) and referred to above.[103] Meinvielle himself stated in a 1946 article that the claim for an "independent politics, a separated politics" was a conception that brought Machiavelli into line with the "great modern liberals." Another author close to Meinvielle, Julio M. Ojea Quintana, made the link in the late 1940s between Machiavelli (via Hobbes) and Carl Schmitt through decisionism. He saw in this (unlike Saúl Taborda's arguments, for example) not a response to liberalism, but a doctrine based on philosophical premises in common with liberalism and, therefore, imperfect or unacceptable (as another variant of modern relativist arbitrariness):

> Machiavelli is logically aligned with the premises of the liberal position [. . .]. He has secularized politics to the exclusion of all religious factors [. . .] he has proposed formulas designed to repair the State artificially by dint of human will and work alone, due to the commitment of the majority, or the sole decision of the strongest.

Here was a judgement that, similarly to what was seen in Casares, focused on the ontological and epistemological rupture of Machiavelli, which associated him, in terms of the forms of government, not only with authoritarianism, but also with democracy.[104]

## Machiavelli as a Reference of Liberalism

Looking at the considerations of Machiavelli displayed in Argentine anti-liberalism between the 1920s and 1940s as a whole, we see that the first obvious conclusion is that there were different, even contrasting, opinions about him: enthusiastic adhesion (Lugones), ambivalence (Palacio, Irazusta), or condemnation and outright rejection (Meinvielle, Legón, Sampay, Casares).

If we take this into consideration, the appropriations of Machiavellian ideas may be understood as an indicator of the differences, if not the tensions, underlying local anti-liberalism regarding its political stances and doctrinal basis. These included the counterpoints between those who became enthusiastic about alternative forms to liberal democracy emerging during this period (such as Fascism); those who conceived of an aristocratic republicanism as the antidote to liberal individualism and universal suffrage; and those who supported the reinstatement of a Christian State, or, from a more moderate perspective, revisited classical natural law as a way of dealing with what they understood to be a modern relativism and its consequent despotic dangers.

At all events, as a way of complementing rather than refuting the above, it is also possible to assert that there were shared traits. Julio Irazusta, Ernesto Palacio, Julio Meinvielle, and Tomás Casares (also Faustino Legón and Arturo Sampay), whose political options and doctrinal positions were not always close to each other throughout their lives, did agree on their dismissal of Machiavelli. This stance reveals the influence of Thomism, or, at any rate, how it materialized in arguments based on this current of thought. From this point of view, the position regarding Machiavelli blurs the distinctions between nationalists and Catholics. From a broader perspective, in one way or another, Argentine anti-liberalism disdained Machiavelli, neither invoking him in any long-lasting way, nor including him among its key references. Lugones, in this scenario, was a dissonant voice.

In Chapter 2, it was underlined that a common reading by the authors of the first half of the twentieth century, different than what was customary until the late nineteenth century, was that Machiavelli shifted from being conceived of as an "ancient" or obsolete, even naïve, author, to being seen as a "modern" and a symbol of present times. This modern character was based, mainly, on the ontology of the politics he had postulated, particularly on its autonomy regarding Christian morality and religion.

The arguments presented in this chapter, may serve to illuminate a key point outlined in Chapter 2: Machiavelli's modernity, derived from his ontology, was subject to different political readings. These different political readings did not take place exclusively between opposing ideological camps, but within the same ones. This may be observed in anti-liberalism, in relation to the afore-mentioned point about the reasons that could link Machiavelli's work to totalitarianism. For some, this connection was based on the fact that his political guiding principles were a frontal response to liberalism. According to others, it was quite the opposite: his ideas exposed, in ground-breaking form, the intrinsic relativism and immanentism of liberalism, which could lead only to totalitarianism. For that reason, according to the latter perspective, fighting Machiavelli was a way of fighting liberalism rather than a remedy for it.

In that sense, a second change can be detected between the readings prevailing until the early twentieth century and those carried out since the 1910s and 1920s. The shift consists of the fact that, inasmuch as he was no longer seen as an ancient author but as a modern one, Machiavelli went from being associated with anti-liberalism to being situated in the history and genealogy of liberalism. For this reason, anti-liberalism, with the exceptions already mentioned, did not refer to him. This shift in the understanding of

Machiavelli's ideas allows the recognition of an agreement between ideological antipodes, which is initially surprising: the fact that nineteenth-century liberalism and twentieth-century anti-liberalism in Argentina mainly considered Machiavelli an adversary.

However, the fact that Machiavelli was largely criticized rather than praised by anti-liberalism was due only in part to the way in which the political and doctrinal affiliation of his ideas was understood. It also sprang from the fact that, during this same period, those related to liberalism valued Machiavelli for the same reasons that he was repudiated by anti-liberalism: that is, for being modern and for advocating freedom (changing the view of him that had prevailed in liberalism until the end of the nineteenth century).

## Notes

1. Halperin Donghi, *Vida y muerte de la República Verdadera*; Halperin Donghi, *La República Imposible (1930–1945)*; Leandro Losada (comp.), *Política y vida pública: Argentina, 1930–1943*, Buenos Aires, Imago Mundi, 2017.
2. Tulio Halperín Donghi, *La Argentina y la tormenta del mundo: ideas e ideologías entre 1930 y 1945*, Buenos Aires, Siglo XXI, 2003, p. 81.
3. See Ellen Kennedy, *Carl Schmitt en la República de Weimar: la quiebra de una constitución*, Madrid, Tecnos, 2012.
4. See L. M. Bassani and C. Vivanti, C. (eds), *Machiavelli nella storiografia e nel pensiero politico del XX secolo*, Milan, Giuffrè, 2006; Laura Mitarotondo, *Un preludio a Machiavelli: letture e interpretazioni fra Mussolini e Gramsci*, Turin, G. Giappichelli, 2016.
5. Leandro Losada, "Liberalismo y derechas en la Argentina, 1912–1943: apuestas interpretativas, posibilidades y límites," *Prismas: Revista de Historia Intelectual*, 24, 2020, pp. 219–25.
6. Astrada, *La Real Politik: de Maquiavelo a Spengler*, p. 22.
7. In some of his writings, Martínez Paz distinguished the Florentine from the German, explaining that "Machiavelli does not deny principles, rather he remembers and recognizes them, but halts them when they are presented as an obstacle in the path of the success of the princes," while "Spengler, instead, elevates whim and arbitrariness to the dignity of system and justifies it invoking who knows what mysterious designs." Martínez Paz, *Sistema de filosofía del derecho*, p. 226. Martínez Paz was a translator of Spengler and organized a tribute to the German thinker at the Universidad de Córdoba in 1923. See Pablo Requena and Ezequiel Grisendi, "Dos eventos de recepción densos en la Universidad de Córdoba: los homenajes a Oswald Spengler (1924) y Henri Bergson (1936)," in *Actas de las V Jornadas de Historia de las Izquierdas ¿Las "ideas fuera*

de lugar"? *El problema de la recepción y la circulación de ideas en América Latina*, Buenos Aires, CeDInCI, 2009.
8. Enrique Martínez Paz, "El retorno de Maquiavelo" [1924], in Martínez Paz, *Sistema de filosofía del derecho*, pp. 283–88.
9. Ibid. pp. 283–4. It is worth pointing out, among other references and influences, the influence of neo-Kantianism on the legal thought of Martínez Paz. See Jorge Dotti, *La letra gótica: recepción de Kant en la Argentina, desde el Romanticismo hasta el treinta*, Buenos Aires, Facultad de Filosofía y Letras, UBA, 1992, pp. 212–13.
10. Martínez Paz, "El retorno," pp. 286–7.
11. Ibid. pp. 286–7.
12. See Roberto Esposito, "Mal," in Roberto Esposito, *Confines de lo politico: nueve pensamientos sobre política*, Madrid, Trotta, 1996, pp. 151–68.
13. Martínez Paz, "El retorno," p. 288. The passage, it is worth highlighting, manifests a counterpoint with the aptitude, and even the viability, of a Catholic criticism of Machiavelli. Later, this topic will be discussed further.
14. Sánchez Viamonte, *Derecho político*, p. 142.
15. Carlos Sánchez Viamonte, "Maquiavelo y Mussolini," in Carlos Sánchez Viamonte, *Jornadas*, Buenos Aires, Samet, 1929, pp. 58–64.
16. Sánchez Viamonte, *Derecho político*, pp. 195–8.
17. Saúl Taborda, "Reflexiones sobre el ideal político en América Latina" [1918], in Saúl Taborda, *Escritos politicos: 1918–1934*, Córdoba, Universidad Nacional de Córdoba, 2008, pp. 30, 38.
18. Saúl Taborda, "La crisis espiritual y el ideario argentino" [1933], in Taborda, *Escritos políticos*, pp. 228–32.
19. Ibid. p. 231; my emphasis.
20. Ibid. pp. 231–2.
21. See Dotti, *Carl Schmitt en Argentina*, pp. 45–8.
22. Lugones, "Elogio de Maquiavelo," pp. 297–301.
23. Ibid. p. 298.
24. Ibid. p. 299. Martínez Paz pointed out that his text was praised by Lugones. *Sistema de filosofía del derecho*, p. 283.
25. Ibid. p. 297.
26. Ibid. p. 298.
27. Ibid. p. 299. In this respect, see also Leopoldo Lugones, "El concepto de potencia," in Leopoldo Lugones, *La patria fuerte*, Buenos Aires, Luis Bernard, 1930, pp. 43–7. The inconsistent distinction, in his opinion, between force and law was the underlying argument in the criticism of Alberdi included in his "Elogio de Maquiavelo": "When Alberdi states: 'the people are not sovereign but of what is just', he thinks he is expressing something relevant and, actually, he is saying nothing. Because the sovereignty of the people, like anything else, is not an expression of justice but of force. Without saying that, he would not know either how to define 'the just.'"

28. Ibid. p. 300.
29. Ibid. p. 299; my emphasis. It can be observed in this passage that Machiavelli and Machiavellianism are the same thing for Lugones, although here he responds to one of the most usual objections to what was called "Machiavellianism."
30. Ibid. pp. 298–300.
31. Ibid. pp. 298–9.
32. Ibid. p. 300.
33. The expression refers to Jeffrey Herf, *El modernismo reaccionario: tecnología, cultura y política en Weimar y el Tercer Reich*, Mexico, Fondo de Cultura Económica, 1990.
34. Leopoldo Lugones, "El tesoro y el dragón," in Lugones, *La patria fuerte*, pp. 22–3.
35. José Ingenieros, a leading intellectual and key figure of the generation identified with the 1918 University Reform, as well as being a companion of Lugones in their youth and sharing his anarchist sympathies, also saw in Machiavelli an important author who repudiated "bourgeois morality," evoking the expression that "the greed of citizens is more harmful for the people than the rapacity of their enemies." It is worth mentioning that here Machiavelli does not represent the behaviors which are the object of repudiation, but a criticism of them, shared by the author: José Ingenieros, *El hombre mediocre* [1913], Buenos Aires, Losada, 2001, p. 155.
36. Sánchez Sorondo, *La clase dirigente y la crisis del régimen*, p. 15.
37. Ibid. pp. 7–22.
38. Marcelo Sánchez Sorondo, "Lo que la guerra representa para la Argentina" [1943], in Marcelo Sánchez Sorondo, *La revolución que anunciamos*, Buenos Aires, Nueva Política, 1945, p. 228.
39. Academic literature has discussed the relation between acting and doing, between art and action, in Machiavelli. See Carlo Ginzburg, "Pontano, Maquiavelo y la prudencia: Algunas reflexiones más," *Anales de Historia Antigua, Medieval y Moderna*, 43, 2011, pp. 115–26.
40. Zuleta Álvarez, *El nacionalismo argentino*, vol. 1, pp. 193–235; Cristian Buchrucker, *Nacionalismo y peronismo: la Argentina en la crisis ideológica mundial (1927–1955)*, Buenos Aires, Sudamericana, 1987, pp. 45–83; Sandra McGee Deutsch and Ronald Dolkart (eds), *La derecha argentina: nacionalistas, neoliberales, militares y clericales*, Buenos Aires, Javier Vergara, 2001; Devoto, *Nacionalismo, fascismo y tradicionalismo en la Argentina moderna*; Losada, "Liberalismo y derechas."
41. Rodolfo Irazusta, "Con motivo del sufragio universal" (28 Apr. 1928), in Julio Irazusta, *El pensamiento político nacionalista, vol. 1. De Alvear a Yrigoyen*, Buenos Aires, Obligado, 1975, pp. 96–104. See also Rodolfo Irazusta, "El aniversario de la Constitución" (5 May 1928), in Ibid, pp. 105–6. Rodolfo was the brother of Julio Irazusta.

42. Devoto, *Nacionalismo*, pp. 169–262.
43. Julio Irazusta, "República y democracia" (15 Mar. 1928), in Irazusta, *El pensamiento político nacionalista*, vol. 1, pp. 79–82.
44. Julio Irazusta, "La forma mixta de gobierno" (31 Jan. 1928), in Irazusta, *El pensamiento político nacionalista*, vol. 1, pp. 55–9.
45. Julio Irazusta, *Tito Livio: o del imperialismo en relación con las formas de gobierno y la evolución histórica*, Mendoza, Universidad Nacional de Cuyo, 1951, p. 287; also pp. 11–20, 179–91. It is worth pointing out that Irazusta dates the end of his work as 1948.
46. Ibid. pp. 286–96.
47. Ibid. p. 81.
48. Ibid. p. 106.
49. Ibid. pp. 17–20, 98–9, 124–6, 163–6.
50. Ibid. p. 130.
51. Ibid. pp. 145–66.
52. According to Palacio, "the perfection of the republican regime requires the existence of a governing class consubstantiated with the public good of a true aristocracy." Ernesto Palacio, *Catilina contra la oligarquía*, Buenos Aires, Rosso, 1935, p. 132.
53. In Sánchez Sorondo´s text, it is worth clarifying, the aristocratic reading of Roman history is not developed in a debate with Machiavelli, but in tune with the elitist and aestheticizing conception of politics that this author attributes to the Florentine.
54. Irazusta, *Tito Livio*, pp. 111–20.
55. Viroli, *De la política a la razón de Estado*, pp. 196–9; Bernard Manin, "Montesquieu, la república y el comercio," in José Antonio Aguilar and Rafael Rojas (eds), *El republicanismo en Hispanoamérica: ensayos de historia intelectual y política*, Mexico, Fondo de Cultura Económica, 2002, pp. 13–56. See also Hulliung, *Citizen Machiavelli*.
56. Irazusta, *Tito Livio*, p. 185.
57. The liberal bias in historiography of the end of the nineteenth century relating to Roman republicanism (among whose members were the authors just mentioned) has been highlighted. See Pierangelo Catalano, "Conceptos y principios del derecho público romano de Rousseau a Bolívar," in *Costituzionalismo Latino: ricerche giuridique e politiche*, Turin, Istituto Universitario di Studi Europei, 1991, pp. 60–74.
58. See Rodolfo and Julio Irazusta, *La Argentina y el imperialismo británico: los eslabones de una cadena, 1806–1933*, Buenos Aires, Tor, 1934. As the title points out, the imperialism denounced here (in relation to the role it had played in Argentine history) was the British one, not the North American.
59. Lugones had also questioned the republic and revindicated the empire. Nevertheless, unlike Irazusta, he had not included Machiavelli among the republican apologists. On the contrary, he exalted Machiavelli for explaining the fall of the empire in his *History of Florence* as a consequence of "the consecutive and combined triumph

of the Church with barbarism": that is, for his anti-clericalism and anti-Christianity (the distortions of the history of Rome, in fact, were also due, according to Lugones, to the "pious fraud" of the Church in documents and writings). Leopoldo Lugones, "Historia del dogma," *Boletín de la Facultad de Derecho y Ciencias Sociales*, I, I, 1921, pp. 51–3, 57–9, 69–74, 82–8 (the whole text, pp. 1–112). On anti-clericalism, see Roberto Di Stefano, *Ovejas negras: historia de los anticlericales argentinos*, Buenos Aires, Sudamericana, 2010.

60. Irazusta, *Tito Livio*, p. 11. In his memoirs, this point is somehow nuanced, pointing out that, when the magazine was created in 1927, he carried out "very careful studies of the political classics," among them Cicero and Machiavelli (he does not mention Livy). If this was the case, he revised his opinions about Machiavelli substantially between that time and the publication of his book on the Roman historian at the beginning of the 1950s. Julio Irazusta, *Memorias (Historia de un historiador a la fuerza)*, Buenos Aires, Ediciones Culturales Argentinas, 1975, p. 179.

61. Palacio, *Catilina*, pp. 168–9; also pp. 7–27. See also Ernesto Palacio, *Historia de Roma*, Buenos Aires, Albatros, 1939. In a similar sense, Joaquín Díaz de Vivar, *Ideas para una biología de la democracia*, Buenos Aires, La Facultad, 1937, pp. 47–65.

62. Fernando Devoto and Nora Pagano, *Historia de la historiografía en la Argentina*, Buenos Aires, Sudamericana, 2009, pp. 201–85. See Tulio Halperín Donghi, *Ensayos de historiografía*, Buenos Aires, El Cielo por Asalto, 1996; Alejandro Cattaruzza and Eujanián, Alejandro, *Políticas de la historia: Argentina, 1860-1960*, Buenos Aires, Alianza, 2003.

63. Zuleta Álvarez, *El nacionalismo argentino*, vol. I, pp. 263–414; vol. II, pp. 423–508. This author classifies Palacio and Irazusta in a "republican nationalism." But this category alludes to the priority given to political action (Argentine republican institutions had to be accepted), rather than a position or a doctrinal reflection. See also Leandro Losada, "Las elites y los 'males' de la Argentina: juicios e interpretaciones en tres momentos del siglo XX," *Desarrollo Económico*, vol. 54, 214, 2015, pp. 387–409; Fernando Devoto, "Acerca de la clase dirigente como problema en el pensamiento de la derecha nacionalista argentina," in Carlos Altamirano and Adrián Gorelik (comps.), *La Argentina como problema*, Buenos Aires, Siglo XXI, 2018, pp. 207–21.

64. Palacio, *Teoría del Estado*, pp. 16, 22, 118.

65. Ibid. p. 49.

66. One of the targets of this criticism is, once again, the Roman tradition: its Ciceronian "legal and regulatory spirit," which "has disturbed all the concepts." Ibid. pp. 86, 119–26.

67. Ibid. pp. 47–59, 61–2.

68. Ibid. pp. 35–45, 71–82, 103–18. Regarding *Catilina* or the *Historia de Roma*, skepticism and criticism of institutional designs persist as

relevant phenomena in the study of politics. One difference is the consideration of the "personal regimes," understood in *Teoría del Estado* as a form of circulation of elites.
69. Palacio, *Catilina*, pp. 178–9.
70. Ibid. pp. 181–2.
71. Irazusta, *Tito Livio*, pp. 100–1.
72. Leonardo Castellani, "Introducción," in Ernesto Palacio, *La historia falsificada*, Buenos Aires, Difusión, 1939, pp. 7 and 24.
73. Julio Irazusta, *La monarquía constitucional en Inglaterra*, Buenos Aires, Eudeba, 1970 (the texts gathered in this volume were written between the 1930s and the 1950s), p. xii.
74. To the authors already mentioned in these pages and the influence of Charles Maurras (addressed in detail by the specialized historiography), Spengler, Toynbee, Ortega y Gasset, Taine, Renan can be added. See, for example, Irazusta, *Tito Livio*, p. 20.
75. Zuleta Álvarez, *El nacionalismo argentino*, vol. II, pp. 441–3, 476–90.
76. Loris Zanatta, *Del estado liberal a la nación católica: iglesia y ejército en los orígenes del peronismo, 1930–1943*, Bernal, Universidad Nacional de Quilmes, 1996; Roberto Di Stefano and Loris Zanatta, *Historia de la Iglesia Argentina: desde la conquista hasta fines del siglo XX*, Buenos Aires, Grijalbo Mondadori, 2000, pp. 412–35.
77. Julio Meinvielle, *Concepción católica de la política* [1932], Buenos Aires, Cursos de Cultura Católica, 1941, p. 45.
78. Ibid. pp. 140–1. More generally, pp. 30–50, 54–8, 137–49.
79. Ibid. pp. 22–30.
80. Ibid. p. 67; see also pp. 137–49.
81. Ibid. p. 56.
82. Ibid. p. 24.
83. All these arguments enable an understanding of why an anti-liberal like Meinvielle kept a doctrinal distance from Fascism. However, it has been pointed out that Meinvielle justified this politically, since as an "economic–political reaction against demo liberalism [. . .] it could be, not only healthy, but also even Catholic." Ibid. p. 27 (footnote). In any case, his distinction between a "Catholic politics" and a "purely right-wing politics," as he expressed it in a controversy with another figure who has already been mentioned in these pages, Marcelo Sánchez Sorondo, was long-lasting. See Dotti, *Carl Schmitt*, pp. 205–6; Zanca, *Cristianos antifascistas*, pp. 58–93.
84. Legón, *Tratado de derecho político general*, vol. I, p. 75; see also 510–13.
85. Faustino Legón, *Cuestiones de política y derecho*, Buenos Aires, Perrot, 1951, pp. 73–4.
86. Sampay, *La crisis del Estado de derecho liberal-burgués*, pp. 12–13.
87. Ibid. pp. 128–32, 156–77, 298–9. Sampay also adopted another widespread reading mentioned in Chapter 2, Machiavelli's association with Nietzsche's "nihilism": p. 209. See also pp. 285–6.

88. Sampay, *Introducción a la teoría del Estado*, pp. 399–400.
89. Ibid. pp. 28–30.
90. Ibid. pp. 464–8. In another text, *La soberanía argentina sobre la Antártida* (1950), Sampay labeled Carl Schmitt a "contemporary Machiavellian." Dotti, *Carl Schmitt*, pp. 135–66, specifically p. 146.
91. Sampay, *Introducción*, p. 465, footnote. A nuance could be included here: there were Catholic intellectuals who, with the purpose of justifying Fascism, connected the negative anthropology of Machiavelli with original sin (and maybe, thus, with a more Augustinian than Thomistic perspective). This is the case with César Pico; Zanca, *Cristianos antifascistas*, p. 81.
92. Tomás Casares, "La política y la moral: a propósito de Maquiavelo (1927)," in Tomás Casares, *Conocimiento, política y moral*, pp. 53–73.
93. Ibid. pp. 72–3.
94. Ibid. p. 62.
95. Ibid. p. 61. In these considerations, throughout the text, the Thomistic distinction between person and individual, reactivated by Maritain, remains (an argument of considerable controversy in the Catholic field; Meinvielle, a critic of Maritain, dismissed it in his text, as mentioned here). It is worth highlighting that the text of Maritain referred to by Casares is one of the most critical for modernity by the French philosopher, *Three Reformers* (1925). See Zanca, *Cristianos antifascistas*, pp. 37–53.
96. Casares, "La política," p. 62.
97. Ibid. p. 61. From this point of view, Machiavelli had had, for Casares, more ground-breaking implications than Kant, since the latter, theorizing "brilliantly about the autonomy of the ethical rule, will say that this autonomous moral law should be erected as a universal rule."
98. Ibid. p. 61.
99. Ibid. pp. 62–3.
100. Ibid. p. 65.
101. Ibid. p. 63.
102. Ibid. pp. 62–3.
103. Sampay, *Introducción*, p. 30. Julio Irazusta also praised Casares's text, qualifying it as "notable": *El pensamiento político nacionalista*, vol. 1, pp. 48–9.
104. The quotes are from Dotti, *Carl Schmitt*, pp. 205–6. More generally, pp. 185–209. It is worth noting the contrast between these arguments and those formulated at that time by figures like Jacques Maritain, who, in the context of the Second World War and criticizing Machiavellianism for being an anti-Christian politics, associated it with totalitarianisms and opposed it to democracy. See Jacques Maritain, "The End of Machiavellianism," *The Review of Politics*, vol. 4, 1, 1942, pp. 1–33.

Chapter 4

# Machiavelli and Freedom

From 1880, the reading of Machiavelli among the intellectuals of Argentine liberalism changed tone and emphasis, compared with the reading in vogue until the mid-nineteenth century among figures such as Sarmiento or Alberdi. He was no longer an author associated with arbitrariness, tyranny, and personal power, or with a way of exercising power that supposed the denial or absence of any regulatory context. Instead, according to authors such as García Mérou or Rizzi, Machiavelli was responsible for creating concepts and instruments in tension with freedom, but not illegal or founded on institutional rupture, as well as strictly defined procedures for government that enabled liberties to be suspended only in exceptional circumstances. Machiavelli was a danger to freedom, but no longer a writer synonymous with an arbitrary personal power, strictly speaking, or even with a substantial denial of freedom. Moreover, because of the objective attributed to his ideas, which was national unification through consolidation of the State (understood as a solution to anarchy rather than a passage to oppression or despotism), his arguments could be linked to individual freedom and security. It is worth recalling García Mérou's words about the State being the "first need of the man."

Certainly, suspicions and misgivings about Machiavelli had not evaporated as concerns preoccupying those linked with the liberal tradition, and not only in Argentina. His relationship with an aggressive form of State, the State-Power, in tension with the rule of law, militarist nationalism, and imperialism — a reading that, as seen in Chapter 1, had become popular in the Western world by the turn of the twentieth century and was, in fact, defined by contemporaries as the reason for a renewed interest in his work and postulates — indicates that the conception of his thinking as a danger for freedom remained valid and persistent.

This idea gathered traction with the outbreak of the First World War and in the post-war scenario, a time when contributions connecting Machiavelli with arbitrariness, violence, and, more specifically, the enemies of liberal democracy, multiplied. It has been seen that this earned the praise of Leopoldo Lugones, even as it was the subject of vigorous debate by university intellectuals of the 1920s, from Enrique Martínez Paz to Carlos Sánchez Viamonte. Similar events may be observed among the intellectuals and leading figures of Argentine liberalism of that time.

## Uncertainty, Indeterminacy, and Freedom

José Nicolás Matienzo (1860–1936) was one of the most eminent constitutionalists of Argentina in the second half of the nineteenth century and early decades of the twentieth. A Professor of Constitutional Law, and also of Civil Law, at the Faculty of Social and Legal Sciences of the Universidad de la Plata (where he was also Dean in the 1910s), he was also Professor and Dean of the Faculty of Philosophy and Literature of the Universidad de Buenos Aires. He played a major role in the public sphere as Argentina's Minister of the Interior in 1923, and was behind a constitutional reform process that eventually foundered.

Matienzo saw in Machiavelli an enemy of freedom, in similar fashion to "founding fathers" such as Sarmiento or Alberdi in the nineteenth century, and made a connection between realism and authoritarianism. In his opinion, realism was invoked by "practical men," disdainful "of those they label theoreticians," to do away with norms and institutions. Constitutional principles were "frequently violated with an expressed sophism of disdain for theory, accompanied almost always by the other concept, as well-known as it is immoral, that the end justifies the means, and with different fallacies as explained in the textbooks of logic."[1]

Nevertheless, other readings were appearing at the same time. Machiavelli, still the object of disdain or reprobation, started to be separated from unequivocal doctrinal positions. Rather than an undisputed and obvious symbol of the dangers threatening freedom, he began to be seen as the author of a work with an open political meaning, a writer who could be invoked for different and even contrasting appropriations. He was an enigma, the architect of indeterminate thought, and likely to be invoked on the basis of all kinds of dissimilar objectives and principles.²

It has been pointed out in Chapter 2 that some intellectuals related realism to uncertainty and indeterminacy, on the one hand, and on the other, to a perspective conducive to accepting things "as they are," and from that, to accepting democracy. Juan Agustín García was an example of the first type of reading: Machiavelli, as an author of "fortune," had taught that the present and future were not determined in advance, but depended on the will (and agency) of human beings. It is important to recall and underline that, in this reading, the importance of fortune in political and historical development was not associated with a validation of strong leadership or exceptional personalities, but strictly with the need to take into account the fact that the present and future were open to what political society was willing to do with them. From this point of view, Machiavelli had highlighted the freedom of action that is constitutive of the human condition.

The second type of reading, instead, became current among those intellectuals linked to liberalism who were disenchanted with the promises of democracy but, at the same time, not very enthusiastic about the authoritarian and anti-liberal proposals of the interwar decades. In these circumstances, Machiavellian realism was invoked to maintain that democracy, in a society like Argentina's, marked from its very beginning by egalitarianism and equality of conditions (a self-portrait with long roots and enduring projections), was an inalterable reality and there were no alternative or effective solutions to its difficulties and setbacks. This approach, besides being a weary acceptance of democracy, prompted or, at any rate, reflected a conservative sensitivity, nervous about the sudden and structural possibilities of change, whatever these might be. In Argentina, this materialized in a conservatism of liberal tone (the legacy to be preserved was the 1853–60 Constitution), which, on occasions, also shone a light on the conservative effects of universal suffrage, meaning its character as an antidote to either left- or right-wing extremism.²

Additionally, a portrayal of Machiavelli as the author of a work with an open political meaning could be found among other liberal intellectuals of the 1910s to 1940s, such as José Bianco. Like the many other figures already mentioned in these pages, Bianco was linked to the 1918 University Reform and was a Professor of Law at the Universidad de La Plata, where he also gave a seminar called "The History of Representative Institutions," whose contents were published in 1919 under the title *Vida de las instituciones políticas*.

In that text, Bianco displayed no interest in the doctrinal affiliation of Machiavelli's ideas, but rather delved into another of the most frequently discussed issues that came up when dealing with his thought: the separation between politics and morals. Bianco, like other authors already mentioned (inscribed within different philosophical perspectives, from Catholic to neo-Kantian), maintained the need for both to converge, proposing a counterpoint with the Florentine author. "Morals and politics, the science of the government and the science of private behavior, cannot be disassociated, no matter the qualification given to them by their exponents in the examination of the facts." As was said in another passage, with a Kantian echo, this separation "invalidates the categorical imperative in the life of institutions."[3] Still, Bianco was not among those who held that the separation between politics and morals in Machiavelli implied a political justification of immorality. On the contrary, he understood that it supposed, strictly speaking, the recognition of the "moral indifference" of politics, and, because of that, its autonomous nature, endowed with a single morality, a "political morality."

Beyond this, the emphasis to be highlighted here is on Bianco's observation that Machiavelli's concepts, especially in *The Prince*, had been recovered as much by the apologists of despotism as the friends of freedom:

> In pages exalted by freedom and despotism at the same time, Machiavelli classifies all the perversions, raising them to the level of indestructible principles guiding nations and rulers. For many, those pages are a reflection of the truth, which the eminent author exhibits with brutal eloquence, intending to provoke, by using contrast, arrogance, and decorum, a sense of righteousness and character. For others, instead, [these pages] were the logical discipline that conquers government with simulation and treachery [...]. From this point of view, Machiavelli is the author that most accurately traces the perimeter of political morality.[4]

As may be seen, Bianco refers to the reading tradition that took *The Prince* as a veiled message denouncing tyrannies, the reason why Machiavelli could be conceived of as an author writing in defense of freedom and no longer only, or not mainly, an author writing in support of power.

In another text from the 1920s, Bianco went further with this argument. This is revealing, as he recognized additionally that, until then, "without knowing him, I used to quote his opinions" due to a "resistance [to reading him] for reasons of prejudice."

Reviewing his point of view prompted him to define Machiavelli as an "immortal spirit seeking freedom with the same procedures he uses to engender dictatorship."

The key to Machiavelli, for Bianco, was that he produced an "enigmatic formula." He was an author riddled with duplicity, not in the sense of hypocrisy, but because he had produced a work of such an open nature. He had a "double personality." He was "a double writer and a double philosopher." *The Prince* was a "double book that may and should be read according to the ideological tenets of the reader." That indeterminate aspect of his work, rather than the fact that he was a symbol of the times (as was maintained by those who had linked Machiavelli to the rise in support for totalitarianism in the interwar period), was what supported his timeliness and validity:

> His books, or rather, his book [*The Prince*] is a book of the present [. . .] Machiavelli is not an author that goes out of date [. . .] Machiavelli has no posterity. Machiavelli lives with you [. . .]. He provides comfort in times of trouble, stimulates political energies, provokes all kinds of rebellion and attains the consecration with which posterity substantiates all those who are overbearing.[5]

Juan Pedro Ramos (1878–1958), a jurist who held the chair of Criminal Law at the Universidad de Buenos Aires shortly after the 1918 University Reform and who became the Dean of the Faculty of Law of this institution, issued a similar judgement. When he completed his reading of *The Prince*, he observed that:

> the enigmatic figure of the great Florentine was on my mind all day long like some huge obsession [. . .]. He surprises me, I admire him, he moves me and I repudiate him at the same time. I am not able to draw the dividing line between the form of the book and the purpose that inspired it. It is magnificent, but it also gives a wicked man the certainty that Machiavelli is on his side. What does it matter if it is not true? I am sure that it is not so.

Mockery of Machiavelli, according to Ramos, stemmed from the fact that,
> when we read him, we admire him or we hate him because we are in the presence of one of the deepest spirits of this wretched humanity which always posited as an irrefutable principle underpinning its norms of social behavior, that the truth is something that should never be spoken.[6]

Another revealing testimony of the shifts in interpretation concerning Machiavelli, or, at any rate, the "open" character of his work, is offered by another previously mentioned author, Ernesto Quesada. In his piece about the government of Juan Manuel de Rosas, published in the last years of the nineteenth century, as explained in Chapter 1, Machiavelli was synonymous with the reason of State (Quesada had discussed the definition of that experience in Argentine political history as tyranny). Instead, in other later texts, anchored in a sociological perspective and focusing on the *Discourses* instead of *The Prince*, Quesada saw in Machiavelli a thinker whose axes of thought concerned individuals and their interests. His main teaching was a "utilitarian and absolutist individualism, which submits social organization to what is convenient, making it dependent on individual interests."[7]

Quesada's example, from this point of view, is symptomatic of a change of register: Machiavelli went from being an author invoked to provide historical legitimacy for an authoritarian political cycle, to being associated with a conception of society structured around individuals and their interests. In other words, the emphasis moved from non-liberal concepts and principles to a representation of society which could be assimilated within a liberal reading.

## Republicanism, Liberalism, and Democracy

It is time to reintroduce the reading carried out by Mariano de Vedia y Mitre. As was mentioned in Chapter 2, De Vedia was a leading figure in Argentine academia following the 1918 University Reform.[8] As a Professor of Political Law at the Universidad de Buenos Aires, he was a pioneer in analyzing Machiavelli's work at the university. Proof of this is a collective volume published in 1927 following a seminar he gave at the Faculty of Law, the first academic book devoted entirely to the analysis of his work in Argentina.[9] De Vedia later focuses sustained attention on Machiavelli between the 1930s and 1950s in his courses on Political Law (which were produced in several editions) and in his *Historia general de las ideas políticas*, the first comprehensive work on this matter in Argentina, published in 1946 in thirteen volumes.[10]

Throughout his texts, De Vedia unfurled a conception of Machiavelli's thought that presented no major changes in interpretation. There were four axes or arguments articulated. First, the Florentine author had been a "genius," the father of modern political thought and modern political science. Second, his stature as an author was unquestionable because he had produced an "immortal" and coherent work, not something disperse, fragmentary, or opportunistic. In this vein, De Vedia considered his main text to be the *Discourses* rather than *The Prince*, as was usually the case in the readings prevailing in Argentina until then. The other two axes supported the doctrinal definition he gave to his thought. Machiavelli had not been an apologist of immorality or despotism. He had, instead, been a champion of freedom and a republican emblem, who had written in the interests of the "people."

For De Vedia, Machiavelli had been a ground-breaking thinker, the founder of modern political science (who, at the same time, provided knowledge on which to base the "art of government") due to "his absolutely original conception of politics as a science independent of morality, which does not respond to preconceptions or established rules."[11] Once again, realism was the foundation used to posit such a separation: "the absolute separation between politics and morals did not appear to be either hypothesis or abstraction, since it was, on the contrary, a real fact."[12] All these reasons construed Machiavelli as the architect able to overcome the medieval conception of politics. More specifically, De Vedia highlighted: "His thought is the antithesis to that of St Thomas."[13]

Based on these considerations, and similarly to what was seen above in the case of Bianco, De Vedia refuted Machiavelli's association with immorality. The accusation was unfair, precisely because morality and politics were vast fields, independent of one another. However, throughout De Vedia's texts, there are at least two other arguments that must be highlighted because they are not devoid of contradictions and, in turn, outline the doctrinal characterization with which he viewed Machiavelli.

The first argument maintained that accusations of immorality were inappropriate because Machiavelli lived in a time that was different than the present where he was judged, a time where moral criteria were quite different than contemporary ones: "It is evident that the morality of our times would turn against the thought of a man who lived, thought and wrote in such an extraordinary political and social context": that is, the Renaissance, where "astuteness and mistrust were the order of the day."[14]

These assertions, which agree with those of Sarmiento or Alberdi, for example, for whom Machiavelli was also a symbol of a controversial historical moment, differ when it comes to the particular version of history underlying them. The "founding fathers" based their criticism on a notion of history as progress that condoned an objection to the past from the present. De Vedia's assertions, instead, are underpinned by a relativist historicism that, in understanding that present and past are immeasurable moments, turned such objections into something inappropriate, if not arbitrary. In fact, a conviction that they were living in times that had managed to dissolve the certainties and expectations of progress sustained De Vedia's assertions as he challenged Machiavelli's critics. "We could wonder what the judgements of times to come will make of these writers who, in the name of today's morality—such an unstable morality as has tolerated the unprecedented events of the 1914 conflagration – condemn Machiavelli's morality."[15]

However, this relativist historicism could also be turned against the defense of Machiavelli since, by definition, it undermined both his "modern" character (or, more precisely, the contemporary aspect of this, as he was from a period that could not be compared with the present) and his status as an author (merely a witness of his times). It challenged the merits afforded to his political science, based on the fact that "men and the elements follow the same rules and wield the same power today as in ancient times." Furthermore, a refutation of the accusations of immorality in the name of Renaissance morality clashed, ultimately, with the vaunted separation between morals and politics. This was because if what was judged as immoral was not so when reintroduced in the context of its time, the actions (and qualities) that Machiavelli taught as political (the case mentioned by De Vedia is Cesare Borgia's "massacre of Sinigaglia") then emerged as products of the morality prevalent in Italy in the fifteenth and early sixteenth centuries.[16]

At all events, in these assertions, there is an aspect that should be highlighted, as it supersedes the ideas of several authors already analyzed in these pages. This is the characterization of Machiavelli as an expression of the Renaissance. In some cases, this was done to emphasize his importance and the relevance of his ideas (regardless of the principles attributed to him). In other cases, the purpose was to debate or even dismiss his relevance. The Renaissance represented the end of the Middle Ages, but, at the same time, enjoyed an ambiguous relationship with modernity (arising from the recovery of classical antiquity that also characterized it). It was also the object of controversy for its relationship with the Protestant Reformation, as the historical moment when the individual and worldliness were vindicated in the face of the transcendent dimension. At the same time, this was a period of history when individualism manifested itself in selfish acts and corruption, in privacy and withdrawal, as well as in vitality and creation, genius and treachery, in artists and *condottieri*. All these traits are given correspondingly greater or lesser importance by the writers discussed to support their appreciations of Machiavelli and the historical relevance of his thought (whether this was about his modernity, immorality, bourgeois character, praise of strong human beings and hierarchies, apostate contents, or "liberalism"). These features were visible in studies of the Renaissance which were repeated in common or transversal bibliographical references, despite the many different political positions and interpretative emphases, particularly in Jacob Burckhardt, Thomas Macaulay, Marcelino Menéndez y Pelayo, or Wilhelm Oncken.[17]

The second argument developed by De Vedia to refute the accusations of immorality leveled against Machiavelli refers more directly to the contents of his work. In this aspect, an accusation of immorality was inappropriate because of recognition of the incommensurability between morals and politics. Even when the political convenience of and need for morally censurable behaviors were pointed out, this should not be used to obstruct the fact that Machiavelli had never written in praise of immorality. De Vedia underlined that the *virtù* of the prince was not moral virtue (nor classical civic virtue). It included learning to be cruel if necessary, and knowing that it was preferable to be feared than to be loved. And it also consisted in a willingness that, as exemplified by Cesare Borgia, allowed one to dominate fortune.

However, in one sense, this advice did not transmit his convictions, but rather his "realism," which taught that human beings were not to be trusted.

> Machiavelli is not the enemy of goodness or sincerity, but neither does he believe that man is faithful to these and, therefore, will not act accordingly towards anyone who proceeds with loyalty and sincerity [. . .]. If he can be good, he should not do otherwise, but in case of dire need, he must.[18]

Machiavelli taught that human beings should learn to be bad, but this does not mean that they should stop being good. He had separated politics and morals, but "nowhere does he praise immorality."[19]

Second, an accusation of immorality against Machiavelli was inappropriate, according to De Vedia, because his political goals included objectives that were moral, not merely political. Morally reprehensible actions were acceptable only when the end sought was beneficial for the majority: "For Machiavelli, the wickedness of the sovereign, or his bad faith, is justified only when an ultimate higher good for the majority of the people is in view."[20]

What was that "higher good"? To create laws and, through them, according to De Vedia, to introduce the notions of good and evil, unknown among human beings due to their constitutive amorality. The negative anthropology of Machiavelli (emphasizing amorality more than immorality) did not justify either arbitrariness or force. In this context, the figure of the prince was that of the great legislator:

> For him [Machiavelli] men are neither good nor bad; they are simply amoral. This does not mean that, for him, men cannot be good, but that, for this to happen, it is necessary that they acquire the awareness that they do not have originally: an awareness of justice, that is, the difference between good and evil [. . .]. This is not acquired but comes about as a consequence of political coexistence, according to what is stated by Machiavelli in the "Discourses." And to say that is tantamount to saying the State, civil life, under the rule of the laws, because it is about them, their application and their knowledge, and from all of this shall be born a moral conscience. Thus it may be deduced, even though Machiavelli [. . .] has not said as much, that the State fulfils a moral purpose.[21]

In sum, De Vedia refuted the accusation of immorality by arguing that the purpose of politics in Machiavelli was not morally neutral, thus blurring the separation between morals and politics, and even moralizing politics. De Vedia himself recognized that it was somewhat forced to attribute to Machiavelli the conception that the State fulfilled a "moral purpose." He did not say as much explicitly, but it could be "deduced" from his work:

> It would seem [. . .] that this [Machiavelli] had conceived of the State as having an end in itself. But, fatally, it would have to contribute to shaping that moral conscience, as it is a natural phenomenon that, ultimately, Machiavelli never denied.[22]

De Vedia put forth similar arguments when he addressed one of the most controversial concepts with which Machiavelli had been associated, reason of State:

> Machiavelli is considered – which is correct – to be the founder of the theory of the "reason of State," according to which abuse of

the rights of others, abuse of morality and good faith, and even life, are justified, when a reason of State exists. And the common phrase that "the end justifies the means" which, as has been said, is the essence of Machiavellian criteria, can be acceptable to him only insofar as the end that justifies the means is a good end, an honest end, an end that ensures the common good.[23]

This "good," "honest end," for De Vedia, was the freedom of the people:

> According to his thought, the reason of State consists of the freedom of the people, the equality of all the inhabitants of the country, and only before this superior objective can the prince break his pledge of faith.[24]

Machiavelli was thus also an author who wrote in support of freedom. This was the case, in addition, because he had been a theorist of the State, even of the reason of State, as a principle of government. The "preservation of the State" that underpinned Machiavelli's advice, according to De Vedia, referred on occasion to the preservation of the "State of the prince," to his staying in power. But it went further, because it also alluded to the preservation of a State in the modern sense, of a legal and sovereign nature, ensuring the freedom (and moral education) of the people. In sum, in De Vedia's opinion, the reason of State in Machiavelli was not a principle that could be deployed by the ruler in extraordinary circumstances to suspend liberties (as Quesada, for example, had argued in *La Época de Rosas*), but quite the opposite: a principle that must be followed in order to defend freedom at all costs.

From this point of view, it may be seen just how distant these considerations are from other previous and contemporary views that have already been analyzed. In this reading of Machiavelli, first of all, politics is not separated from moral horizons. The reason for this was, on the one hand, that the separation of politics and morals did not imply an incompatibility between them, nor the validation of immorality. On the other hand, it also could be seen in the fact that Machiavelli's politics, according to De Vedia, were not "morally indifferent" (to use José Bianco's expression), but pursued ends, and not only processes, which could, and even should, be both political and moral at the same time. This was his understanding of the legislative action taken by the prince, and freedom.[25] It is worth recalling that this had not been emphasized by other authors who had praised Machiavelli for reasons similar to De Vedia's. For García Mérou and Rizzi, for example, Machiavelli, by proposing the consolidation of the State or specific government procedures in exceptional circumstances, had postulated political solutions to strictly political problems. From the opposite angle, denouncing Machiavelli as the author who advocated evil was not merely supported by moral arguments (which could be judged to be inappropriate due to the amorality of politics). Machiavelli had been objected to for reducing politics to "effectiveness" or for expressing uniquely political ills, as, in fact, was the case with those who condemned him for exposing, through his realism, a "natural politics" defined by force and violence, or for being a key author for authoritarianism.

Second, for several authors analyzed here, Machiavelli had been a theorist – even a foundational one – of the modern State, a crucial figure for sovereignty and an exponent of the reason of State. This is also the case with De Vedia.[26] His counterpoints, therefore, are evident as regards those who associated Machiavelli exclusively with a reprehensible form of government such as tyranny, attaching to it, in turn, the reason of State. In fact, De Vedia criticized the way the Generation of 1837 had understood the Florentine author.[27] But his arguments also clash with those who had portrayed him as a theorist of the State. In this counterpoint, two axes may be differentiated.

The first is the relation between State and freedom. In De Vedia's reading, there is no tension between one and the other, as posited, for example, by Alberdi, who was criticized by De Vedia for the arguments that he expounded in works such as *La omnipotencia del estado es la negación de la libertad individual*.[28] His point of view stands opposed, in another sense, to the inexorable "statolatry" arising from the irresolvable modern aporia that aspired to freedom through a State based on an immanent politics, proposed by key figures of Catholic thought such as Tomás Casares. It is worth recalling that, for this jurist, the consolidation of State omnipotence and the appearance of liberalism were associated, inasmuch as they were possible thanks to the autonomization of politics from a transcendent dimension. But ultimately, State and freedom were incompatible and this made despotism unavoidable. However, for De Vedia, the consolidation of sovereignty and the State was a necessary condition for freedom (his position, in this sense, is closer to the one mentioned in connection with García Mérou). In this line of argument, he took a step away from writers like Sánchez Viamonte, who saw in sovereignty the root of arbitrariness and demanded, in consequence, that the pillars of State action be reformulated as a public service.

These controversies are manifestations of the broader debate taking place in Argentine political and legal thought during the 1920s and 1930s, which concerned the relation between State and society.[29] This debate featured, prominently, the criticism of sovereignty on the basis of arguments and principles that were very different to each other, ranging from classical iusnaturalism to public service associated with jurists like León Duguit. De Vedia was a critic of all those perspectives that objected to sovereignty, whether this was "individualistic liberalism" (as he labeled nineteenth-century classical liberalism, in which he included Alberdi), or Duguit himself. Similarly, he considered the work of Thomas Aquinas to have been overtaken by that of Machiavelli, defined by "the incoherence [. . .], the contradiction in the foundation of institutions," whose distinctions between eternal law, natural law, human law, and divine law were irrelevant for the present: "This classification [. . .] would probably not enter into any current classification made of the law, even by the most deeply religious spirits."[30] In the face of all this, De Vedia y Mitre adhered to legal positivism, in line with the theory of self-limitation of State sovereignty. In his opinion, this cleared away any danger of arbitrariness (that is, from a perspective also opposed to that formulated by Lugones, for whom State sovereignty and legal positivism could "suspend personal guarantees" if "necessity" demanded it). The controversies around Machiavelli as the founder (or not, depending on the case) of the modern concept of the State and its relation with freedom were a dimension not only of the debates about his work and his thought, but also of the discussions taking place about the State and its foundations and its limits.[31]

In this area, a second counterpoint between De Vedia and other – not only Argentine – writers, who defined Machiavelli as a theorist of the State, is that his considerations about this matter were at odds with those of intellectuals and scholars with whom he otherwise shared certain perspectives and references. This is the case with the Spaniard Adolfo Posada. Like De Vedia, Posada linked State with freedom, and the German theory of the self-limitation of State authority was a theoretical reference to be found in both men's writings. Also evident was the influence of Krausism, a current of thought inspired by the German philosopher Karl Christian Friedrich Krause (1781–1832), which had a great impact on Spanish and Hispanic-American political and legal thinking, and featured a search for convergence between morality, politics, and justice.[32]

From this point of view, attributing to Machiavelli the notion of a State with a moral purpose could be connected with the Krausist influences in De Vedia. However, this was not the case for another Krausist like Posada. It is worth recalling that, according to the Spanish jurist, Machiavelli was the author of a reprehensible model of State: the State-Power or State-Force, which lacked all ethical purpose and represented a threat to freedom. In this context, De Vedia's reading appears as a very personal interpretation, which may be seen in his observation that the conception of a State with moral ends may be "deduced" from the work of Machiavelli, instead of being an explicit postulate.[33]

However, other arguments he made are similar to those postulated by the historian José Luis Romero. As was seen in Chapter 2, Romero had both objected to the way in which "Machiavelli" was characterized and given moral meanings to the Florentine's work. He asserted that the author of the *Discourses* had clashed with the "politics of concealment," and that his writings had been guided by a clear purpose: "to call things by their name."[34]

Romero also pointed out that Machiavelli's prince was a great legislator and a founder of the State ("he is basically the sage of Greek tradition, the philosopher–king to whom Plato aspired"), whose laws "educated" individuals by promoting the common good and inhibiting selfish passions. The prince "ensures the '*vivere civile*' and forestalls a natural human tendency to 'corruption,' which is nothing but the prevalence of selfish impulses over the demands of the 'common good.'"[35] For Romero, then, the prince was a constructive, rather than a destructive, figure, and thus he did not see in Machiavelli's reasoning any contradiction between *virtù* and moral virtue, but between *virtù* and fortune: that is, "between human will and the forces beyond his power."[36]

A similar appreciation had been proffered earlier, in the 1910s (Romero's book is from the 1940s), by Nicolás Bessio Moreno (1879-1962). In his opinion, morality, virtue, and freedom were blended to portray Machiavelli as someone who had fought against feudalism and proposed violence in order to achieve good:

> Machiavelli's morality consists of proclaiming the existence of virtue, as long as its exercise is advantageous for man and society, and he prescribes violence to achieve good. His doctrine is another correction to the morality we commented on; he combats feudalism as the enemy of freedom, since, for him, this can only be born of equality.[37]

In doctrinal terms, but as a corollary to the disquisitions concerning the relationship between morals and politics, and the characteristics of the figure of the prince, De Vedia defined Machiavelli as the stronghold of republicanism. That meant, in his reading, that he was an author writing in support of freedom. That is, he was a stronghold of republicanism for his conception of the State, which proposed a convergence between State authority and freedom, as well as for his political sympathies and the form of government he lauded. These considerations were based on a reading which raised certain original points when compared with those prevailing in Argentina until then. One is the relative importance attributed to his main texts. The second is the conception of the ideas or arguments that, according to De Vedia, articulated Machiavelli's republicanism: patriotism, freedom, and mixed government (to which may be added the central role played by the law – which, in Vedia's view, was an instrument of moral education and freedom, not of oppression – in the thought of the Florentine).

Regarding the first point, De Vedia conceived of the *Discourses* as the main text and *The Prince* as a complement to this. This consideration was based on a singular interpretation of the latter. Its objective (as is clear from what has been seen so far) was not the justification of arbitrariness or immorality, but the achievement of Italian unification through the construction of a sovereign State: "it is clear and forthright [. . .] that 'The Prince' in itself is merely the chapter of the 'Decades of Titus Livy' that Machiavelli devoted to the ideal of Italian union."[38] For that reason, its key chapter was not one of those most frequently alluded by the thinkers objecting to Machiavellianism, such as Chapters XVII or XVIII, but the last one, Chapter XXVI, which contains "the exhortation to free Italy of the barbarians."[39]

According to De Vedia, in *The Prince*, Machiavelli had discussed an exceptional situation and his maxims were, therefore, those necessary for extraordinary circumstances. In the *Discourses*, instead, he produced a general reflection on politics, and thus, this was where the genuine Machiavelli, a republican committed to freedom, appeared:

> the essential train of his thought is contained in the *Discorsi*, where he reasons about the way the people achieve freedom and are governed by it; in *The Prince*, he discusses the means to find a new and absolute monarchy in order to achieve independence and national union.[40]

Furthermore, De Vedia y Mitre underlined that "as Machiavelli was a republican, ideas of a republican cast roam freely through the pages of *The Prince*."[41]

In consequence, the two works were neither unconnected nor dedicated to portraying opposing problems. The subject of *The Prince* was union, while freedom was the main issue in the *Discourses*. Both were linked by an intimate bond. A joint reading of these texts unveiled the author's political ideas, reflecting his true visage: that of a republican for whom political union and freedom were principles or objectives which were not antagonistic but mutually necessary. Machiavelli wrote about power and freedom at the same time because power was not an end in itself, but a means to consolidating freedom.

In addition, those objectives condensed another distinctive trait of his thought, criticism of Christianity and the Church:

> Machiavelli believed, however, that the State should be independent of religious morality and should thus be independent from, and supersede, the Church. For Machiavelli, there should be no other sovereignty than national sovereignty, to whom all corporations, including the Church, should be subordinate. In this sense, he is a harbinger.[42]

As is observed in this paragraph, Machiavelli's concern for Italian political unification projected his texts towards the future. His commitment to the problems of his time, and his patriotic nature, neither invalidated nor diminished his works (as posited by Casares, Sampay, Astrada, and even Romero); on the contrary, these qualities turned him into an author of universal scope.

Besides, Machiavelli's patriotism, even though it initially required a strong (but not arbitrary) government, was intimately linked to freedom. It was not connected to greatness and militarism, as had been posited by Lugones. According to De Vedia, patriotism was one of the aspects that made Machiavelli "passionate for freedom."[43] Throughout his texts, he emphasized "the maintenance of freedom as a cardinal goal of government."[44]

However, what type of freedom did he exalt? The expressions De Vedia repeats most frequently are "freedom of the homeland" and "freedom of the people." These are linked to self-determination, a united Italy freed from the barbarians. From this perspective, De Vedia infers that Machiavelli's disruptive character was aimed at restoring the classical notion of freedom in the Christian world. The

Machiavelli of the *Discourses* appears in general as a commentator of Titus Livy, more than as the author of a contribution that breaks with notions of classical republicanism. Nevertheless, there are also other nuances, since, in his own words, there was a "liberal thought" in Machiavelli.[45]

In fact, in asserting "the maintenance of freedom as the cardinal goal of government," Machiavelli suggests something more than the country's search for self-determination. Freedom was also "equality among all inhabitants": that is, the absence of any internal relations of domination. In the afore-mentioned words of Bessio Moreno, Machiavelli was an author for whom freedom sprang from equality. Moreover, De Vedia highlighted Machiavelli's considerations about the priority human beings gave to freedom, seen as the safety of their goods and person (a position that is certainly a familiar element in the "sociological" reading of Quesada, according to which the axis of Machiavelli's thought was the individual and his interests).[46]

However, De Vedia did not attribute much importance to the possible frictions between "the freedom of the homeland" (understood, in addition, to be the reason of State or common good) and individual liberties. Other authors, inscribed in the liberal tradition, did observe this. José Luis Romero, for example, also portrayed a republican Machiavelli, but pointed out the possibility that the freedom of the homeland, understood as the common good, was invoked precisely in order to undermine individual liberties:

> Astuteness, the artful concealment of plans, the use of force and deception acquire the category of fair means if the ends are guided by the idea of the "common good," a notion that encompasses the idea of patriotism, on the one hand, but also anticipates the modern *raison d'état*. However, not only is the submission of current moral criteria lawful; to subordinate for political purposes all forms of life that, in other circumstances, may be considered ends in themselves is also lawful. Above all, freedom, wherein, as Machiavelli suggests, an inoperative appearance is sufficient to satisfy the people, as Cosimo de Medici must have thought. This is because the freedom of the individual may be considered a manifestation of a "selfish or utilitarian conscience" rather than a moral one, which must be subordinate to the demands of the "common good" through the coercion of the State.[47]

Thus, Romero questioned the importance of freedom for Machiavelli (stating that he stressed that an "inoperative appearance" was sufficient) and identified the possible tensions lying between certain republican topics (like patriotism) and individual liberties. In much the same way as Alberdi or, from another standpoint, Julio Irazusta or Ernesto Palacio had pointed out in their intellectual output, for Romero, Machiavelli could be an author in favor of authoritarianism due to his republicanism – but not for being an apologist of tyranny, proposing the reason of State in favor of the prince, asserting the need to concentrate power in exceptional circumstances, or being a harbinger of Fascism.

De Vedia, on the contrary, proposed a Machiavelli in whom republicanism and liberalism (and democracy) were aligned. To understand this point, a third element that, in his opinion, articulated his republicanism was crucial: mixed government. His adherence to this approach was another inference of his political realism. The realization that there were no pure or optimal forms had turned him into a "determined supporter of mixed government, where three classical forms coexist, and where each power implies a deterrent of the abuses of the other two." De Vedia y Mitre saw in Machiavelli a theorist writing about mixed government which broke with classical forms (even while raising the issue that, in this category, he juxtaposes social groups and institutions), at least in the version coined by Polybius. If, for the latter, the keys were union and cooperation between the parties, for Machiavelli, conflict was the decisive element spurring its (virtuous) dynamics.[48]

On the other hand, mixed government did not require either the sovereignty of the people as its foundation or the homogeneity implicit in the idea of one person, one vote. The equality on which freedom was founded meant an egalitarian participation in public affairs, combined with a recognition of social diversity. But this did not mean a consecration of deferential hierarchies or aristocratic descent, such as that posited by Irazusta or Palacio.

It is worth reproducing *in extenso* how De Vedia interpreted the well-known passage in the fourth chapter of the first book of the *Discourses*, which posits "That the disunion between the people and the senate made that republic free and powerful":

> He takes as an example the government of Rome and says: the republic in Rome pitted the Senate against the government of the consuls, but the people, who did not feel represented in the Senate, were a constant and permanent source of public danger, of conspiracies and seditious movements against the established authority. Machiavelli adds that Rome owes its republican liberties to this dissent between the people and the Senate. If the people had not been alert, with an awakened thought and longing for freedom,

if they had not finally achieved the creation of the tribunes of the people in order to exercise control over the acts of the Senate, the republic would not have happened, and democracy would not have emerged.[49]

As may seen, particular importance is given to conflict, and its relationship with freedom is emphasized. Here, perhaps, is one of the most original contributions made by De Vedia in the context of Argentine readings of Machiavelli. Conflict is not associated with a "biological" politics, nor with a fight for survival where force is imposed, nor with a functional role for the consolidation of arbitrariness (as Martínez Paz, Sánchez Viamonte, or Taborda had held); nor is it associated with the danger of political society falling apart, as, for example, may be read in Romero.[50] For De Vedia, the attention Machiavelli pays to conflict is another reason why he is an author writing in favor of freedom.

He also underlines that, along with the struggle between the great and the people, the democratic element, the existence of democratic institutions (the "tribunes of the people"), is the guarantor of freedom in a republic. That is, the peoples themselves are a cause of freedom. It could even be asserted, following the emphasis of the text, that this a cause that rises above conflict. That is why De Vedia saw Machiavelli as a democratic author: "His thought is essentially democratic."[51] The Florentine author had thought of politics from the perspective of the interests of the people, not of the prince: "Machiavelli does not have in his sights, when he expresses his thought, the interest of the prince, he always bears the interest of the people in mind."[52] This aspect of his thought is further thrown into relief when De Vedia observes that he alerted his readers to the danger of aristocracies for the republic:

> he stays true to the principle that the greatest hindrance to the fortune of the State arises from the behavior and actions of the privileged classes [...]. He states that, while tycoons occupy the State, there cannot be a regime of freedom and equality.[53]

Therefore, Machiavelli was not talking about the opposition between republic and democracy, as posited by Irazusta or Palacio on certain occasions. Neither was he writing in praise of an aristocratic republic. On the contrary, and this is another break with the classics according to De Vedia, he was the first author to conceive of the republic in its modern sense, as a "popular government," just as he did at the beginning of *The Prince*. This assertion shows, once again, that, for De Vedia, the current of Machiavelli's republicanism ran through his two major works.[54]

At the end of the analysis, the lesson De Vedia found in Machiavelli emerges with clarity. He was not a harbinger of Fascism or of an anti-liberal republicanism. In him there was, in fact, a convergence between republicanism, liberalism (in the words of De Vedia himself, in allusion to a commitment to society's external and internal freedoms), and democracy. This mitigated the insufficiencies inherent to each of these traditions taken separately, or at least curtailed their dangers, such as the "individualism" of liberalism or the despotic potential of popular sovereignty.[55]

It is worth highlighting this last argument. In De Vedia's opinion, Machiavellian democracy eclipsed the characterization of Machiavelli as a supporter of an elitist republicanism. However, in turn, the democratic aspects of his work had the singularity of highlighting democratic participation without appealing to the sovereignty of the people. This concept, according to De Vedia, is a harmful one due to its potential for liberticidal projections. For this reason, as will be seen in detail further on, De Vedia insisted throughout his work on drawing a distinction between legal and political notions of sovereignty – whether monarchic sovereignty or popular sovereignty – and vindicated the former over the latter.[56]

De Vedia's contribution is relevant not only because of his arguments, but also because of its more academic approach (which can be traced in his texts and in the syllabi of the course he taught on Political Law), in which he provides information about the sources underlying his arguments.[57] For one thing, and despite the fact that local editions of Machiavelli's works began to be published in the 1930s, the references made by De Vedia allude to Spanish editions. The most quoted among these are the *Obras políticas* translated by Luis Navarro, with editions in 1914 and 1923 (he also refers to the edition of *El príncipe* translated by José Sánchez Rojas, in 1924).[58] De Vedia's scholarly bibliography is a minimal but suggestive indicator of two aspects: that access to Machiavelli's texts in Spanish had already been consolidated, and that the circulation of local editions was still a limited affair, even in those (university and legal) spheres more directly interested in his thought and his work. For that reason, and beyond any academic factors, the consultation of editions in other languages continued to be a feature (the quotations in Romero, for example, referred to Italian editions).

Regarding the references on which his arguments are based (which does not mean, of course, that they were not the result of a direct reading of Machiavelli's texts), these were mostly in works by nineteenth-century Italian and German authors, among many others, as well as more contemporary output. These included writings by Charles Benoist (*Le Machiavélisme de l'anti-machiavel*, 1915 edition), Francesco Ercole (*La política di Machiavelli*, 1926), and Louis de Villefosse (*Machiavel et nous*, 1937). The importance of the Italian and German bibliography deserves to be highlighted, since, in both countries, as was pointed out in Chapters 1 and 3, there was, throughout the nineteenth century, a renewal of interest in Machiavelli's work which was at odds with the views associating him with immorality and tyranny (in Germany, this line of interpretation could be traced back to Hegel and Fichte). There was also a reactivation of interest in his work during the Weimar years and, in Italy, in times of Fascism.

The quotations in De Vedia include exemplary authors and studies on Machiavelli carried out during the Italy of the Risorgimento. This is the case with a critical edition of his works drawn up by Luigi Passerini, Gaetano Milanesi, and Pietro Fanfani, published in the 1870s; the *Historia de la literatura italiana*, by Francesco de Sanctis, of 1870–1871; *La vita e gli scritti di Niccolò Machiavelli nella loro relazione col machiavellismo*, by Oreste Tommasini (two volumes published between 1883 and 1911); and Pasquale Villari, who had highlighted Machiavelli's republicanism and his character as a harbinger of Italian patriotism in his three-volume work published between 1870 and 1880.[59] Then there was Vittorio Emmanuele Orlando, a prominent jurist and Prime Minister of Italy in the second half of the 1910s, to whom De Vedia attributed the view of Machiavelli as the father of the modern notion of State.[60] National union as the main subject of his work (and, therefore, the central aspect of the last chapter of *The Prince*), the consolidation of the State, and his association with the formulation of the concept of reason of State (as well as the afore-mentioned relationship between his works and Renaissance corruption) were common topics in the nineteenth-century German historians quoted by De Vedia. These included Leopold von Ranke and the afore-mentioned Heinrich von Treitschke. In addition, De Vedia referred to Ludwig von Rochau, who coined the expression *Realpolitik*.[61]

The influence of these German references (which were not unknown in Argentina before De Vedia launched his own intellectual production, as shown by the writings of Ernesto Quesada, discussed in Chapter 1) may be related to two points which have already been raised.[62] On the one hand, the influence of Krausism on his education as a jurist may be important: as was stated previously, this could be the reason for some of his considerations about Machiavelli. On the other hand, there was his interest in the historical and legal formation of the rule of law, and his appreciation of the theory of self-limitation of the State sovereignty. This was typical of continental European legal thought in the second half of the nineteenth century, specifically in those countries where the national State had been a recent creation: that is, Italy and Germany. Such a concept justified the so-called "liberal rule of law," by proposing that the conditions for freedom could be met in a legal regime created by a voluntarily self-limited sovereign State. This involved distancing oneself from criticism of the sovereignty of constitutionalism or meta-legal (or iusnaturalist) notions of individual rights, as well as the "political" notions of sovereignty, including the sovereignty of the people affirmed since the French Revolution.[63] The exponents of this current of legal thought are referred to in De Vedia's work (and include Carl Friedrich von Gerber, Georg Jellinek, Rudolf von Ihering, and the Frenchman Raymond Carré de Malberg); some, such as the Italian Vittorio Orlando, as was pointed out, had postulated Machiavelli as the harbinger of the modern notion of State.[64]

There are certain conclusions to be drawn from all of this. In the first place, De Vedia y Mitre's reading indicates the substantial qualitative change in the resources available to those seeking to study Machiavelli in Argentina since the 1920s (influenced, as has been said, by the renewal of university studies in Law and promoted mainly by foreign rather than national editions).

Second, it reflects a judicious and relatively informed bibliographical selection of the debates on Machiavelli's work. To mention two contemporary parameters, different in interpretative terms: round about the same time as De Vedia's first book about Machiavelli was published in 1927, Friedrich Meinecke published *Die Idee der Staatsräson in der neueren Geschichte* (1924) and Hans Baron produced a study introducing the notion of civic humanism, *Leonardo Bruni Aretino: Humanistische-philosophische Schriften mit einer Chronologie seiner Werke und Briefe* (1928). In addition, De Vedia translated and published Mussolini's 1924 text on Machiavelli.[65]

Third, the references of De Vedia y Mitre, more detailed and extensive than those in the other texts discussed here, point to a set of shared and transversal readings, although there are interpretative contrasts indicating more than just his specific preferences. First of all, and in relation to Machiavelli himself, the allusions to *The Prince* are combined with more frequent references to other texts, mainly the *Discourses*, by writers such as Casares, Sampay, Legón, and Romero, although De Vedia stands out in this sense with his proposition of a reading of Machiavelli beginning with the *Discourses*. Regarding commentators and scholars from other latitudes (as well as others such as Astrada), who wielded a different relative weight according to the case in point, these include Villari (to whom Rizzi referred), De Sanctis, Maurice Joly and his *Dialogue aux enfers entre Machiavel et Montesquieu ou la politique de Machiavel au XIXe siècle* (1864, also published in 1898), and the afore-mentioned group of writers consisting of Macaulay, Burckhardt, Ercole, Benoist, and, once again, Treitschke.[66]

Fourth, but in line with the previous point, De Vedia's reading suggests a change in interpretation of Machiavelli, even though there are shared bibliographical references. As may be inferred by what has been said hitherto, the most prominent case is linked to German output at the end of the nineteenth and beginning of the twentieth centuries. Treitschke, as seen in Chapter 1, played a bridging role between Machiavelli and German militarist nationalism. Besides, the consideration of Machiavelli as an author of the State was reflected in how he was attributed a form of the State at odds with the rule of law, State-Power. These arguments were made by writers known in Argentina, whose intellectual references were close to De Vedia's, such as the Spaniard Posada. De Vedia, instead, took his cues from German historiography (including Treitschke himself) and its theory of the State, especially the theory of the self-limitation of State, to portray Machiavelli as a key figure for the rule of law and freedom.[67]

## A Machiavellian Moment in the Spanish-Speaking Atlantic World

It is time for an overview of the issues covered in this chapter and the previous one. It should be said in that respect that it is possible to postulate the existence of a "Machiavellian moment" in Argentina, between the 1920s and the 1940s. This expression has two possible interpretations. On the one hand, it defines a scenario of uncertainty and crisis that fostered political and doctrinal reflection. More literally, on the other hand, it simply refers to the existence of an interest in Machiavelli. The issues covered hitherto sustain both meanings. Interest in the author of the *Discourses* was far greater than in the past (as was the possibility of access to his work, thanks to significant material and institutional changes). Evidence of this is provided by contemporary testimonies emphasizing his "return," his "actuality," and his "validity," as well as the controversies and readings raised by his texts, from many perspectives, from the epistemological to the doctrinal.

However, if one takes an overview of the readings of Machiavelli during this period, it becomes clear that both positive and negative assessments of his writings and thought were sustained by coincidental rather than opposing readings. Individuals from the liberal tradition (like Mariano de Vedia y Mitre and José Luis Romero) joined some of the most representative voices of anti-liberalism (from Ernesto Palacio to Julio Irazusta, including Tomás Casares and Julio Meinvielle) in presenting similar portraits of Machiavelli. He was a symbol of the separation between politics and religion, a key figure in the period ending the "Middle Ages" (statements to which Leopoldo Lugones also subscribed), and an author who was part of the genealogy of liberalism and, in any case, whose work revolved around freedom.

These two last expressions should not be confused, as they do not mean the same thing and may even enter into tension, which was pointed out by many of the writers mentioned. In fact, Romero and De Vedia y Mitre labeled Machiavelli a republican rather than a liberal. It did not go unnoticed, especially for the former, that the freedom of the homeland and individual freedom could clash, leading to the latter being sacrificed in the name of the former. These considerations are telling in themselves because they are a sign (along with some of the observations made by Alberdi or the approaches taken by the nationalists at certain moments, always limiting the field of study to those writers discussed in this book) that liberalism and republicanism were recognized as different political and doctrinal currents. In this respect, it was also pointed out that the relation between them could be vulnerable to tension and did not necessarily tend towards compatibility. Nevertheless, this was not the emphasis that most concerned Argentine scholars writing about Machiavelli between the 1920s and the 1940s. When they addressed his thought, the predominant issue was the overlapping of republicanism and liberalism.

This overlap was supported by different arguments, depending on the case, and these should be differentiated. For some, like Meinvielle or Casares, the main axis was Machiavelli's conception of politics in itself: when he defined this as an autonomous field, he revealed the foundations underpinning liberal thought. His republicanism, in this sense, was a political option (which was not only recognized but given greater importance than his sympathy for "principalities"), which played a subordinate or secondary role in his thought.

From other points of view, this overlap arose instead from the fact that there were no substantial doctrinal differences between republicanism and liberalism. Nationalist authors like Palacio or Irazusta had concluded (starting from inverse premises) that the relation between Roman republicanism and liberalism was one of continuity rather than rupture.[68] According to De Vedia y Mitre, freedom as an essential principle of Machiavelli's work justified the compatibility of, rather than opposition between, his republicanism and his liberalism.

Once again, these comparisons should not overlook important details. One of these is that Machiavelli, as a republican, was understood in general as a revivalist of Roman tradition rather than the creator of an original contribution. Only De Vedia y Mitre made some remarks in this direction, mainly concerning mixed government. This reading, on the other hand, was not conceived of as contradictory to the affirmation of his radical modernity in other domains, whether because of his denial of the transcendence in political life or his character as a theorist of the modern State. Also, the degree of compatibility between republicanism and liberalism turned on a discussion about liberalism in moments of instability, as well as on authoritarianism, both currents flowing through the 1920s–1940s period.

De Vedia y Mitre himself exemplifies these discussions because he distanced himself from the postulates of nineteenth-century "individualist liberalism" and raised, instead, the possibility of convergence between State authority and freedom (a convergence that, certainly, was not original as regards liberal thought in general, particularly in the Argentine one, although De Vedia held that this was so). He pursued this line of thought even as he distanced himself from criticisms of State sovereignty and the theory of self-limitation expressed from perspectives that differed significantly, like Thomism or the work of León Duguit. He was also opposed to those who claimed that the principle of sovereignty was compatible with the suspension of individual liberties, like Lugones. From De Vedia's perspective, Machiavelli's republicanism offered up elements to prompt a renewed reflection on freedom in troubled times, based on realistic thought and not on speculative abstraction, without losing scientific rigor.

From this point of view, republican freedom was not, for De Vedia, an ancient freedom incompatible with modernity, but a notion of freedom that could be reintroduced in contemporaneity: a repertoire useful for dealing with the liberalism inherited from the nineteenth century without breaking with the liberal tradition. This approach was based on another of the lessons found in Machiavelli (and in classical writers, such as Polybius). History did not follow a steadily ascendant and progressive course but was ruled by cycles or even by uncertainty (a cyclical notion offered the possibility of some kind of order). This undermined any conception of the past as obsolete and out of date, or of the present as projected towards a future where nothing that was already known was likely to recur.

Finally, from De Vedia's perspective, Machiavelli also entertained a notion of democracy without appealing to the sovereignty of the people. In his opinion, this argument was attractive as it permitted expression of the reservations aroused by the modern foundation of democracy (particularly because of its potential projection for oppression, in the name of the will of the majority), without needing to turn to an explicitly anti-democratic vocabulary.

## Notes

1. José Nicolás Matienzo, *Nuevos temas políticos e históricos*, Buenos Aires, La Facultad, 1928, pp. 495, 497.
2. Leandro Losada, "Conservadurismo y democracia en Argentina. Formulaciones intelectuales y reflexiones políticas en el pensamiento liberal, 1912–1943," *Cuadernos de Historia Contemporánea*, 2022, 44, pp. 155–74.
3. In this respect, see also the considerations on "political ethics" formulated by another important intellectual and scholar of the first half of the twentieth century, Rodolfo Rivarola (founder and director of the *Revista Argentina de Ciencias Políticas*): "Moralidad de los medios y moralidad de los fines" (1898) and "Los problemas de la moral política: necesidad y posibilidad de estudios universitarios sobre ética política" (1912), both in Rodolfo Rivarola, *Escritos filosóficos*, Buenos Aires, Instituto de Estudios Filosóficos, Facultad de Filosofía y Letras, UBA, 1945, pp. 51–67, 175–88. See Dotti, *La letra gótica*, pp. 154–61.
4. José Bianco, *Vida de las instituciones políticas*, Buenos Aires, Librería Mendesky-Augusto Sabourin e hijo, 1919, pp. 283–5.
5. José Bianco, *Mis lecturas*, Buenos Aires, Librería Mendesky-Augusto Sabourin e hijo, 1920, pp. 231–7.

6. Juan P. Ramos, *Fragmentos de vida*, Emecé, Buenos Aires, 1946, pp. 175–6.
7. Ernesto Quesada, *Las doctrinas presociológicas*, Buenos Aires, Librería de J. Menéndez, 1905, pp. 30–1.
8. Héctor José Tanzi, "La enseñanza de Derecho Constitucional en la Facultad de Derecho de Buenos Aires," *Academia: Revista sobre Enseñanza del Derecho*, 17, 2011, pp. 85–112.
9. de Vedia y Mitre, *Maquiavelo*. See Miguel Ángel Speroni, "Los argentinos y Maquiavelo," in Miguel Ángel Speroni, *Maquiavelo*, Buenos Aires, Santiago Rueda, 1971, pp. 191–3.
10. Mariano de Vedia y Mitre, *Curso de Derecho Político*, Buenos Aires, 1926; *Curso de Derecho Político*, 2 vols, Buenos Aires, Biblioteca Jurídica, 1934; *Derecho Político General*, 2 vols, Buenos Aires, Kraft, 1952.
11. De Vedia y Mitre, *Maquiavelo*, pp. xx-xxi.
12. Ibid., p. xxiii.
13. De Vedia y Mitre, *Derecho Político*, 1934, vol. 1, p. 279.
14. Ibid. p. 281.
15. Ibid. p. 287.
16. It is worth saying that these arguments also clashed with the moral relativism being claimed: the Renaissance was not comparable with the present, but its morality was judged "immoral."
17. De Vedia, for example, appealed to Macaulay for a contrast between the present day and the Renaissance, referring his observations to the judgements dealt out to the Shakespearean characters Othello and Iago. If, nowadays, one's empathy lies with the first, for the people of the Renaissance age Iago was the condensation of cunning and skill. De Vedia y Mitre, *Maquiavelo*, p. xviii.
18. De Vedia y Mitre, *Historia general de las ideas políticas*, vol. 5, pp. 325–6.
19. De Vedia y Mitre, *Derecho Político*, 1934, vol. 1, p. 280.
20. Ibid. p. 277.
21. De Vedia y Mitre, *Historia general*, vol. 5, pp. 387–8.
22. Ibid. p. 388.
23. De Vedia y Mitre, *Derecho Político*, 1934, vol. 1, p. 278.
24. Ibid. p. 286.
25. On this topic, see Isaiah Berlin, "La originalidad de Maquiavelo," in Isaiah Berlin, *Contra la corriente: ensayos sobre historia de las ideas*, Mexico, Fondo de Cultura Económica, 1992, pp. 85–143.
26. The association of Machiavelli with sovereignty comes from his portrayal as a theorist of the State, as well as his decisive role in the autonomization of politics, more than from the definition or the theoretical development of the concept itself, in the manner of Bodin and Hobbes. Certainly, there were authors who relativized or disputed his inaugural stature regarding specifically the paternity

of the modern notion of State: Legón, *Tratado de derecho político general*, vol. 1, pp. 34–5; Arturo Sampay, *Introducción a la teoría del Estado*, p. 369. The latter, in previous texts, had established a more direct bond between Machiavelli and the modern notion of State: *La crisis del Estado de derecho liberal-burgués*, pp. 156–8. It is worth specifying that, in these two authors, one dimension of the criticism of the modern notion of sovereignty discussed its originality compared to the "Aristotelian-scholastic" notion of "perfection": Sampay, *Introducción*, pp. 393–400; Legón, *Tratado de derecho político*, vol. 2, pp. 201–15. See Fernando Segovia, "El derecho entre iusnaturalismo, decisionismo y personalismo: Arturo Sampay lector de Carl Schmitt," *Anales de la Fundación Francisco Elías de Tejada*, 20, 2014, pp. 133–56. On Machiavelli and the modern notion of State, see, for example, Corrado Vivanti, *Maquiavelo: los tiempos de la política*, Buenos Aires, Paidós, 2013, pp. 191–216.

27. De Vedia y Mitre, *Historia de las ideas*, vol. 13, pp. 52–3.
28. Ibid., pp. 165–73.
29. Eduardo Zimmermann, "Constitucionalismo argentino, siglos XIX y XX: poderes y derechos," in Catherine Andrews (ed.), *Un siglo de constitucionalismo en América Latina (1917–2017)*, Mexico, CIDE-Secretaría de Relaciones Exteriores-Archivo General de la Nación, 2017, pp. 1–32.
30. De Vedia y Mitre, *Derecho político*, 1934, vol. 1, pp. 233–4. He also understood that there was a "contradiction" in his considerations about the forms of government and only alluded to the "long prestige" of his work for the "doctrine of freedom," which De Vedia saw in his "repudiation of tyranny," pp. 238–9. On Duguit, *Derecho político*, 1934, vol. 1, pp. 78–81, 136–41; *Derecho político*, 1952, vol. 2, pp. 331–4, 373–8, 427–34.
31. Leandro Losada, "El Derecho Político y las controversias acerca de la soberanía: Argentina, 1910–1940," *Cuadernos del Instituto Antonio de Nebrija - Revista de Historia de las Universidades*, vol. 24, 2, 2021, pp. 167–96; Leandro Losada, "Soberanía y libertad: balances y diagnósticos de Mariano de Vedia y Mitre sobre el liberalismo (Argentina, 1920–1950)," *Anuario IEHS*, 33, 2, 2018, pp. 39–60.
32. On Krausism in De Vedia y Mitre, Raúl Arlotti, "Las primeras lecciones de Derecho Político en la Facultad de Derecho y Ciencias Sociales de la UBA," pp. 125–49. See also Arturo Andrés Roig, *Los krausistas argentinos*, Puebla, Cajica, 1969; Dotti, *La letra gótica*, pp. 72–94.
33. De Vedia argued with Posada in his writings. *Derecho Político*, 1934, vol. 1, 95–100; *Derecho Político*, 1952, vol. 2, 451–53.
34. Romero, *Maquiavelo historiador*, p. 18.
35. Ibid. p. 73.
36. Ibid. p. 93. More generally, pp. 89–96. Certainly, the "constructive labor" of the prince and the "will" were attributes that, for their

intrinsic ambiguity, could well be emphasized from other political coordinates. In fact, those who read Machiavelli in an authoritarian key or as a harbinger of Fascism – for example, Lugones or Sánchez Sorondo – did so.

37. The text appeals to Kant for a proposal for a convergence between morality and freedom, and therefore includes Machiavelli among the authors who contributed to that. Nicolás Bessio Moreno, "El sistema filosófico de Agustín Álvarez," in Agustín Álvarez, ¿Adónde vamos?, Buenos Aires, La Cultura Argentina, 1915, p. 25. On Álvarez and this book in particular, Oscar Terán, Positivismo y nación en la Argentina, Buenos Aires, Puntosur, 1987, pp. 27–36. On Bessio Moreno and his references to Kant, Dotti, La letra gótica, pp. 114, 143–4. Certainly, the positive recovery of Machiavelli from an author who appeals to Kant contrasts with the critical judgements of other authors already seen who also fed on the philosopher of Königsberg and, more generally, on German idealism (with arguments that also differ from each other, like Martínez Paz, Astrada, or Bianco himself).
38. De Vedia y Mitre, Derecho político, 1934, vol. 1, p. 291.
39. De Vedia y Mitre, Maquiavelo, p. xlvii.
40. Ibid. p. xlviii.
41. De Vedia y Mitre, Derecho político, 1934, vol. 1, p. 275. Belisario Montero had praised the Discourses because he identified in that text the core of Machiavelli's patriotism: Ensayos sobre filosofía y arte (de mi diario), pp. 172–80. For the rest, and unlike what was held by authors like Rizzi, the concentration of power (even with the goal of political union) was not the doctrinal center of Machiavelli's thought, but an adjoining, circumstantial dimension to his genuine, republican core.
42. De Vedia y Mitre, Historia general, vol. 5, pp. 287–8. At the same time, De Vedia pointed out the importance that Machiavelli had given to religion to achieve political union. As stated in one of the papers from the 1927 volumes, patriotism was the "civic" religion that should occupy the place of a corrupt Christianity: "The homeland, for him, is a deity superior to all morality and all law [. . .] for the preservation of the homeland there is nothing illegal," De Vedia y Mitre, Maquiavelo, p. 532.
43. De Vedia y Mitre, Derecho político, 1934, vol. 1, p. 286.
44. De Vedia y Mitre, Maquiavelo, p. xliv. Also De Vedia y Mitre, Historia general, vol. 5, p. 302.
45. De Vedia y Mitre, Derecho político, 1934, vol. 1, p. 275.
46. De Vedia quotes a passage from Chapter XXI of The Prince about the prince having the duty of "honoring those who stood out in some profession [. . .], so they do not refrain from improving their farms out of fear that other will take them away, and, out of fear of taxes, other citizens do not want to open new channels to trade," Derecho político, 1934, vol. 1, p. 280.
47. Romero, Maquiavelo historiador, pp. 77–8.

48. It is worth saying that De Vedia did not mistake mixed government with the separation of powers or moderate government, according to Montesquieu: "mixed government is not what Montesquieu seems to be promoting, but a moderate government [. . .]. The separation of powers can exist in a simple form of government, and conversely the powers may be mixed up in a mixed government, as existed in republican Rome." De Vedia y Mitre, *Derecho político,* 1952, vol. 1, pp. 442–3. Cf. Norberto Bobbio, *La teoría de las formas de gobierno en la historia del pensamiento político,* Mexico, Fondo de Cultura Económica, 2012, pp. 64–79.
49. De Vedia y Mitre, *Maquiavelo,* p. xliv.
50. In his opinion, "the natural hostility between the nobility and the people" is synonymous with a factional struggle, which is key, since it pits "those who want to acquire against those who want to preserve" (a singular reading, taking into account the "over-estimation" of politics in human life that Romero attributed to Machiavelli). The conflict, in sum, exposes the "disappearance of the ideal of the 'common good'" and the prevalence of particular interests and a "selfish conscience." Romero, *Maquiavelo historiador,* pp. 80–1.
51. De Vedia y Mitre, *Derecho político,* 1934, vol. 1, p. 272.
52. Ibid. p. 290.
53. Ibid. p. 275.
54. De Vedia y Mitre, *Historia general,* vol. 5, pp. 306–9.
55. De Vedia y Mitre, *Derecho político,* 1934, vol. 1, pp. 136–41; De Vedia y Mitre, *Historia de las ideas,* vol. 10, pp. 273–80.
56. Losada, "Soberanía y libertad."
57. Mariano de Vedia y Mitre, *Programa de Derecho Político: carrera de abogacía,* Buenos Aires, Facultad de Derecho y Ciencias Sociales, Universidad de Buenos Aires, Imprenta de la Universidad, 1929 and 1944.
58. De Vedia y Mitre, *Derecho político,* 1934, vol. 1, p. 27.
59. Claude Lefort defines Villari as "one of the most serious interpreters": Lefort, *Maquiavelo: lecturas de lo político,* p. 65.
60. De Vedia y Mitre, *Derecho político,* 1952, vol. 2, pp. 138–9.
61. See Ernesto De Cristofaro, "Letture di Machiavelli nella cultura di area tedesca tra fine Ottocento e inizio Novecento: Burckhardt, Treitschke, Meinecke," in Carta and Tabet (eds), *Machiavelli nel XIX e nel XX secolo,* pp. 125–43.
62. See also Ernesto Quesada, *La enseñanza de la historia en las universidades alemanas,* La Plata, Facultad de Ciencias Jurídicas y Sociales, 1910; Rodolfo Rivarola, *Filosofía, política, historia: lecturas en la Facultad de Filosofía y Letras y en la Junta de Historia y Numismática,* Buenos Aires, Librería La Facultad de J. Roldán, 1917.
63. Maurizio Fioravanti, *Los derechos fundamentals: apuntes de historia de las constituciones,* Madrid, Trotta, 2009; Michael Stolleis, *Public Law in Germany, 1800–1914,* New York, Berghahn, 2001.

64. The legal references of De Vedia may explain other aspects of his works, like his counterpoints with Hans Kelsen or his disinterest in Carl Schmitt.
65. It is worth highlighting that De Vedia did not base his reading of Machiavelli on Mussolini. It is enough to contrast his appreciations with those of Leopoldo Lugones or remember what has already been explored in these pages: De Vedia understood that Machiavelli considered the concentration of power in exceptional circumstances to be a legitimate but not permanent regime. He portrayed him as a key figure of the republic and freedom (with all the ambiguities that, certainly, encompassed this formula, as has been pointed out). However, none of this prevented De Vedia from being the target of criticisms for having translated and disseminated Mussolini's text: for example, according to another writer mentioned here, Viamonte: "Maquiavelo y Mussolini."
66. About the influence of De Sanctis on the Argentine reception of Italian literature, Alejandro Patat, *Un destino sudamericano: la letteratura italiana in Argentina (1910–1970)*, Perugia, Guerra, 2005. It is worth saying that there are no allusions to Benedetto Croce in the works of De Vedia or Romero discussed here (in the latter, his recurring references are Federico Chabod and Felice Alderisio, also referred to in De Vedia's texts). This is a point to mention not only because Croce was referred to by others (for example, Enrique Martínez Paz), but also because he was a reference for other works of Romero and was himself concerned with the relation between politics and morals through Machiavelli, in connection with the Italian political scenario during Fascism. In fact, one of his contributions was motivated by Mussolini's text, which, as has been seen, was known in Argentina (and translated and published by De Vedia himself). De Vedia only mentions Croce in passing and in another context, as a "debtor" of Giambattista Vico. See De Vedia, *Derecho político*, 1952, vol. 2, p. 369; Benedetto Croce, "Maquiavelo y Vico: la política y la ética," in Benedetto Croce, *Ética y política*, Buenos Aires, Imán, 1952, pp. 217–21. About this text (originally published in 1924), its context (established, among other events, by the killing of the socialist representative Giacomo Matteoti), and its place in Croce's work, Carlo Ginzburg, "Maquiavelo, la excepción y la regla: líneas de una investigación en curso," *Ingenium: Revista de Historia del Pensamiento Moderno*, 4, 2010, pp. 5–28, specifically pp. 16–17. In another sense, it is worth adding that, in later works (Romero, Legón, Sampay, De Vedia himself), mentions of Wilhelm Dilthey, Ernst Cassirer, and Hermann Heller appear, and one text frequently alluded to sustain criticism of Machiavellianism is James Burham, *Los maquiavelistas* (1943). Several of these titles were available at the library of the Faculty of Law and/or that of the Faculty of Philosophy and Literature of the Universidad de Buenos Aires (there

were Italian and French editions of authors like Burkhardt, Gierke and Treitschke, a fact that maybe made their reading easier). By 1925, also, the National Library had the *Florentine Histories*, *Castruccio Castracani*, and the *Discourses*, all of them in Italian editions. As was already mentioned, *The Prince* is not found. See *Catálogo metódico de la Biblioteca Nacional. Vol. VI. Historia y geografía*, p. 871.
67. It is worth recalling, as was indicated in Chapter 1, that other authors addressed here discussed the criticisms of Treitschke and German nationalism at the beginning of the twentieth century, as well as their relation with Machiavelli: Orestes Ferrara, *La guerra europea: causas y pretextos*, New York, D. Appleton and Co., 1915.
68. In Irazusta, it is worth recalling that this was a compatibility resting on an imposture, on deliberate concealment, since Roman republicanism, in his opinion, had relied on conquest and war, instead of on constitutionalism and freedom (a judgement that was certainly close to the one Alberdi issued in his time).

Chapter 5

# The Hispanic and North American Reception of Machiavelli in Comparative Perspective

The previous chapters featured a reconstruction of how Machiavelli was read in Argentina by liberal and anti-liberal political thinkers in the period running from 1880 to 1940. This reconstruction allows two major conclusions to be drawn. First, the critical voices in the nineteenth century were mostly to be heard in the liberal camp, while in the twentieth century, the majority of the objections issued from writers belonging to the anti-liberal field. This change in Machiavelli's critics mirrored another aspect: he went from being understood as an "ancient" to being conceived of as "modern" and even as a "liberal." The strongest objection to him in Argentina during the first half of the twentieth century was not to do with the fact of him being associated with tyranny and violence, but with him being considered responsible for the beginning of the modern era and inscribed in the genealogy of liberalism.

Second, the name of Machiavelli can be used to reconstruct a sequence of the way in which the relationship between republicanism and liberalism was considered. On the one hand, it highlighted how republicanism was incompatible with liberalism. From a liberal perspective, an incompatibility was pointed out emphasizing the danger of republicanism for individual liberties, due to its militarist character or the centrality given to political freedom. From an anti-liberal perspective, the incompatibility stemmed from understanding republicanism as a justification for an elitist and even authoritarian order facing the inconsistencies of liberal democracy.

On the other hand, and mainly during the first half of the twentieth century, republicanism started to be seen as convergent with liberalism, and even with democracy. Liberal as well as anti-liberal authors arrived at this conclusion, the latter after a substantial revision of their arguments, since at first, as outlined in the previous paragraph, some of them had associated republicanism, through their readings of Machiavelli, with elitist and anti-liberal principles.

Taking into account the results of this historical inquiry, it is important to formulate a few questions: what characterization can be drawn up about these readings of Machiavelli in a broader context? Did they have singularities – and, in that case, which ones? Or, instead, did they recognize similarities with the ways of reading Machiavelli in other intellectual geographies?

To that end, in the following pages, Argentine readings will be put in dialogue with two other types of register: a historical one and a theoretical one. First, they will be compared with the interpretations made in Spanish political thought. The results of this inquiry will offer elements to outline, at least initially, what type of readings of Machiavelli were made in the Spanish-speaking Atlantic world, and what similarities and differences can be recognized within it. Second, the readings in the Spanish-speaking Atlantic world (Argentine and Spanish) will be compared with the ways that Machiavelli was read in the English-speaking Atlantic world.

A second register refers to possible dialogues between the results of this historical research and political theory and philosophy: that is, how to conceptualize or conceive of the readings of Machiavelli seen in this book from the perspective of the contributions offered by debates cutting across the political philosophy and theory dedicated to the study of the author of *The Prince*, and through this, the characteristics and relations between republicanism, liberalism, and democracy. Next, and in quite a different approach to the first question, do the arguments drawn from the historical reconstruction made here offer any contributions, questions, or precisions to the afore-mentioned theoretical discussions?

## Readings of Machiavelli in Spanish-Speaking and English-Speaking Atlantic Worlds

In previous chapters, there were references to the considerations of Machiavelli made by three outstanding Spanish intellectuals and academics who had similar biographical trajectories (prestigious jurists and university professors) but differing political convictions: Adolfo Posada (1860–1944), Luis Legaz y Lacambra (1906–80), and Francisco Javier Conde (1908–74). It is time to talk about these men more systematically. In this approach, it is worth recalling some details that allow them to be contextualized with certain elements for the purposes of analysis.

In the first place, let us look at some general features of Machiavelli's reception in Spain. One of these, as seen in Chapter 1, was how deeply rooted the negative and condemnatory perception of him had become, an attitude which turned anti-Machiavellianism into a key trait of Spanish political thought from the seventeenth century onwards. This combined, certainly, with a quest to offset the notion of a "Christian prince" against Machiavelli's "impious prince," which was the reason why the criticism took the form of repudiating the behaviors and principles displayed, but not necessarily the way of exercising power. A second feature, which could be seen as a form of rejection or, at the very least, of disinterest, was the lack of Spanish translations of *The Prince* until the beginning of the nineteenth century.

On the other hand, the profiles of Posada, Legaz y Lacambra, and Conde indicate that, in Spain, a similar phenomenon to that in Argentina was developing. This had to do with an interest in the study of Machiavelli's works, without sidestepping political controversy but reaching beyond this dimension in favor of more rigorous reflection, and was connected to the consolidation and expansion of university studies in Political Law.[1] This may be the explanation for why Machiavelli's work too was addressed and thematically analyzed in a similar way (for example, in relation to the theory of the State, as will be seen later), although, despite that, there were a number of singularities and differences to be identified, as will also be proposed in the following pages.

Regarding Posada, it is worth saying that he was one of the most prominent jurists of Spain between the end of the nineteenth century and first half of the twentieth. Among other things, his biographical and intellectual trajectory reveals a close link to Krausism, an intellectual movement that had a major impact in Spain in the second half of the nineteenth century. Krausism infused life into social and reformist liberalism and revived academic and intellectual discussion, leading to clashes with the Catholic Church, and even the separation of leading Krausist figures from the university system. As a result, in 1876 they created the Instituto Libre de Enseñanza, which lasted until the end of the Spanish Civil War in 1939.[2]

Posada was also a key figure in the development of Spanish Political Law and university life, and his work pursues several weighty topics. These include the relation between morality and law, the nature and characteristics of the State, legal pluralism, and the theory of the self-limitation of State sovereignty, according to which the State self-limited its sovereignty in order to establish a legal regime. This meant that it assumed, in consequence, the character of rule of law, compatible, in turn, with the "legal recognition of the – individual and collective – personalities within the State."[3] At the same time, regarding his political positions, Posada referred to the afore-mentioned reform-oriented liberalism inspired by Krausism. The correlation between these interests and perspectives in the political context of turn-of-the-century Spain, marked specifically by the consolidation of a State based on liberal principles, in the framework of the so-called Bourbon Restoration (1875–1931), should be highlighted. Later on, Posada played a significant role in the design of the Constitution of the Spanish Second Republic which was adopted in 1931 (it is worth recalling, also, that he visited Buenos Aires in the 1910s and 1920s).[4]

Considering these biographical and intellectual particularities, it is necessary to restate Posada's main considerations about Machiavelli. First of all, it should be said that there was a notable increment in his interest and references to the Florentine author throughout his work, even though the opinion he held of him remained largely unchanged, as did the topics and issues that Posada associated with him.

On the one hand, the Spaniard valued realism as a necessary perspective for political study but entertained a dismissive assessment of its Machiavellian version. In his opinion, Machiavelli did not offer any valuable ontology or political knowledge. His work was empiricist but lacked ethical purposes, and thus had an authoritarian projection, an example of the "empiricism that makes people veritable herds of slaves." In addition, that same empiricist approach undermined its scientific status: "Machiavellian practices are the most perfect expression of this anti-scientific politics of circumstances. The man whose actions are inspired by the principles exposed by the famous writer in his Prince has lost all notion of what is just."[5] This statement certainly has points in common with the thinking of one of Posada's teachers, Francisco Giner de los Ríos, also a key figure for Spanish Krausism. According to Giner, political science should be subordinate to legal science:

> that is why Politics, the science of the State, is a branch, important as they all are, but subordinate to the general science of the Law, and all that has been done to try to wrench it from its main

trunk has led to the disastrous essays by Machiavelli and modern positivists, which are equally lethal for both life and thought, because it is difficult for it to flourish when bereft of its own matter and content.[6]

In other texts, Posada expounded his most enduring characterization of Machiavelli, already mentioned in previous chapters, as the harbinger and intellectual father of imperialist and militarist nationalism, and of a particular form of State – State-Power. The arguments contained in this characterization and the conceptions supporting it should be highlighted. According to Posada, Machiavelli was a patriot writing in the interests of national political union and even of the formation of the State. But none of these aspects, in Posada's reading, connected Machiavelli with liberalism. On the contrary, he was a key figure for a form of State that Posada differentiated from the rule of law and from a variant of nationalism which was also in tension with liberal nationalism, due to its militarist ingredients. Posada developed these arguments in several texts published in the 1910s and 1920s, and did not conceal his rejection of these phenomena, to the point of defining as "catastrophic" the process that had given rise to the State-Power, because its most eloquent result was the First World War.[7]

Second, for Posada, Machiavelli was not writing in favor of freedom, although neither was he, strictly speaking, writing in favor of tyranny. According to the Spanish jurist, it is worth underscoring that Machiavelli occupied an eminent place in the historical development of the theory of the State but had postulated a state form that was ultimately pernicious. In addition, in Posada's opinion, Machiavelli may have been a theorist of the State, but he was not an exponent of sovereignty. His relevance lay in having identified the specific "political event" that heralded the possibility of the theoretical elaboration of the foundations of the power of the State at the end of the sixteenth century and throughout the seventeenth:

> Two moments may be distinguished in the elaboration of the theory of sovereignty: one occurring prior to the determination of the idea and its consideration as a political category. The political fact is stated, but there is no understanding of its distinctive qualities and the critical interpretation of the phenomenon. The other moment occurs when there is a reasoning, through either a mechanical, ethical, or metaphysical – transcendental – explanation of political power, and it is attributed to its own subject. The proposed solutions to the problems of the elaboration of these explanations lay the grounds for the doctrines of sovereignty.

According to this analysis, then, Machiavelli embodied the first moment, while Jean Bodin started the second.[8] According to Posada, the Florentine had reflected on a personal form of government (the principality), which offered elements for a theoretical reflection on the first modern expression of sovereignty, absolutism, as the political basis for modern States.

At the same time, according to Posada, Machiavelli's writing was relevant to a consolidation of monarchic sovereignty inasmuch as it had forestalled the expansion of popular sovereignty at the beginning of modernity:

> Represented in the fourteenth and fifteenth centuries by prominent writers, the popular origin of Power becomes, thanks to the internal complications triggered by the Reformation in the Western States, an instrument of struggle against secular power, which is also an oppressor of individual consciousness. But, in response to such important movements, those currents which prompt favorable reactions to the power of the prince, synthesized in absolute monarchy, are intensified. A study of specific precedents would identify as a priority the representation made by Machiavelli, in whose work *The Prince* the power of the State is concentrated in the King as the ultimate aim of civil society.[9]

Indeed, Posada pointed out that "in *The Prince* there are many more indications than those arising from the doctrine of power for power's sake."[10] He recognized the singularities of his contribution to the theory of the forms of government, in the form of the distinction between the principality and the republic, and his version of a mixed government (wherein Posada identified the attention Machiavelli dedicated to conflict).[11] However, in perspective, the Spanish jurist entertained a negative consideration of Machiavelli's work, based on two principal aspects: his political ontology and the type of political study he promoted (an anti-scientific yet authoritarian empiricism), in addition to the political meaning of his writings. As regards the latter, Posada saw the Florentine author as linked to the history of absolute monarchy, a reprehensible form of State (the State-Power), and to a militarist and aggressive nationalism, and thus paid very little attention to the relationship between Machiavelli and republicanism.

Unlike Posada, Luis Legaz y Lacambra, also a renowned jurist with a remarkable academic career (a Professor of Philosophy of Law, Rector of the Universidad de Santiago de Compostela, and Dean of the Faculty of Law at the Universidad de Madrid), had anti-liberal sympathies and convictions, which were not only heterogeneous but also changed throughout his life. He was variously labeled a Fascist, a Catholic, and a national syndicalist, and was a member of the Falange, the political space which gave rise to the Francoist regime. In his legal thought, we can see an interest in the work of Hans Kelsen and Carl Schmitt, as well as the influence of natural law and Thomism.[12]

Legaz y Lacambra's interest in Machiavelli was focused mainly on his ontology, his notion of politics. As was discussed in Chapter 2, according to Legaz, the statement of the autonomy of politics had two possible projections: to present a dimension of human life or to identify a specific form of knowledge.

> In this problem of politics, two quite different topics are involved. The first, that of the recognition of politics as science or art with its own formal object which is thus subject to its own rules, that cannot be reduced merely to theological or moral precepts. The other recognizes politics as a regulatory order governing human behavior, which cannot be reduced to other normative orders such as the moral and legal ones. This implies the assumption that certain human actions would not be moral or legal, but "political" and thus justified according to this specific regulatory context which is autonomous and irreducible to the others.[13]

For Legaz, the first stance was not open to censure because it had enabled a precise outline of political science. However, on the other hand, conceiving of politics as an autonomous and self-sufficient dimension was censurable, since

> we cannot elevate the political to something with autonomous value, of the same rank as the value of morality. Nor should we believe, therefore, that there is a system that can order the rules of human behavior called "politics," and be coordinated with a system of legal and moral norms.

It was crucial to signal one's opposition to "any 'sanctification' of politics, a spiritual attitude based on the overvaluation of action for action's sake."[14] In sum, "politics must be subordinated to morality."[15]

It is worth noting that Legaz y Lacambra accompanied all these objections with other statements, which, although still critical of such projections of Machiavelli's work, recognized that his "technical" conception of politics was not, strictly speaking, an amoral one. Politics as technique had an ethics, its own notion of good (which Legaz, of course, did not share):

> Morality, according to Machiavelli, is, then, the ability to achieve good at all costs, understood as one's own utility and that of others. And this is exactly what politics is [. . .] Thus, any moral action is a technical action, even though not any technical action is a moral one.

It follows from this that

> the concept of "virtue" in Machiavelli would be a complex concept, of both an ethical and a technical nature, an expression of the complex fact of professional morality. This is not an abstract but a concrete concept, expressed differently in the politician and in the writer, in the family man and in the citizen, but which makes specific demands in each case.[16]

Legaz thus highlighted that one of the reasons why Machiavelli was so controversial was his idea about the existence of different possible ethics (a formulation that, certainly, has similarities with that developed by Isaiah Berlin).[17] In consequence, Legaz's main criticism of Machiavelli was his relativist implication, which displaced the centrality of Christian morality, about which the Florentine had come up with a wrong or simplistic conception:

> Machiavelli presupposes a double morality: one, of the evangelical-Christian, which is "what there should be" if men actually were as if defined this way. The other one involves the reality of human nature, a morality which is the "political" one described by Machiavellianism.

Legaz underlined that "naturally, Machiavelli makes the mistake of admitting that evangelical morality presupposes that man is something different to what he really is, which is equivalent to declaring it a false morality, since it stems from a mistaken assumption."[18]

In addition, Legaz y Lacambra did not pay attention to, or even detect, the republican vein running through Machiavelli's thought, although he did state certain considerations similar to those of Posada regarding his place in the history of European political thought. He had "sensed" the notion of sovereignty and developed the notion of the "reason of State," whereby the State could be conceived of as different then the Law.[19] Accordingly, his work was associated with a certain notion or form of State, the "State of Power," which was different than, and indeed opposed to, the rule of law, revived at the turn of the twentieth century by the German State and linked in that sense with the work of Treitschke.[20]

Finally, it is worth revisiting the considerations of Machiavelli made by another bastion of Spanish anti-liberalism, Francisco Javier Conde.[21] In his reading also, the main aspect of Machiavelli's thought was not republicanism. For Conde, the central axis of the Florentine's work was order, not freedom. At the same time, Conde posited that he had been a foundational figure of modernity in a specific area by expounding the close relationship between political and military orders. Finally, as pointed out in Chapter 2, Machiavelli had postulated a "positive, technical, and pragmatic" form of knowledge:

> Machiavellian knowledge does not pursue a transcendent objective, nor is it sanctioned ultimately by the idea of a Providence that rules all things and human affairs. Wisdom lies in fully understanding human movements, predicting the course of political events and managing them as perfectly as possible. That is why the "wise" prince is governed neither by faith or by promise, and must forego both when the reasons moving him to provide these are lacking. The positive, technical, and pragmatic character of Machiavellian knowledge neutralizes the sphere of knowledge, separating it from moral and religious values at the outset.[22]

In this quotation, the separation between politics and Christianity, according to Conde, had implied, not immorality, but a neutrality in terms of value. "The words good and bad lose their autonomous and substantial moral content to become neutral terms belonging to a mathematical function."[23] This is why Machiavelli's knowledge is defined as "technical." At the same time, this neutrality was related to another trait underlying his thinking: "rationality." Rationality and technique turned Machiavelli into a foundational theorist of the modern State:

> The political order will then be a highly rational one, where everything may be rationally predicted and calculated. In this passage by Machiavelli, we witness the birth of the modern State as an ultra-rational form of political organization, with a tendency to rational centralism in the face of traditional feudal law.[24]

The rationalism Conde found in Machiavelli, however, coexisted with an "irrational" aspect which was just as important in his work, condensed in the notion of *virtù*. Conde stated (in a discussion with writers such as Friedrich Meinecke) that Machiavelli's virtue, understood as the ability to foresee and anticipate events, to dominate Fortune, had persuasion as its most distinctive trait, not violence: "Machiavellian virtue does not consist merely of commanding with violence and ferocity, it also means 'persuading'"; "*virtù* is, after all, that outstanding quality of intelligence that allows man to master the movement of all things human."[25]

In another sense, Machiavelli's relation with the modern State did not connect him with liberalism. On the contrary, according to Conde, the objectives or goals of the author of the *Discorsi* are clear: he was a theorist writing about order, stability, and discipline, even about "stillness" and command, whose model for political order was a military one. Rather than a concern about corruption, his thought turned on the issue of stability. Instead of praising the turmoil in Roman life, his attention focused on stability:

> Political or civil life is the opposite of living in corruption. But there is still another Machiavellian expression that reveals with greater precision the meaning of "political life" for Machiavelli. This is the word "stillness," "*vivere quietamente*." True political life means living in utter stillness [. . .] Machiavelli's problem [. . .] is, precisely, that of "stability" [. . .]. The main task pursued by political wisdom is how to "halt" the movement of human nature, which is as worthy as curbing human passions.[26]

Therefore, "the '*vivere quietamente*' is based, then, on coercion."[27] Hence, Machiavelli's modern trait is "the essential link between political and military order"; "the specifically 'modern' aspect is that Machiavelli introduces military order into the heart of politics, according the State the monopoly of the military."[28]

In Conde's reading, then, Machiavelli seems much closer to (and perhaps anticipates) the work of Max Weber rather than Carl Schmitt.[29] His "wisdom" consisted of having proposed rationality and monopoly of legitimate violence as attributes of the State, and of observing the importance of non-rational aspects in political leadership (it does not seem unreasonable to see a connection between Conde's interpretation of Machiavellian virtue and Weberian charisma). Certainly, order and stability could be understood as specific traits of the Florentine author connecting him with liberalism. Conde, in fact, linked Machiavelli to Descartes, stating that

> when Machiavelli has asked himself the question of what is the ultimate purpose of politics, he has managed to give only one answer, the same that will later be elevated by Descartes to the axis of "modern" metaphysics: safety.[30]

This is not Conde's emphasis, however. In his reading, Machiavelli is an author concerned primarily with the ends that political life must achieve, not about forms of government – and those ends are order and stability. The election of the form of government is thus subject to these objectives, and depends on another aspect raised by the Florentine, the "wisdom of proportion": that is, the relative importance of corruption at a certain point in time in a specific society. If this prevails, then the option is the principality. If not, the choice will be the republic. In other words, when Machiavelli offers the option of the republic, this is neither ideological nor doctrinal, but pragmatic, in line with his "technical knowledge." According to Conde, for Machiavelli, "frankly, there are only two possible ways of politically ordering human reality as a perfect figure: *'il vero principato e la vera repubblica.'*"[31] Republic, in fact, "means a global order."[32]

In sum, for Francisco Conde, Machiavelli wrote mainly about order and the State. Not in favor of tyranny or emergency powers, but through the convergence of military and political order (a point that, it is worth repeating, defined the modern aspect of Machiavelli), he offered arguments to justify an authoritarian or, at all events, disciplinarian exercise of power. This reading could be related to other visible and enduring concerns in his work, such as the search for ways in which to link personal and charismatic leaderships with representation and rationality.[33]

In another sense, according to Conde, Machiavelli had built solid foundations for political authority by conferring on it a neutrality of values; for this reason, the separation between Christian and political morality does not undermine leadership but strengthens it. Finally, republicanism, or the idea of the republic, was a secondary aspect in Machiavelli's work, which, in addition, had no connection with either freedom or liberalism. On the contrary, the horizon of Machiavelli's republic was focused on order, command, discipline, and stability, not freedom.

The readings of Machiavelli made by Posada, Legaz y Lacambra, and Conde, as well as the Argentine sources and bibliography analyzed in the previous chapters, offer the opportunity to compare and contrast different approaches. For example, it could be highlighted that the opinions on Machiavellian realism, as seen in the Argentine case, cannot be classified according to theoretical perspectives or political sympathies. Posada and Legaz y Lacambra both objected to him (with different emphases – authoritarianism and relativism, respectively) because they agreed on a line of questioning for a notion of politics that lacked ethical purpose (whatever their foundation – religion, natural law, or morality). However, Conde issued a more positive assessment, and it is revealing that his portrayal of realism was similar to that which inspired the criticism of another anti-liberal, Legaz y Lacambra (realistic politics as technical knowledge). In this sense, the criticism made by Legaz y Lacambra has parallels with those identified among Argentine Catholics, although the objections made by the Spanish jurist are more moderate, as he pointed out that the separation between morals and politics had enabled the emergence of a political science. Still somewhat unconvincing for Legaz y Lacambra, this contained its own ethical framework rather than being an amoral or immoral form of knowledge, strictly speaking. These statements are deserving of emphasis if we recall the long anti-Machiavellian tradition of Spanish thought. In this context, Legaz's objections also provide an impression of moderation.[34]

In this sense, Conde's affirmation that the separation between politics and morals strengthened political leadership stands in contrast to the legacy of Spanish anti-Machiavellianism, as well as to the conclusion of Argentine anti-liberals exploring this subject: for example, Ernesto Palacio (who was not, it is worth recalling, an orthodox Catholic thinker), for whom the division between politics and morals weakened leadership instead of strengthening it. Conde's judgement, in this sense, was far closer to that stated by Leopoldo Lugones, although his notion of politics in Machiavelli also differed. For Conde, Machiavelli was synonymous with rationalism, while Lugones stressed his non-rational qualities, such as force and violence. These were attributes that Conde himself, even as he recognized the non-rational dimension in the Florentine's work, either nuanced or, regarding the place of military power, took as an expression of State rationalism as promoted by Machiavelli.

A point alluded to in Chapter 4 should be revisited here. In Argentina, the conception of Machiavelli as a theorist of the State did not foster an understanding of him as an author writing about a form of State foreign to liberalism, like the State-Power or the State-Force. That was the view taken by Catholic thinkers who defined him as the forerunner of an immanent conception of politics that enabled modern "statolatry," caused by the aporias of liberalism.[35] But this was also the case with liberal authors such as Martín García Mérou or Mariano de Vedia y Mitre. They linked Machiavelli to a theory of the State and a form of State that, by attempting to secure the freedom of the homeland in the face of foreign enemies, as well as the individual liberties of its citizens, coincided with the rule of law. Machiavelli's patriotism was not associated with either expansionist militarism or aggressive nationalism, but with a call to national union, skewed in favor of freedom and liberty through the formation of the State.[36] At some point, an anti-liberal like Conde, who linked Machiavelli to a State displaying certain Weberian features, was closer to a liberal such as De Vedia y Mitre in his considerations about Machiavelli and the State than Posada, who associated Machiavelli with the State-Power (De Vedia, in fact, discussed Posada in his texts). In any case, Conde, Posada, and Legaz y Lacambra highlighted the link between militarism and the State in Machiavelli (a less visible argument among Argentine writers), but their assessment of this link differed as it was related to his considerations about the autonomy of politics. Conde linked rationalism, technique, and militarism together, while Posada and Legaz y Lacambra understood militarism to be the result of a politics stripped of either ethical or religious frameworks, implications that both authors deplored, despite their different approaches.[37]

In sum, the possible comparisons could be multiplied. However, it is interesting here to draw another type of distinction, based on the identification of distinctive topics, or prevailing problems, in the Spanish and Argentine readings. To summarize the aspects just mentioned, there are two affirmations to be made. For one thing, one salient aspect common to both Spanish and Argentine readings is the connection established between Machiavelli and the State. This can be attributed to a phenomenon mentioned earlier: the fact that the reception of Machiavelli in both countries gained depth and rigor with the consolidation of Political Law in the academic field, a phenomenon also connected to the political context of the two countries at the end of the nineteenth century. This was defined by the affirmation of a liberal model of State (during the Bourbon Restoration initiated in 1874 in Spain and the consolidation of the national State in Argentina in 1880).[38]

These common points, nevertheless, must not overlook the essential differences springing from the association of Machiavelli with different forms or notions of State. Linking Machiavelli to oppressive forms of State power (whether absolutist, militarist, amoral, or impious) was more common among the Spanish writers, despite their differences and opinions about those forms of State power.[39]

This point should be highlighted particularly for the Spanish anti-liberals, as Machiavelli's association with authoritarian State models did not evoke an enthusiastic vindication of his work and thought among them. The portrayal of Machiavelli as an author in favor of a militarist State drawn up by liberal figures like Posada could, in itself, have been a reason to see him in a positive light. Also, it is worth taking into account the fact that, unlike in Argentina, anti-liberalism had enjoyed political success in Spain and, therefore, the construction of a political order and an anti-liberal State was a political objective, and not just an intellectual or speculative one. Furthermore, Machiavelli had been invoked by contemporary experiences that served as political and doctrinal references, such as Italian Fascism. This may be a reason for the more moderate tone of their criticisms compared with that of the Argentine anti-liberals. But the truth is that neither Conde nor Legaz y Lacambra (who both dedicated specific works to thought on the subject of the State, and flirted with Nazi Fascism at certain points during their public career) appealed principally to Machiavelli for these reasons; in fact, they criticized him and repudiated him as an intellectual figure.[40] This fact deserves to be emphasized because it can be seen as yet another indication of the long trail left by Spanish anti-Machiavellianism, and also highlights that one of the underlying rejections of Machiavelli was a reaction to his ontology, the absolutization of politics. This was so significant that it obstructed efforts to reinstate him, in doctrinal or ideological terms, as an author in favor of authoritarianism.[41] However, in Argentina, without leaving aside exceptions but looking at the way he was portrayed in general terms, Machiavelli was associated with the liberal State (once again, irrespective of positive or negative judgements).

Second, but in relation to what was said above, the association of Machiavelli with freedom, and even with liberalism, is more visible in Argentine readings than in Spanish ones. More precisely, among the Argentines Machiavelli's close relationship with freedom and liberalism was visible, thanks not only to the notion of State attributed to him, but also to his characterization as a republican author. Machiavelli's republicanism was as a subject less thematized by the Spaniards. In any case, Machiavelli's republic was linked, overwhelmingly, with order, not with freedom, as raised by Francisco Javier Conde (with an additional emphasis on the fact that forms of government were a subordinate theme in his work). In fact, the limited attention paid to the republic and republicanism, or relating republicanism to order or "conservation," rather than freedom, is a diagnosis that would gather strength if a greater number of writers and texts were studied.[42]

On the other hand, republicanism as a leading trait of Machiavelli's thought was a recurrent issue among the Argentines and also an object of controversy.⁴³ It is worth recalling that, according to some readings, he had favored an anti-liberal and anti-democratic form of republicanism (a topic detected in some passages by Conde, as noted above). However, according to another perspective prevalent mostly during the first half of the twentieth century and common to both liberal and anti-liberal writers, Machiavelli was a symbol of a liberal republicanism (one tinged even with democratic projections) and, in a broader sense, a part of the historical genealogy of liberalism.

In sum, within the Spanish-speaking Atlantic world between 1880 and 1940, the evidence in this book enables the conclusion that the conception of Machiavelli as a republican writer was a singular or particularly visible axis of reading in the Argentine reception.⁴⁴ This deserves to be highlighted because, on the one hand, it can be related to a previously mentioned point, which is that the tradition of reception in Spain was based on *The Prince* rather than on the *Discourses* and, therefore, Machiavelli was associated with arbitrariness or with absolutism, rather than with the republic and freedom.⁴⁵

On the other hand, the distinction should be emphasized in the political contexts prevalent in both countries, rather than in relation to the reception of Machiavelli. It could be said that, at first glance, the greater prominence given to Machiavelli's republicanism had a degree of correspondence with a republican Argentina as it faced a monarchic Spain. However, this would not be a convincing argument, since it would mean ignoring the weight of republicanism in Spain, in both politics and political thought, which was because of, not in spite of, monarchy.⁴⁶ It may be speculated, though, that the different degrees of visibility of the republican Machiavelli in Spain and Argentina (at least as deduced from the writers studied in this book) bear some relation to the characteristics of republicanism in the two countries.

In Spain, republicanism (at least until the early twentieth century) was found in many different expressions, both in the form of its doctrinal foundations and in the degree of political moderation or radicalization, although it was, in general terms, closer to liberalism rather than opposed to it, its enduring principles being freedom and citizen participation. In this sense, its differences with liberalism were more of degree than of nature, and referred mainly to republican demands for a democracy with popular content. This was particularly the case in the context created by the Restoration of 1875, after the Democratic Sexennium of 1868–74, when the ephemeral experience of the Spanish First Republic took shape, between 1873 and 1874.⁴⁷

Along with all this, especially in those versions on which Krausism had greatest influence, Spanish republicanism was defined by its reformist positions (rather than by its revolutionary impetus) and by a harmonic representation of society (of an organicist hue), before which rose a State understood as an arbitrator of sectorial interests. This perspective exposes the similarities between these currents of Spanish republicanism and the social and reformist liberalism widespread in Europe at the turn of the twentieth century, from the French Third Republic to new Anglo-Saxon liberalism, without forgetting, of course, the German National Liberal Party.[48] Moreover, beyond anti-clericalism and the opposition to the Church that also characterized Spanish republicanism, this perspective highlights the deep Christian traits underlying this tradition.[49]

Bearing all of this in mind, it comes as no surprise to see how infrequent it is to find a republican reading of Machiavelli, whether as a key figure for a republicanism pursuing freedom through conflict or, in an opposite version, as a symbol of a republicanism antagonistic to liberalism. Similarly, it is also not surprising to see the association of his work with an aggressive and militarist form of the State in an author like Adolfo Posada, an exponent of the Spanish liberal and Krausist field. In fact, it is noteworthy that Posada, a key figure involved in drafting the 1931 Constitution, the foundation of the Spanish Second Republic, showed no interest at all, at least in his academic writings, in the republican aspect of Machiavelli's work.[50]

Still, the greater visibility of the republican reading of Machiavelli in Argentina can be associated only at a superficial level with the republican nature of the politics there since it broke with Spain in 1810. On the contrary, the consolidation of the republic as the political order when the country reorganized itself at constitutional level in the mid-nineteenth century did not imply that conceptions about republicanism were unequivocal, or that its political projections pursued one sole direction or a definitive, enduring content. The readings of Machiavelli may be seen as a singular testament to this fact.

This topic will be re-examined in the next section, but before that, the second comparative exercise mentioned at the beginning of the chapter must be addressed. This concerns the nature of the relationship – what similarities, what differences – that can be established between the readings made in the Spanish-speaking Atlantic word and those in English-speaking Atlantic countries.

As regards the latter, there is plentiful, well-known literature, at least relating to a specific period in the reception of Machiavelli, against the backdrop of the 1776 American Revolution and the federal organization established by the 1787 Constitution of Philadelphia. In this respect, it has been amply proved that Machiavellian republicanism – along with, in a broader sense, Italian Renaissance republicanism (or civic humanism) – was well known to both federalists and anti-federalists, although more particularly the latter. The reception of Machiavelli as a republican author, rather than the "Machiavellian" writer who legitimized the personal power wielded by princes, was, in turn, an offshoot of the readings made in Britain since the seventeenth century by authors such as James Harrington. In any case, historiography revealed that the conventional representation of the ideological roots of the North American republic as lying in the prevalence of liberalism was unsatisfactory, because it ignored the weight and relevance of republicanism and some of its core principles, including political freedom and the opposition between virtue and corruption as the axes articulating political struggle.[51]

However, this historiography, as well as other studies which were more firmly rooted in a theoretical or doctrinal approach, even highlighting the differences between republicanism and liberalism, and underlining the importance of the former, also showed a tendency to converge in the design of the North American federal republic. That is, instead of tension, there was a virtuous synthesis between liberalism and republicanism. In this sense, research has identified new topics and problems where the weight and influence of republicanism, and more specifically of Machiavelli, can be observed in the foundational stages of the North American republic. This includes, for example, connections or similarities noted between Machiavelli's formulations about the possibilities of a territorially extended republic and proposals made by federalists, especially James Madison. In these studies, Machiavelli is even postulated as a distant forerunner of federalism, especially in his writings about the "composite" monarchy of the France of his time, or his suggestions about how Florence could become the engine of an expanded republic in the center and north of Italy.[52]

Another specific period signaling heightened interest in Machiavelli in the English-speaking Atlantic world was pointed out at the beginning of this book. This was a time when controversies arose about his link to late nineteenth-century imperialism, defined by the specialized literature as a revival of attention to Machiavelli in those geographies.[53] By relating the interpretations of that time with those prevailing at the foundation of the North American republic at the end of the eighteenth century, it may be concluded that there was a resignification in the characterization of Machiavelli and his work between one period and the other. The first was defined by a republican reception which, unlike liberalism, would, at all events, have been a decisive ingredient in the forging of a liberal republic such as that consecrated by the Constitution of Philadelphia. Yet, a century later, Machiavelli was largely read as an author who exalted imperialism, nationalism, and militarism, a reading that, without necessarily revisiting the more common places of "Machiavellianism," did constitute a critical and condemnatory view.[54]

What can be said, then, about the subjects studied in these pages, taking into account the reception in the English-speaking Atlantic world?

A first conclusion is that, in times of independence and constitutional organization, the reception of Machiavelli in the Spanish-speaking Atlantic world achieved less relevance than among its English-speaking counterparts. This has already been pointed out in Chapter 1. The Hispanic American republican tradition did not, at the time, have any significant doctrinal source in Italian Renaissance republicanism. The anti-Machiavellianism sentiment underpinning Hispanic political thought since at least the seventeenth century was by no means a minor factor in this. Indeed, several different versions (classical, Catholic, and Hispanic, influenced by the French and North American revolutions) and a multitude of references (Rousseau, the Italian Enlightenment, Spanish Thomism, the law of peoples of Northern Europe) in Spanish American republicanism at the time of revolution have been detected.[55] In this aspect, superficial or limited intellectual knowledge of republicanism, and of Machiavelli in particular, even prompted the conclusion that there was an "epidermal republic" taking shape in Hispanic America, meaning the adoption of the republic as a form of political organization (additionally based on liberal principles), without this being accompanied by any appropriately thorough reflection on the republican tradition.[56]

As has been already developed in this book, the opinions prevailing in Spain and in Argentina until well into the nineteenth century ratify this diagnosis. In fact, examples abound among the leading intellectuals of nineteenth-century Hispanic America, reflecting similarities and topics typical of the long tradition of "anti-Machiavellianism."[57] However, if attention is brought to bear on the specific period chosen here, that between 1880 and 1940, it cannot be said that Machiavelli's reception in the Spanish-speaking Atlantic world was either superficial or unimportant, nor that it was limited to the repetition of commonplace points of view. This makes it necessary to review and clarify other points outlined throughout these pages.

First, the influence of Catholic thought may have fostered a rejection or contemptuous reading of Machiavelli, but not disinterest or superficiality when approaching his work. The Catholic intellectuals described in this book, both Argentine and Spanish, studied Machiavelli with interest and attention; their writings may have been largely critical, but were never trivial. It is worth adding, also, that these authors observed the similarities between "Machiavellianism" and the Spanish anti-Machiavellian political thought based on scholasticism: for example, when they drew parallels between Machiavelli and authors like Diego Saavedra Fajardo (who praised the Christian prince as a counter-example of the Machiavellian prince).[58] The contrast between a Protestant English-speaking Atlantic space and a Catholic Spanish-speaking Atlantic one as an argument explaining the different receptions of Machiavelli or, at least, a less rigorous understanding of him, is unconvincing. Furthermore, such an affirmation would mean ignoring the anti-Machiavellianism of Protestant tradition, which was every bit as widespread as the Catholic one.

Second, it has been shown here that common interpretations in the English-speaking Atlantic space were familiar to Hispanic American and Spanish intellectuals and scholars who commented on and discussed them, such as the link between Machiavelli and imperialism at the end of the nineteenth century. As was seen in Chapter 1, and mentioned again above, writers such as Adolfo Posada referred to these readings to draw negative conclusions about Machiavelli, while others, like the Argentine Ernesto Quesada, took a positive approach in the name of political realism. Still others, such as the Italian–Cuban Orestes Ferrara, examined the objection to German nationalism as well as its association with Machiavelli. It should not be forgotten, in addition, that allusion to an expansionist nationalism inspired by Machiavelli was sometimes employed to draw attention to North American expansion in Latin America.

Finally, and recapitulating a number of previously developed arguments, it cannot be said that the republican reception of Machiavelli has been exclusive to the English-speaking Atlantic space. If this affirmation, as pointed out earlier, is justified in the context of the Revolution for Independence and constitutional organization (and, notwithstanding, there are suggestions of possible allusions to Machiavelli in Hispanic America at that time[59]), it is, however, inconsistent as regards the period between 1880 and 1940. Throughout those years, a republican reading of Machiavelli can be seen in the Spanish-speaking sphere, especially in Argentine readings.

In fact, regarding this matter, it can be said that the interpretations of and controversies around Machiavelli's republicanism in the Spanish-speaking Atlantic world concerned aspects that are less visible in the English-speaking world. These refer to a point touched on earlier: the republican Machiavelli was referred to in order to characterize a liberal (and democratic) republicanism, but also to posit an anti-liberal and authoritarian republicanism, and both characterizations can be found in liberal and anti-liberal authors alike. It is time, then, to explore this issue in greater depth.

## Historiography and Political Theory: Dialogues and Counterpoints

Although political theory has pursued a long-lasting interest in Machiavelli, it is possible to see that this attention has grown over the last few years, as manifested in the appeals made to Machiavelli when discussing the republic, conflict, citizen participation, or democracy rather than power, political decision-making, or the State. In current political theory, if a panoramic diagnosis is made, Machiavelli is seen as synonymous with republic, freedom, and democracy rather than authoritarianism.[60]

In addition, this interest has many sources. One of them, whose roots can be traced back to the crises which affected structuralism in the 1960s and 1970s, is the potential offered by Machiavelli for a study of politics and social conflicts without social or material overdeterminations.[61] A second reason is the impact, and its repercussions, of the historical research undertaken by writers such as Quentin Skinner, John Pocock, or Gordon Wood (Skinner developing even more strictly theoretical formulations on the basis of his historical findings) on political theory and political philosophy.[62] Third, the renewed interest in Machiavelli also came from a critical, even gloomy, diagnosis of the present situation affecting several liberal democracies, mainly due to elitist (or oligarchic) torsions and the ensuing deficits of participation. This fact, meaning that the study of Machiavelli recognizes as one of its triggers a concern about the present rather than an interest in his work itself, has prompted critical comments about methodological procedures and thence about the consistency of some of arguments posited in recent works on the Florentine author.[63] Finally, another indicator of the increased interest in Machiavelli is that it can be seen in a range of different intellectual and academic milieus. The debates in the English-speaking world (exemplified in the afore-mentioned references) are complemented by the controversies raging around the so-called "Italian theory," which gives pride of place to a Machiavelli conceived of as a radical theorist of politics.[64]

One of the axes articulating this theoretical output, which is also the object of controversy, has already been mentioned in this book on several occasions, and concerns the definition of a Machiavellian approach to the characteristics and links between republicanism, liberalism, and democracy. It is no exaggeration to say that Machiavelli has been the source *par excellence* for contemporary political theory examining these problems, of which there are two main interpretations.

On the one hand, there is the conception that republicanism, inasmuch as it could be restored through Machiavelli, would reveal concurrences and points in common with liberalism in its core principles (freedom), but would also offer more substantial versions of these, enabling the workings of liberal democracy to be optimized. This perspective conceives of republicanism as an optimization of liberalism, rather than its alternative or opposite.[65]

Other formulations critical of the one mentioned above have underscored the differences, even the antinomy, between republicanism and liberalism. In some cases, these differences have been emphasized through the principles and concepts articulating the political language of one versus the other. In these approaches, republicanism defines itself by the opposition between virtue and corruption, and politics is conceived of as a communal and even existential experience, faced with a liberalism populated by a legal vocabulary and individualism.[66]

A second criticism of republicanism, especially in the version outlined by Skinner or Philip Pettit, involves pointing out that despite the much-vaunted distinction between republicanism and liberalism, the differences between them end up by being highly nuanced, and republicanism is thus absorbed into liberalism. An additional reason to criticize this "liberal republicanism" is its elitist or aristocratic character, which protects the interests of the elite to the detriment of the majority.[67]

The study of Machiavelli has been both the source and setting of these controversies. For those objecting to republicanism according to Skinner or Pettit, the thought of the Florentine should be defined as pursuing democratic rather than republican lines. However, this conclusion has not produced any consensus about Machiavelli's characteristics as a democratic author, a characterization that, as was indicated earlier, has been also the object of criticism for methodological and heuristic reasons.

In some formulations, "Machiavellian democracy" has been associated with the attention Machiavelli paid to the institutions enabling and channeling popular participation. From this point of view, he offered institutional models aimed at overcoming the deficit of participation in contemporary democracies, a deficit sidestepped by elitist republicanism.[68] However, in other readings, Machiavelli's conceptions of the political role of the "people" have led to him being portrayed as a radical political theorist, since popular participation, driven by a "humor" of rejection for all forms of domination, would be, by definition, antithetical to all regulatory order. In this sense, the republic would be an especially dense moment of political life, defined by the challenges brought against institutional order.[69]

How should the readings analyzed in this book be seen in the context of these theoretical discussions? This question may be answered in two different, yet possibly complementary rather than antagonistic ways, whereby theory and history are made to dialogue. One option is to use contemporary theoretical discussions to characterize or analyze the historical accounts given here. Another option is to identify whether certain arguments in these historical accounts can contribute anything further to contemporary theoretical discussions.

A first point to note, to state the obvious, is that the reception of Machiavelli in the Spanish-speaking Atlantic world between 1880 and 1940 reveals a series of topics and controversies similar to those addressed in current political theory. This is in addition to what was pointed out in the previous section concerning the similarities in reception as analyzed in the English-speaking Atlantic world. However, this does not mean that either the answers or the arguments agree (this topic will be discussed shortly), nor that their rigor and richness are comparable. Neither is there a proposal for a genealogy able to nuance the originality or singularity of current discussions. The sole interest at this point is to indicate that there are clear similarities between the problems and the axes of reflection defining the reading of the Spanish-speaking Atlantic world in the period studied in this book, and those running through a good part of current output in the sphere of political theory devoted to Machiavelli.

In this sense, and second, it has been noted that there were readings that identified and emphasized Machiavelli's democratic arguments, as was the case, for example, with Mariano de Vedia y Mitre. According to this Argentine intellectual, Machiavelli connected freedom and people when he revisited Roman history and even highlighted the role played by conflict between the people and the elites as a reason for freedom. Machiavelli had coined the modern notion of the republic as a "popular government."

However, De Vedia y Mitre did not see (and possibly did not try to, either) Machiavelli as a writer who supported the intensification of popular participation which would thus enable the functioning of liberal democracy to be optimized. It is worth recalling that De Vedia developed an interest in the Florentine author when liberal democracy in Argentina, and not only in Argentina, was under threat. Neither did De Vedia y Mitre envisage popular participation as a challenge (one that was furthermore both desirable and necessary) to the established order: that is, as an expression of political radicalization that was healthy for freedom.

Instead, for De Vedia y Mitre, the main appeal of Machiavelli's arguments arose from the fact that his conception of mixed government offered democratic principles, institutions, and actions an important place, without requiring people's sovereignty to be the substantial and exclusive principle of political order. Machiavelli offered the possibility of considering democracy without resorting to its modern foundation. In other words, he was an author whose democratic arguments could be approached from a perspective defined by caution or even by criticism of democracy.

In sum, De Vedia y Mitre's reading envisages a possible form of the reception of Machiavelli's democratic postulates which is different than, if not opposed to, those formulated by contemporary theoretical proposals. Rather than justifying a radical version of democracy (both for aiming to achieve greater popular participation and for confronting the liberal regulatory order), they were able to sustain arguments which sought to mitigate the place of and role played by democratic participation (even if this took place in a mixed government defined by conflict instead of consensus). Machiavelli, as a democratic writer, could offer a moderate alternative to democracy based on people's sovereignty.

However, the readings of Machiavelli made by intellectuals such as De Vedia y Mitre cannot be defined as an elitist form of republicanism. On the contrary, this writer, inscribed in Argentine liberalism, highlighted how, for Machiavelli, the main threat to the republic came from the elites, not the people. Indeed, those who were in favor of an elitist or aristocratic republic, or, similarly, of a republic based on order rather than freedom, were anti-liberal authors. This was visible in the work of Argentine authors like Julio Irazusta and Spanish ones like Francisco Javier Conde.

In parallel, the accusation that liberal republicanism was elitist or aristocratic was particularly prevalent among anti-liberal authors. One of the forms in which liberalism encountered repudiation, as seen in this book, was through its association with the established elites, who were the object of criticism for being corrupt and displaying anti-national tendencies. However, it must be said that this criticism was not made in the name of a more radical democracy free from a liberal format largely because of renewed popular political participation.

On the contrary, criticism of the elitist nature of liberal republicanism stemmed from support for an authoritarian and anti-liberal political order based, for example, on a direct bond between an exceptional leader and popular majorities. Anti-elitism was not enshrined in calls for radical democracy, but in an authoritarian regime which relied on popular support: according to Ernesto Palacio, in the name of a "democratic dictatorship." In this sense, it should be noted that those who voiced such arguments in Argentina adhered (at least at some point in their public career) to Peronism (such as Ernesto Palacio himself). At a more general level, these arguments were in tune with the revalidation of personal leaderships running from the 1920s to the 1940s in the Spanish-speaking Atlantic world. These were based on doctrines that naturally transcended any possible appropriations of Machiavelli's work, which, as stated earlier, was the case with Francisco Conde and his analysis of the leadership of Francisco Franco.

To sum up, the tendency to criticize liberal republicanism by labeling it elitist was clear in arguments close to what could, in simplistic but illustrative fashion, be defined as democratic Caesarism, or populism. It is true that, in present times, populism has ceased to be seen as a downgraded version of democracy (with regard to the ideal model supposed by liberal democracy), and is now understood as its possible and even legitimate form.[70] It is equally verifiable that in contemporary political theory, Machiavelli has been linked to populism, with a positive rather than condemnatory appreciation.[71] At all events, it may be highlighted that, in the sources studied here, the point of departure for criticism of liberal republicanism in favor of populist experiences was a conviction nursed by anti-liberal authoritarianism, rather than by demands for radical democracy.

Lastly, it has been pointed out that one of the key issues, especially in Argentine readings, was the convergence, as well as the divergence, between republicanism and liberalism. It was indicated above that the tension, or at least the distinction, between republicanism and liberalism is a central axis of contemporary political theory. This distinction has been drawn on the basis that republicanism would offer a more substantial political life (because of its emphasis on civic participation, providing the stimulus to recreate communal political experiences, even those of an existential character) in comparison to liberalism. Republicanism would propose, in sum, an experience of freedom superior to that of liberalism.

Argentine readings of Machiavelli reveal a register of differences between liberalism and republicanism which took different paths to those emphasized by these theoretical proposals. One of the points that has been most commonly explored as an indicator of this tension, visible among both liberal and anti-liberal authors, was the authoritarian projection of republicanism. In the name of republican principles such as virtue, inequality and hierarchy could be justified before the egalitarian individualism of liberal democracy and its postulate of one person, one vote. Besides, its main principles (even if, in addition to order and virtue, freedom or the common good was included) were opposed to modern freedoms and could thus constitute the foundation for authoritarianism.

These arguments, as already noted, are less visible among the Spanish authors mentioned here. The possibility of an authoritarian republicanism as a threat to modern freedoms seems to have found less favor in a political culture where republicanism shared elements in common with liberalism, starting with its controversies over the issue of the monarchy. For this reason, it was, in general terms, a radicalized variant of liberalism due to its appeals to democracy, although it adopted a reformist tone enhanced by a harmonic conception of society and its dynamics (at least until the first few decades of the twentieth century).

Although with a few differences, this convergence also occurred, of course, in the United States, where the classical republicanism prevalent at the time of the American Revolution, not without its tensions, culminated in the synthesis represented by the liberal republic enshrined in the 1787 Constitution. The political affirmation of that synthesis can be seen as undeniably laborious and conflictive (compared with other classical visions) if the time frame is extended to include the 1860–5 Civil War, or if the distinction between liberalism and republicanism is contemplated as a way of characterizing the frictions and differences between the federal government, in whose design prevailed the liberal principles of limited government, and the states, which entertained long-lasting republican principles justifying greater attributions to those accepted for the federal government.[72]

In Argentina, however, the distinction, in terms of opposition, between republicanism and liberalism was consolidated in the historiography portraying the country's political history. On the one hand, this can be seen in the statement that there were republican foundations for non-liberal governments and political experiences. The most important political cycle of the first half of the nineteenth century, led by Juan Manuel de Rosas (repudiated by the Generation of 1837 liberals, who called him Machiavelli), featured popular support, an authoritarian cast, and an appeal to republican principles to legitimize authoritarianism, such as order and virtue.[73]

At a more general level, Argentine political life in the nineteenth century has been defined as republican (instead of liberal), due to traits that, in addition to electoral participation and public mobilization, included resorting to arms as an accepted way of resolving conflict. Violence as a legitimate form of politics had recourse to the "citizens up in arms" for justification.[74] Once the State was consolidated in 1880, armed insurrection against State authority, fueled by the argument that it was about defending the Constitution against a bad government, lasted and even changed its *raison d'être*. Instead of justifying armed uprisings in the name of federalism and the autonomy of the provincial States (as happened up until the 1880s),[75] it became a language used to rationalize the actions of political forces that claimed to represent general interests (even those of the nation itself). This was the case with the movement that ended up becoming one of the most important political parties of Argentina, the Unión Cívica Radical (whose name, by the way, has strong republican echoes).[76]

This style of republican language, although it chose as its target the government and not the State, objected to one of the distinctive traits of the modern State, which was its monopoly of legitimate violence, and went up against a State based on liberal principles.[77] The fact that liberalism in Argentina has been directed at the State-building process (meaning a liberalism of government, not of the opposition, aimed at building institutions rather than expanding freedoms) laid the ground for an appeal to freedom based on republican arguments, against the excesses of power as wielded by a liberal State.[78] In fact, similar arguments (the armed uprising against a bad government) were revived on the occasion of the first coup which took place in twentieth-century Argentina, in 1930. This episode was supported and accompanied by anti-liberal public figures and intellectuals who have already been mentioned in this book and who were at the time interested in republicanism as an alternative to liberal democracy, such as Julio Irazusta and Ernesto Palacio.[79]

None of this should ignore the fact that Argentina had its own version of a liberal republican synthesis in its 1853–60 Constitution, or the existence of a broad and enduring consensus (at least until the 1930s) on the matter. Neither does it imply forgetting that the distinction between republic and democracy was reiterated in layers of Argentine liberalism which were reluctant to entertain the notion of the expansion of political rights, or that the elites identified with the liberal project of nation saw themselves as "republican aristocracies."[80] That is, the elitist declension of republican language was not exclusive to anti-liberalism. But this does not conceal the fact that, in Argentina, republican language was able to justify, according to the case in question, the arbitrary exercise of power, or appeals to the people and civic participation which were in tension with, when not in opposition to, liberal democracy, individual liberties, and the authority of the liberal State. In this context, then, the readings of Machiavelli in Argentina can be understood as specific expressions of this oscillating relationship between republicanism, liberalism, and democracy.

At all events, if the focus is turned towards the political theory discussions mentioned at the beginning of this section, the readings of Machiavelli in Argentina can be presented as a historical case revealing the tensions lying between republicanism and liberalism, different than those which attracted the most attention in these theoretical productions/formulations. Rather than a counterpoint that turns on freedom (that is, balancing between two traditions that made freedom their core principle, where republicanism would offer the fullest version), the Argentine texts studied here reveal another possibility: republicanism as the doctrinal source for an authoritarian repertoire, or for the institutional rupture of the State and liberal democracy.[81]

## Notes

1. See López García, *Estado y Derecho en el franquismo: el nacionalsindicalismo*.
2. Manuel Suárez Cortina, "El republicanismo institucionista en la Restauración," *Ayer: Revista de Historia Contemporánea*, vol. 39, 3, 2000,

pp. 61–81; Manuel Suárez Cortina, *Los caballeros de la razón: cultura institucionista y democracia parlamentaria en la España liberal*, Madrid, Genueve, 2019.
3. Adolfo Posada, *Tratado de Derecho Político. Vol. I*, Madrid, Librería General de Victoriano Suárez, 1923, pp. 341–2.
4. Francisco Ayala, Eduardo L. Llorens, and Nicolás Pérez Serrano, *El derecho político de la Segunda República*. Preliminary study, ed. and notes by Sebastián Martín, Madrid, Universidad Carlos III, 2011.
5. Adolfo Posada, *Principios de Derecho Político*, Madrid, Imprenta de la Revista de Legislación, 1884, pp. 248–9. See also p. 241.
6. Francisco Giner de los Ríos, *Estudios jurídicos y políticos*, Madrid, Imprenta de Julio Cosano, 1921, p. 186.
7. Posada, *Tratado de Derecho Político. Vol. 1*, pp. 279–80. See also Posada, *La idea del Estado y la guerra europea*; Posada, *Teoría social y jurídica del Estado*.
8. Posada, *Tratado de Derecho Político. Vol. 1*, p. 345.
9. Ibid. pp. 379–80.
10. Ibid. p. 281.
11. Ibid. pp. 543–4. See also p. 380, note 1, where he states: "Machiavelli's thought [. . .] is too complex to reflect in either a condemnatory or approving formula."
12. See López García, *Estado y Derecho en el Franquismo*, pp. 127–71; García Manrique, *La filosofía de los derechos humanos durante el franquismo*, pp. 179–85, 223–36; Rodríguez, *Filosofía Política de Luis Legaz y Lacambra*, pp. 85–141, 203–40; Rivaya, *Filosofía del Derecho y primer franquismo (1937–1945)*, pp. 34–8, 50–75, 95–108, 200–4, 209–11, 230–4, 336–45, 386–95, 446–9; Rivaya, *Una historia de la filosofía del derecho española del siglo XX*, pp. 87–9, 114–29, 153–9; Nicolás Sesma Landrín, "Sociología del Instituto de Estudios Políticos: un 'grupo de elite' intelectual al servicio del partido único y del Estado franquista," in Miguel Ángel Ruiz Carnicer (ed.), *Falange, las culturas políticas del fascismo en la España de Franco (1936-1975). Vol. 1*, Zaragoza, Institución Fernando el Católico, 2013, pp. 253–88.
13. Legaz y Lacambra, *Introducción a la Ciencia del Derecho*, p. 243.
14. Ibid. p. 245.
15. Ibid. p. 252.
16. Ibid. pp. 248–9.
17. Isaiah Berlin, "La originalidad de Maquiavelo," in Berlin, *Contra la Corriente*, pp. 85–143.
18. Legaz y Lacambra, *Introducción a la Ciencia del Derecho*, p. 249.
19. Luis Legaz y Lacambra, *Filosofía del Derecho*, Barcelona, Bosch, 1953, p. 345.
20. Ibid. pp. 646–9. A similar argument could be read in Luis Izaga, *Elementos de derecho político. Vol. 1*, Barcelona, Casa Editorial Bosch, 1952, pp. 256–7.

21. Conde has been defined as the expression of a "falangism rooted in Ortega" (in reference to the philosopher José Ortega y Gasset). See Nicolás Sesma Landrín, "Sociología del Instituto de Estudios Políticos," pp. 253–88, especially p. 275; López García, *Estado y Derecho en el franquismo*, pp. 79–126.
22. Conde, *El saber político de Maquiavelo*, p. 154.
23. Ibid. p. 171.
24. Ibid. p. 198. Other authors also detected Machiavelli's "rationalism" but repudiated it, linking it with immorality (not neutrality as a value) and individualism: for example, Fernando Mellado, *Tratado elemental de Derecho Político*, Madrid, Manuel G. Hernández, 1891, pp. 135–6.
25. Conde, *El saber político*, pp. 179–80. See also pp. 172–7. Conde explains here that the "irrational dimension" of Machiavelli's politics does not mean that his doctrine has a relation with the "theory of 'exceptional cases' or states of necessity. [Because this] is equivalent to transplanting into his work notions and concepts that only have a reason within the confines of the political theory of the nineteenth and twentieth centuries."
26. Conde, *El saber político*, pp. 162–3.
27. Ibid. p. 164.
28. Ibid. p. 201.
29. Legaz y Lacambra drew a parallelism between Machiavelli and Schmitt. In his opinion, the ontology of the Florentine and the concept of "the political" of the German author shared an "absolute" conception of politics.
30. Conde, *El saber político*, p. 204.
31. Ibid. p. 196.
32. Ibid. p. 188.
33. Ismael Saz, "Franco, ¿caudillo fascista? Sobre las sucesivas y contradictorias concepciones falangistas del caudillaje franquista," *Historia y Política*, 27, 2012, p. 43 (pp. 27–50). In this text, Saz points out that Machiavelli was not particularly valued by Conde, as he was an author about whom he entertained much ambivalence, in particular at the point in his public career when this text was written: the second half of the 1940s. By then, Conde had devoted himself to highlighting the specifically Spanish character of Francisco Franco's "*caudillismo*," thus distancing himself from references to Nazism and Fascism, whose connection with Machiavelli Conde himself had postulated on some occasions. In fact, in a text immediately prior to the one quoted here, Conde's considerations about Machiavelli had a more visibly critical tone. They basically underlined that the "appearance of truth," which, according to Conde, was enough in Machiavelli to guarantee the public order, led to the non-creation of a "political community," meaning the "appearance of community, a despotic community": Francisco Javier Conde, *La sabiduría maquiavélica: política y retórica*

*(1947)*, in Conde, *Escritos y fragmentos políticos, Vol. I*, pp. 117–43 (the passage referred to is on pp. 142–3).

34. Legaz y Lacambra's legal and philosophical training, as well as his changing political positions, have been an object of controversy among scholars, precisely because of their variety and mutations throughout his career (natural law, Kelsen, Schmitt), so it is reveling to consider Legaz's "moderation" of Machiavelli from this perspective. In fact, the primacy of politics and power over morality and law in Legaz has already been pointed out: López García, *Estado y Derecho en el Franquismo*, pp. 136–9, 150–2.

35. Statements that may certainly be found in Spanish authors: for example, Enrique Gil Robles, *Tratado de Derecho Político según los principios de la filosofía y el derecho cristianos*, Salamanca, Imprenta y Encuadernación Católica Salmanticense, 1909, pp. 192–3, 210.

36. An interpretation similar to that of García Mérou or De Vedia is found in the Italian–Cuban Orestes Ferrara, *Maquiavelo*, pp. 199–234.

37. Legaz y Lacambra was a critic of Krausism. López García, *Estado y derecho en el franquismo*, pp. 162–3.

38. It has been seen that there were intellectual references concerning this subject in common between Argentine and Spanish writers, despite the counterpoint between them, like the German theory of the State. For example, the author Georg Jellinek was quoted by Posada and De Vedia y Mitre when relating Machiavelli to the modern notion of the State.

39. In fact, Machiavelli was sometimes associated with tyranny rather than absolutism because the latter corresponded to the "Christian prince." "Absolute monarchy, despite everything, admits some moderations: those of an ethical character [. . .] For this special situation of the absolute king, restrained, not by legal attachments, but merely by moral ones, the vital importance given in times of absolute regimes by writers to the Christian training and education of kings is implicit. This is the result of the almost unanimous rejection voiced by the writers of the time, in reaction to the Machiavellian theory advising the Prince to step out of the moral domain for reasons of State and political need or convenience. First of all, the King must be adorned with the moral virtues Christianity preaches for all men." Izaga, *Elementos de derecho político*, vol. 2, pp. 39–40.

40. Some considerations of those authors about other subjects are also revealing when considering the resistances to and caution displayed about Machiavelli: for example, the postulates of Legaz y Lacambra about the relation between the State and the single party. He defined the party as a Party-Church and conceived its relation with the State by taking as a reference the relation between the State and the Catholic Church in the Spanish Old Regime (as an autonomous organization enshrining the purposes that the State should pursue,

but also subordinate to it in that task). In addition, the Movimiento Nacional (the Francoist party, whose civil religion, for Legaz, had as its main ingredient the Catholic religion) was conceived of as a contemporary version of the role played by the Society of Jesus. Luis Aurelio González Prieto, "La concreción teórica del partido único español franquista," *Revista de Estudios Políticos (nueva época)*, 141, 2008, pp. 41–68; Rivaya, *Filosofía del Derecho y primer franquismo*, pp. 102–8.

41. In this respect, it is worth taking into account the characteristics that have generally been attributed to Spanish anti-liberalism. These feature the tensions between Fascist tendencies (represented by the Falange and subsequently by the Falange JONS - Juntas de Ofensiva Nacional Sindicalista, the space where the groups recognizing pro-Fascist tendencies merged in 1934) and national-Catholic tendencies. Both merged in 1937 in the FET (Falange Española Tradicionalista) of the JONS, in an unstable relationship in which the national-Catholic sectors prevailed. Such characterization, it is worth recalling, along with the priority of political action over doctrinal orthodoxy, is also valid, in a broad sense, for Argentine anti-liberalism, as seen in Chapter 3. For the rest, given the time when the texts seen here are located, it is necessary to remember a point mentioned above in the discussion of Conde's considerations. These were published in the second post-war period and, therefore, at a time when the intellectuals close to Francoism moderated their pre-war sympathies because of Spain's alignment with the West in the Cold War context. The justification for Francoism in an anti-totalitarian, nationalist, conservative, and Catholic key (which did not completely eradicate the historical tensions between Falange and the regime) deepened over that time. Ismael Saz, "Las culturas de los nacionalismos franquistas," *Ayer: Revista de historia contemporánea*, vol. 71, 3, 2008, pp. 153–74; Sesma Landrin, "'La dialéctica de los puños y de las pistolas,'" pp. 51–82.

42. See, for example, J. Maury Mateos, *Ensayo de un estudio acerca de Nicolas Maquiavelo y principalmente de su obra El Príncipe*, Málaga, Tip. A. Castro, 1915; Rodríguez Aniceto, *Maquiavelo y Nietzsche*; Recaredo F. de Velasco, *Referencias y transcripciones para la historia de la literatura política en España; la razón de estado; el tiranicidio; el derecho de resistencia al poder; bibliografía de la literatura política*, Madrid, Editorial Reus, 1925; Edmundo González Blanco, *Introducción a El Príncipe: comentado por Napoleón Bonaparte*, Madrid, Ediciones Ibéricas, 1933, pp. 4–247.

43. It is worth saying that a recurring topic among Spanish authors, which is less visible among the Argentines, is the link between Machiavelli's republicanism and the revolutionary terrorism of Jacobin origins. See the authors mentioned in the previous note. In Argentina, only

Ernesto Quesada turned to Machiavelli to justify terror, but this was a terror applied by power, not revolutionary terrorism.

44. It is worth underlining once more that this distinction is not intended to be conclusive or to ignore nuances, but is an initial characterization that, at least, enables certain axes or reading topics prevailing in different intellectual geographies in the Hispanic Atlantic world to be established. Republic and State, besides, were far from being mutually exclusive, even in works by the same author, as is exemplified by the case of De Vedia y Mitre himself. Or, to mention another Hispanic American figure, Orestes Ferrara, who emphasized Machiavelli's republicanism but stated that the core of his thought was the State (in its modern sense, inasmuch as it was a legal regime designed to consolidate external and internal freedom), and the theme of forms of government was a secondary or subordinate concern. See Ferrara, *Maquiavelo*, pp. 36, 201, 263, 274–5.
45. Arbulu Barturen, "La fortuna de Maquiavelo en España," pp. 3–28. See Chapter 1.
46. Ángel Duarte, "Los significados históricos del republicanismo," in Nicolas Berjoan, Eduardo Higueras Castañeda and Sergio Sánchez Collantes (eds), *El republicanismo en el espacio ibérico contemporáneo: recorridos y perspectivas*, Madrid, Casa de Velázquez, 2021, pp. 9–23.
47. Ángel Duarte and Pere Gabriel, "¿Una sola cultura política republicana ochocentista en España?," *Ayer: Revista de Historia Contemporánea*, vol. 39, 3, 2000, pp. 11–34.
48. Manuel Suárez Cortina (ed.), *Libertad, armonía y tolerancia: la cultura institucionista en España*, Madrid, Tecnos, 2008.
49. Ángel Duarte, "Los republicanos del ochocientos y la memoria de su tiempo," *Ayer: Revista de Historia contemporánea*, vol. 58, 2, 2005, pp. 207–28.
50. On the other hand, the limits to anti-liberal republicanism in Spain have been pointed out: for example, in the research into the Falange, the Spanish political Fascist space, as a consequence of the prevalence of a democratic and liberal (parliamentary) conception of republic (conceived of by the 1931 Second Republic). Also, in this context, the relation between the monarchy and the Francoist regime has been underscored to explain the lack of anti-liberal versions of republicanism. See Nicolás Sesma Landrín, "El republicanismo en la cultura política falangista: de la Falange fundacional al modelo de la V República francesa," in *Espacio, Tiempo y Forma*, Serie V, Historia Contemporánea, vol. 18, 2006, pp. 261–83.
51. Pocock, *El momento maquiavélico*; Gordon Wood, *The Creation of the American Republic, 1776–1787*, Chapel Hill, University of North Carolina Press, 1969; Bernard Baylin, *Los orígenes ideológicos de la revolución norteamericana*, Madrid, Tecnos, 2012.

52. Alissa Ardito, *Machiavelli and the Modern State: The Prince, the Discourses on Livy, and the Extended Territorial Republic*, New York, Cambridge University Press, 2015.
53. Price, "L. Arthur Burd, Lord Acton, and Machiavelli."
54. To these two moments a third could be added, in the middle, in the context of the Civil War and around the figure of Abraham Lincoln as a republican dictator. See Phillip Shaw Paludan, "'Dictator Lincoln': Surveying Lincoln and the Constitution," *OAH Magazine of History*, Vol. 21, 1, 2007, pp. 8–13; Thomas E. Cronin, "Machiavelli´s Prince: An Americanist´s Perspective," in Timothy Fuller (ed.), *Machiavelli´s Legacy: The Prince After Five Hundred Years*, Philadelphia, University of Pennsylvania Press, 2015, pp. 127–55.
55. Tulio Halperín Donghi, *Tradición política española e ideología revolucionaria de Mayo*, Buenos Aires, Prometeo, 2010; Frank Safford, "Politics, Ideology and Society in Post- Independence Spanish America," in Leslie Bethell (ed.), *The Cambridge History of Latin America, Vol. III. From Independence to c. 1870*, Cambridge, Cambridge University Press, 1985, pp. 347–422; Ambrosio Velasco Gómez, "Republicanismo anticolonial y republicanismo nacionalista en el Renacimiento," in Moisés González García and Rafael Herrera Guillén (eds), *Maquiavelo en España y Latinoamérica: del siglo XVI al XXI*, Madrid, Tecnos, 2014, pp. 267–89; Aguilar and Rojas, *El republicanismo en Hispanoamérica*; Rafael Rojas, *Las repúblicas del aire: utopía y desencanto en la revolución hispanoamericana*, Buenos Aires, Alfaguara, 2010; David Brading, "El republicanismo clásico y el patriotismo criollo: Simón Bolívar y la Revolución Hispanoamericana," in David Brading, *Mito y profecía en la historia de México*, Mexico, Vuelta, 1988, pp. 78–111; Silvana Carozzi, *Las filosofías de la revolución: Mariano Moreno y los jacobinos rioplatenses en la prensa de Mayo: 1810–1815*, Buenos Aires, Prometeo, 2011; Gabriela Rodríguez Rial (ed.), *República y republicanismos: conceptos, tradiciones y prácticas en pugna*, Buenos Aires, Miño y Dávila, 2016; Gabriel Entin, "Catholic Republicanism: The Creation of the Spanish American Republics During Revolution," *Journal of the History of Ideas*, vol. 79, 2018, pp. 105–23.
56. José Antonio Aguilar, "Dos conceptos de república," in José Antonio Aguilar and Rafael Rojas (eds), *El republicanismo en Hispanoamérica: ensayos de historia intelectual y política*, Mexico, Fondo de Cultura Económica, 2002, pp. 57–85.
57. For example, statements like "This immoral and disastrous work is worthy of the most serious censorship" (Juan Vicente González, *Manual de Historia Universal*, Caracas, Rojas Hermanos, 1869, p. 593); or "Great monarchies triumph, restoring national union, which was good, but strengthening administrative despotism, which is an ill. The philosopher of this school is Machiavelli; his last word

is the Prince. Up to then Politics had been subordinate to Religion; Machiavelli made it independent of Religion and Morality and reduced it completely to skill" (José Victorino Lastarria, *La América*. *Vol. 1*, Madrid, Editorial La América, 1917, pp. 140–1; also, the definition of the Chilean Diego Barros Arana about *The Prince* as "the most infamous and immoral code of tyranny," in *Obras Completas. Vol. IV: Nociones de Historia Literaria*, Santiago de Chile, Imprenta Cervantes, 1908, p. 329.

58. Giner, *Estudios jurídicos y políticos*, p. 186 (footnote); Azorín, *El Político* [1919], Biblioteca Nueva, Madrid, 2007, pp. 147–53; Juan P. Ramos, "Don Diego de Saavedra Fajardo," in Juan P. Ramos, *Ensayos hispánicos*, Buenos Aires, Institución Cultural Española, 1942, pp. 157–79.

59. Silvana Carozzi and Maximiliano Ferrero, "El siglo XIX rioplatense y el ensayo liminar de una nación republicana," in Gabriela Rodríguez Rial (ed.), *República y republicanismos: conceptos, tradiciones y prácticas en pugna*, Buenos Aires, Miño y Dávila, 2016, pp. 227–44.

60. See Boris Litvin, "Mapping Rule and Subversion: Perspective and the Democratic Turn in Machiavelli Scholarship," *European Journal of Political Theory*, vol. 18, 1, 2019, pp. 3–25; Jérémie Barthas, "Machiavelli in Political Thought from the Age of Revolutions to the Present," in John N. Najemy (ed.), *The Cambridge Companion to Machiavelli*, Cambridge, Cambridge University Press, 2010, pp. 256–73. Another field of interest in contemporary Machiavellian studies is the relationship between politics and the emotions. See, for example: Nicole Hochner, "Machiavelli: Love and the Economy of Emotions," *Italian Culture*, vol. 32, 2, 2014, pp. 79–84; Mark Hoipkemier, "Machiavelli and the Double Politics of Ambition," *Political Studies*, vol. 66, 1, 2018, pp. 245–60; Manuel Knoll, "The Role of Emotions, Desires and Passions in Politics: Machiavelli's Political Psychology of Motivation," *Lo Sguardo: Rivista di Filosofia*, vol. 27, II, 2018, pp. 49–59.

61. Lefort, *Maquiavelo*.

62. Skinner, *La libertad antes del liberalismo*. See also Hans Baron, *The Crisis of Early Italian Renaissance: Civic Humanism and Republican Liberty in an Age of Classicism and Tyranny*, Princeton, Princeton University Press, 1966; Felix Gilbert, *Machiavelli and Guicciardini: Politics and History in Sixteenth Century Florence*, Princeton, Princeton University Press, 1965; Harvey Mansfield, *Machiavelli's New Modes and Orders*, London, Cornell University Press, 1979; James Hankins (ed.), *Renaissance Civic Humanism Reconsidered*, Cambridge, Cambridge University Press, 2000.

63. See Catherine H. Zuckert, "Review Essay: Machiavelli: Radical Democratic Political Theorist?," *The Review of Politics*, 81, 2019, pp. 499–510; Jean Fabien Spitz, "The Reception of Machiavelli in

Contemporary Republicanism: Some Ambiguities and Paradoxes," in David Johnston, Nadia Urbinati, and Camila Vergara (eds), *Machiavelli on Liberty and Conflict*, Chicago, University of Chicago Press, 2017, pp. 309–29.
64. Pier Paolo Portinaro, *La apropiación de Maquiavelo. Una crítica de la Italian Theory*, Salamanca, Guillermo Escolar Editor, 2021. See Roberto Esposito, *Pensamiento viviente: origen y actualidad de la filosofía italiana*, Buenos Aires, Amorrortu, 2015.
65. Skinner, *La libertad*; Philip Pettit, *Republicanismo. Una teoría sobre la libertad y el gobierno*, Barcelona, Paidós, 1999; Maurizio Viroli, *Republicanismo*, Santander, Ediciones Universidad Cantabria, 2015.
66. Pocock, *El momento*; John G. A. Pocock, "Virtudes, derechos y manners: un modelo para historiadores del pensamiento político," in John G. A. Pocock, *Doce estudios*, Madrid, Marcial Pons, 2002, pp. 317–37; Hannah Arendt, *La condición humana*, Madrid, Paidós, 2005. See Joyce Appleby, *Liberalism and Republicanism*, Cambridge, MA, Harvard University Press, 1992.
67. Spitz, "The Reception of Machiavelli in Contemporary Republicanism."
68. John McCormick, *Machiavellian Democracy*, Cambridge and New York, Cambridge University Press, 2011.
69. Miguel E. Vatter, *Between Form and Event. Machiavelli's Theory of Political Freedom*, Dordrecht, Kluwer Academic, 2000. See also Filippo del Lucchese, Fabio Frosini, and Vittorio Morfino (eds), *The Radical Machiavelli*, London, Brill, 2015; Christopher Holman, *Machiavelli and the Politics of Democratic Innovation*, Toronto, University of Toronto Press, 2018; Ronald J. Schmidt, Jr, *Reading Politics with Machiavelli*, New York, Oxford University Press, 2018; Yves Winter, *Machiavelli and the Orders of Violence*, Cambridge, Cambridge, University Press, 2018.
70. Ernesto Laclau, *On Populist Reason*, London, Verso, 2002; Cas Mudde and Cristóbal Rovira Kaltwasse, *Populism: A Very Short Introduction*, New York, Oxford University Press, 2017.
71. Sandro Landi, "Multitud, pueblo y populismo en Maquiavelo: un enfoque histórico," *Revista Argentina de Ciencia Política*, vol. 1, 27, 2021, pp. 1–28; Diego von Vacano, "American *Caudillo*: Princely Performative Populism and Democracy in the Americas," *Philosophy and Social Criticism*, vol. 45, 4, 2019, pp. 413–28; Diego von Vacano, *The Art of Power: Machiavelli, Nietzsche and the Making of Aesthetic Political Theory*, Lanham, MD: Lexington Books, 2006; John McCormick, *Reading Machiavelli: Scandalous Books, Suspect Engagements, and the Virtue of Populist Politics*, Princeton, Princeton University Press, 2018.
72. Gary Gerstle, *Libertad y coacción. La paradoja del gobierno estadounidense desde su fundación hasta el presente*, México, FCE, 2017. Regarding the classical vision, Louis Hartz, *La tradición liberal*

*en los Estados Unidos: una interpretación del pensamiento político estadounidense desde la Guerra de Independencia*, Mexico, FCE, 1995. See Robert E. Shalhope, "Toward a Republican Synthesis: The Emergence of an Understanding of Republicanism in American Historiography," *William and Mary Quarterly*, 29, 1972, pp. 49–80; Rodgers, "Republicanism: The Career of a Concept,"pp. 11–38.
73. Myers, *Orden y virtud*.
74. Hilda Sabato, *Republics of the New World: The Revolutionary Political Experiment in Nineteenth-Century Latin America*, Princeton, Princeton University Press, 2018; Hilda Sabato, *Buenos Aires en armas: la revolución de 1880*, Buenos Aires, Siglo XXI, 2008; Hilda Sabato, *La política en las calles: entre el voto y la movilización. Buenos Aires, 1862–1880*, Buenos Aires, Sudamericana, 1998.
75. Similarly to other process of State building, the formation of an army subordinate to the national authority and the weakening or elimination of militia formations linked to local authorities (the National Guards) were decisive processes in nineteenth-century Argentina. See Lucas Codesido, *El Ejército de Línea y el poder central: guerra, política militar y construcción estatal en Argentina, 1860–1880*, Buenos Aires, Prohistoria, 2021.
76. Paula Alonso, *Between Revolution and the Ballot Box: The Origins of the Argentine Radical Party in the 1890s*, Cambridge, Cambridge University Press, 2000.
77. In fact, in 1890 an armed uprising took place, known as the "1890 revolution" (an episode from which the Unión Cívica Radical would emerge), among whose characteristics was the fact that the officers of the national army were divided between those who stayed subordinate to the State authority and those who joined the "revolution."
78. Halperin Donghi, *Proyecto y construcción de una nación (1846–1880)*; Botana, *La tradición republicana*; Darío Roldán, "La cuestión liberal en la Argentina en el siglo XIX: política, sociedad, representación," in Beatriz Bragoni and Eduardo Míguez (eds), *Un nuevo orden politico: provincias y estado nacional, 1852–1880*, Buenos Aires, Biblos, 2010, pp. 275–91; Palti, *El momento romántico*.
79. It is worth recalling, in this sense, a point mentioned above regarding some Spanish readings of Machiavelli: the connection between Machiavellian republicanism and revolutionary politics, in a critical sense, associated with Jacobin terrorism or, at least, institutional rupture. Significantly, this topic has not been observed in Argentine readings, and it is worth adding that, in nineteenth-century Argentine political language and until the first half of the twentieth century at least, the notion of revolution – for example, in 1890 and also in 1930 – was used in its classical (or ancient) sense: that is, as a restoration, not a rupture. Leandro Losada, "El ocaso de la 'Argentina liberal' y la tradición republicana: reflexiones en torno a los discursos

públicos de Agustín Justo, Roberto Ortiz y Marcelo T. de Alvear, 1930-1943," *Estudios Sociales*, 54, 2018, pp. 43-66.

80. Leandro Losada, "Aristocracia y democracia: representación política y distinción social en la Argentina, 1810-1930. Un ensayo de interpretación," *Revista Economía y Política*, vol. 4, 1, 2017, pp. 5-36. These formulations, in addition, were not exclusive of the Argentine elite as the answer to the consolidation of the democratic society. See Bernard Manin, *Los principios del gobierno representativo*, Madrid, Alianza, 1998.

81. Similar observations, certainly, have been leveled against liberalism (the anti-democratic position of liberalism is a characterization widely expounded in historiography). See Jorge Nállim, *Transformación y crisis del liberalism: su desarrollo en la Argentina en el período 1930-1955*, Buenos Aires, Gedisa, 2014; David Rock, *La Argentina autoritaria: los nacionalistas, su historia y su influencia en la vida pública*, Buenos Aires, Ariel, 1993. Without going into the consistency of this characterization, here it is merely held that the convergence between republicanism and authoritarianism is historically verifiable, and that this verification is revealing in relation to a theoretical output focused on the connection between republicanism and freedom.

# Epilogue and Overview: Machiavelli in Spanish-Speaking Political Thought

In order to analyze the circulation and reception of Machiavelli's ideas in the Spanish-speaking Atlantic world, this book has reconstructed how his works were read, discussed, and understood in Argentina between 1880 and 1940. At the same time, it proposes different scales of analysis, through study of the chosen national case, on the one hand, and Spain and its former colonies, on the other. This enables an in-depth look at the modulations and problems differentiating these readings from those prevalent in the English-speaking world.

The affirmation that Argentine and Spanish sources (those studied in a more systematic way in these pages), offer evidence characterizing the reception of Machiavelli's work in the Spanish-speaking Atlantic world does not mean that these sources have aspects that can be generalized and applied to the whole, but rather that there are certain tendencies that deserve to be highlighted. Irrespective of whether they can be generalized or not, Argentine and Spanish readings provide evidence of the ways in which Machiavelli was interpreted in Spanish-speaking Atlantic countries. In addition, there is an extensive range of readings and invocations that reveal attitudes which are very different to those considered typical: disinterest, prejudice, and banal repudiation, arising from an anti-Machiavellian tradition of a Catholic cast. This can be related to some particularities in both cases, which is precisely what motivated their choice. It is worth recalling these briefly.

Argentina has been defined, among the American nations that were formerly Spanish colonies, as a country where liberalism enjoyed an early hegemony, cutting across political and ideological differences, throughout the nineteenth century and until the first few decades of the twentieth, from Catholicism to socialism. This was a long-lasting phenomenon, to the point where it has been affirmed that, despite the crisis of liberalism raging in the country (in tune with the rest of the West) since the first post-war period, and more emphatically since the 1930s, liberalism continued to be valid trait in Argentine politics and political thought. These features made the Argentine case, *a priori*, a revealing one for a study of the reception of Machiavelli, since the prevalence of liberalism implied less influence issuing from the legacies of the Old Regime, one of which was, precisely, a negative consideration of Machiavelli's work, largely due to Catholic influence.

Spain, in turn, was relevant mainly for obvious reasons related to its weight and influence in the Spanish-speaking Atlantic world. Besides, it was the driver of anti-Machiavellian Catholic tradition. However, at the same time, it was also defined by certain political and doctrinal tendencies that, since the nineteenth century and the beginning of the twentieth, opened up the possibility of identifying ways of invoking and reading Machiavelli that went beyond Catholic anti-Machiavellianism. These tendencies are, specifically, republicanism and the transformation, growth, and consolidation of anti-liberalism, whose expressions included certain modulations inspired by sources different than traditional ones, such as those provided by Italian Fascism or German National Socialism. Spain is also an example of the incomparable political success achieved by anti-liberalism in the context of the Spanish-speaking Atlantic world: the regime of Francisco Franco, which lasted almost forty years. Both aspects (the republican tradition, and the renewal and success of anti-liberalism), then, were political and intellectual features that justify the question of whether they had had an influence on the reception or interest in Machiavelli. And, if they had, what relation could be established between them and the anti-Machiavellian legacy prevalent in Spanish thought since the seventeenth century?

In sum, on the one hand, a country that was "born" liberal, and thus singular for that reason in the Hispanic American context, and on the other, a nation that, in addition to being a *sine qua non* in the Spanish-speaking Atlantic world, displayed certain features relating to Machiavelli in its political and intellectual history, ranging from revulsion to disinterest, as well as attraction and even a positive reception. These features made Argentine and Spanish readings pertinent and relevant cases for study, to examine how Machiavelli was read between 1880 and 1940, a period defined by the consolidation, crisis, and decline of liberalism. From this exploration, then, some general conclusions may be drawn as a balance and epilogue, beyond casuistry; some of these concern the history of intellectual thought while others are connected to political history.

Regarding the former, one point to be highlighted is that, precisely, the reception of and interest in Machiavelli in the Spanish-speaking Atlantic world were extremely important. The weight of anti-Machiavellian tradition was not translated into disinterest, outright rejection, or the reiteration of commonplace platitudes. Although these phenomena existed, they were accompanied by others at the same time, with particular attention being paid to reflection about the meaning and impact of Machiavelli's ideas on Western political thought, as well as about the controversies and debates around his doctrinal and ideological meanings.

In this area, readings, debates, and interpretations worthy of note in other intellectual and political geographies, like the English-speaking Atlantic world, were also the object of discussion in the Spanish-speaking Atlantic space. Machiavelli was understood not only in a "Machiavellian" key as a leading author for tyranny, immorality, or arbitrariness, for both Argentine and Spanish intellectuals analyzed topics such as the relation between him and imperialism, his place in the theory of the State, or the republican content of his thought, and the connection between this and liberalism and democracy. On the subject of the latter, it is worth underlining that the distinction between republicanism and liberalism existed historically in the political thought of the Spanish-speaking Atlantic world, meaning that these are not historiographic or theoretical categories employed to classify the accounts in the historical sources, but that there was an effective distinction between them.

This does not mean, however, that it is not possible to identify the topics or problems most prevalent in Spanish-speaking readings. Machiavelli was extensively studied, quoted, and referred to as regards his ideas about the State and in relation to republicanism. The first of these could be attributed, in part, to the intellectual and academic context in which a more systematic and scholarly approach to the work of Machiavelli emerged: Political Law. It could also be attributed to the broader political scenario at the beginning of the period, defined by the consolidation of a liberal model of State, both in Argentina and in Spain. Regarding the second topic, a distinctive feature was that Machiavelli's republicanism was invoked to delineate a republicanism of a conservative and even authoritarian and anti-liberal cast, or, in another sense, to paint a critical and disparaging portrait of liberal republicanism. Machiavelli was the symbol for a conservative or anti-liberal republicanism, or, in an opposite view, the key figure for a liberal republicanism which was negatively portrayed with an emphasis on its intrinsic impostures and treacheries. In sum, he was useful in both senses to outline the distinction between republicanism and liberalism (regardless of the type of judgement), and could even serve as a basis to discuss, confront, or even refute liberal republicanism. The version of Machiavelli as a crucial author for a liberal republicanism with a positive assessment existed mainly in Argentina, but this was by no means the majority view in the other cases studied in this book.

It has been pointed out that the historical versions examined in this book posit arguments about these topics which are different than those usually emphasized in contemporary political theory. At least three deserve to be highlighted. First, the appeal to the democratic aspects of Machiavelli's thought could justify an alternative conception of democracy, critical of the concept of democracy based on the people's sovereignty, and thus not a radical theory of democracy. Second, Machiavelli enabled the construction of a critical view of liberal republicanism opposed not by democratic republicanism but by an authoritarian version, or at least a hierarchical one. Only in the context of that primacy of hierarchy did some versions take the popular element into account. Third, there were anti-liberal versions of republicanism (as noted earlier, some of them invoking the people and thus employing democratic declensions), as well as anti-liberal and anti-democratic ones. In other words, republicanism was not always or necessarily synonymous with freedom and civic participation; nor was it an expression of dissatisfaction with liberalism in the name of freedom. It was the expression of an authoritarian, elitist, and anti-liberal repertoire, one enabling the separation between liberalism and democracy.

This is where the evidence provided by intellectual history can be connected to political history. Invoking Machiavelli as a way of conceiving of the State or of authority rather than freedom, painting a negative picture of liberal republicanism, or postulating anti-liberal or anti-democratic versions of republicanism, plus the exceptional, infrequent character of the versions expounding the virtues of the convergences between republicanism and liberalism, can be taken together as an indicator of a topic that is well known in historiography. This concerns the singularities of liberalism in the Spanish-speaking Atlantic world, especially in Hispanic America or, on a more general level, the elusive thematization of freedom or of an intellectual and doctrinal synthesis between republicanism, liberalism, and democracy.

In this regard, it must be remembered that appealing to Machiavelli when considering the role of authority and the State, rather than freedom, was quite common among liberal writers, and not only among those who associated him with a non-liberal model of State (like the State-Force or the State-Power). The relationship between the author of *The Prince* and the rule of law, a relation that did not assume any condemnatory notion of his thought (that is, did not link it with limitless power or authoritarianism), can be connected to a central theme at the turn of the twentieth century. This was the construction and consolidation of the liberal State, a topic which was present, with some differences, in both Argentina and Spain. Similarly, the versions proposing a convergence between republicanism and liberalism through Machiavelli, formulated by liberal authors, also contained an appeal to Machiavellian democracy as a moderate alternative to democracy based on popular sovereignty, as it was inscribed in a theory of mixed government. Finally, such formulations, which were not, strictly speaking, elitist versions of republicanism as such, enabled criticism of liberal republicanism in the name of democratic Caesarism.

However, in parallel to this, the readings of Machiavelli also offer indications about the singularities of anti-liberalism. Certainly, a point to highlight in this sense is that the identification of a "liberal" Machiavelli was more common among anti-liberal writers than liberal ones, particularly Catholic authors or those with neo-Thomist and scholastic influences, and this was the reason for their condemnatory portrayal of the Florentine. This may be connected with the points made in the previous paragraph. That is, the "liberal" definition of Machiavelli used as an argument to condemn him is an expression of the antipathy and repudiation leveled at liberalism in general in the first decades of the twentieth century. Furthermore, the criticism of liberalism based on or enabled by Machiavelli's ideas insisted on holding this political tradition responsible for the emergence of totalitarianism. This indicates, in addition to the underlying Catholic view that liberalism and totalitarianism were linked by an immanent conception of politics, a form of criticism acceptable only in countries where liberalism had played a leading role in the construction of the State – in other words, a criticism of liberalism made in the name of freedom and based on a consideration that it was synonymous with power.

A second point to be stressed is that the anti-liberal intellectuals who turned to Machiavelli to justify authoritarianism were, by and large, the exception, even though the liberal legacy relating to the Florentine author was of a condemnatory nature, which was the case, for example, with Alberdi's considerations in Argentina or Posada's views in Spain. The infrequent nature of the appeals to Machiavelli in order to justify authoritarianism should also be underscored, considering that, throughout the first half of the twentieth century, the new variants of anti-liberalism – particularly Fascism, which had adopted Machiavelli as its key figure– had an impact on Argentine and Spanish anti-liberalism. In other words, the infrequent references to Machiavelli in favor of authoritarianism are a significant indicator of the main characteristics of this form of anti-liberalism, meaning the weight of Catholic perspectives, without ignoring the range of diversities and tensions, and the subordinate role played by doctrinal or theoretical concerns. Caution, inconstancy, and even a blatant rejection of Machiavelli in anti-liberalism emerge as testimony of the survival of the Catholic anti-Machiavellian tradition in the Spanish-speaking Atlantic world. And all of this shines a light on another feature to be highlighted. The anti-liberal rejection of Machiavelli was not based on doctrinal concerns, but on his ontology: he made politics independent and, thus, "absolutized" it. The rejection of his ontology was the main issue preventing any possible doctrinal recovery (meaning that he could be invoked as an author writing in support of authoritarianism).

This point leads to two last observations. On the one hand, anti-Machiavellianism in the Spanish-speaking Atlantic world did not entertain purely Catholic modulations. There was a Catholic anti-Machiavellianism and there was a liberal one. These phenomena bore a certain relation to doctrinal readings (as they were associated with liberalism and authoritarianism, respectively), but the real reason underlying them was quite different, and it was something they shared. This is the second observation to be highlighted.

The main reason why Machiavelli was rejected, irrespective of ideological distinctions, lies in the derivations of his ontology: that is, in politics understood as both autonomous and conflictive. Criticism of Machiavelli was frequently based on a rejection of the fact that he stripped politics of its ethical bases or purposes (whether these had to do with morality, religion, or natural law). Even praise and positive assessments were made possible by subordinating or shifting away from these axes of his thought. Thus, it could be said that his politics was not, *per se*, stripped of its ethical horizons, or that it meant, strictly speaking, a neutrality of values (that amorality was not, in fact, immorality). In another area, it was also posited that Machiavelli presented arguments and recommendations for solving rather than sustaining conflict, such as the State, exceptional leadership, hierarchy, and authoritarianism.[1]

This aspect allows us once again to link the clues provided by intellectual history with others from political history. These are that restraint, rejection, or even acceptance of Machiavelli by sidestepping the crux of the conflict indicates the degree of resistance to, or the difficulty in, understanding politics – and particularly democratic politics – as intrinsically conflictive. From this point of view, not only authoritarian recipes, but also those postulating a moralization of politics, arguments which gained visibility in the readings of Machiavelli in the Spanish-speaking Atlantic world as well as in the discussions prompted by his work, can be conceived of as indicators of the difficulties in facing the challenges posed by democratic society and politics.

## Note

1. It is worth recalling that the author who most explicitly saw Machiavelli as an author of conflict, as well as the positive role he attributed to it, the Argentine Mariano de Vedia y Mitre, subordinated this trait by emphasizing that the people (within a mixed government), rather than conflict, were the engine of freedom.

# Bibliography

Acha, Omar, *La trama profunda: historia y vida en José Luis Romero*, Buenos Aires, El Cielo por Asalto, 2005.
Acton, John Dalberg (Lord Acton), "Introduction to L. A. Burd's Edition of *Il Principe* by Machiavelli" (1891), in John Dalberg Acton, *The History of Freedom and Other Essays*, London, MacMillan, 1907, pp. 212–31.
Agüero, Ana Clarisa and Alejandro Eujanián (eds), *Variaciones del reformismo: tiempos y experiencias*, Rosario, Universidad Nacional de Rosario, 2018.
Aguilar, José Antonio and Rafael Rojas (eds), *El republicanismo en Hispanoamérica: ensayos de historia intelectual y política*, Mexico, Fondo de Cultura Económica, 2002.
Aguilar Rivera, José Antonio, *En pos de la quimera: reflexiones sobre el experimento constitucional atlántico*, México, Fondo de Cultura Económica, 2000.
Alberdi, Juan Bautista, *El crimen de la guerra*, in *Escritos póstumos de Juan Bautista Alberdi*, Bernal, Universidad Nacional de Quilmes, 1997.
Alberdi, Juan Bautista, *Escritos póstumos. Vol. XII: Miscelánea. Propaganda revolucionaria*, Buenos Aires, Imprenta Juan Bautista Alberdi, 1900.
Alberdi, Juan Bautista, *Obras completas*, Vol. VIII, Buenos Aires, La Tribuna Nacional, 1887.
Alberdi, Juan Bautista, *Peregrinación de Luz del Día*, in Juan Bautista Alberdi, *Obras completas, Vol. VII*, Buenos Aires, Imprenta de La Tribuna Nacional, 1887.
Alberdi, Juan Bautista, *Bases y puntos de partida para la organización política de la República Argentina*, in Juan Bautista Alberdi, *Obras completas, Vol. III*, Buenos Aires, La Tribuna Nacional, 1886.

Alberdi, Juan Bautista, *Sistema rentístico y económico de la Confederación Argentina* en *Organización de la Confederación Argentina*, Vol. II, Buenos Aires, Casa Editora de Pedro García, 1858.

Alonso, Paula, *Between Revolution and the Ballot Box: The Origins of the Argentine Radical Party in the 1890s*, Cambridge, Cambridge University Press, 2000.

Altamirano, Carlos, "Entre el naturalismo y la psicología: el comienzo de la 'ciencia social' en la Argentina," in Federico Neiburg and Mariano Plotkin (eds), *Intelectuales y expertos: la constitución del conocimiento social en la Argentina*, Buenos Aires, Paidós, 2004.

Appleby, Joyce, *Liberalism and Republicanism*, Cambridge, MA, Harvard University Press, 1992.

Arbulu Barturen, María Begoña, "La fortuna de Maquiavelo en España: las primeras traducciones manuscritas y editadas de *Il principe*," *Ingenium: Revista de Historia del Pensamiento Moderno*, 7, 2013, pp. 3–28.

Ardito, Alissa, *Machiavelli and the Modern State. The Prince, the Discourses on Livy, and the Extended Territorial Republic*, New York, Cambridge University Press, 2015.

Arendt, Hannah, *La condición humana*, Madrid, Paidós, 2005.

Arlotti, Raúl, "Faustino J. Legón: la primera comunidad epistémica del Derecho Político en Argentina y la introducción del Derecho Político en la Universidad Nacional de La Plata," *Revista Anales de la Facultad de Ciencias Jurídicas y Sociales*, 47, 2017, pp. 653–68.

Arlotti, Raúl, "Las primeras lecciones de Derecho Político en la Facultad de Derecho y Ciencias Sociales de la UBA," in Tulio Ortiz (ed.), *Nuevos aportes a la historia de la Facultad de Derecho de la Universidad de Buenos Aires*, Buenos Aires, Facultad de Derecho, UBA, 2014, pp. 47–82.

Armitage, David, "Tres conceptos de historia atlántica," *Revista de Occidente*, 281, 2004, pp. 7–28.

Astrada, Carlos, *La Real Politik: de Maquiavelo a Spengler*, Córdoba, Estudio Gráfico Biffignandi, 1924.

Ayala, Francisco, Eduardo L. Llorens, and Nicolás Pérez Serrano, *El derecho político de la Segunda República. Estudio preliminar, edición y notas de Sebastián Martín*, Madrid, Universidad Carlos III, 2011.

Azorín, *El Político* [1919], Biblioteca Nueva, Madrid, 2007.

Bacolla, Natacha, "A propósito de Rafael Bielsa: semblanza para una historia de la ciencia política en Argentina en los inicios del siglo XX," *Araucaria*, 38, 2017, pp. 545–73.

Bagno, Sandra, "'Maquiavélico' versus 'maquiaveliano' na língua e nos dicionários monolíngües brasileiros," *Cadernos de Tradução*, vol. 2, 22, 2008, pp. 129–50.

Baldini, Enzo (ed.), *Botero e la ragion di Stato*, Florence, Olschki, 1992.

Barbuto, Marcelo, "El momento maquiaveliano: propuesta de un nuevo vocablo para el Diccionario de la Lengua Española (DRAE)," *Desafíos*, vol. 25, 2, 2013, pp. 15–33.

Baron, Hans, *The Crisis of Early Italian Renaissance: Civic Humanism and Republican Liberty in an Age of Classicism and Tyranny*, Princeton, Princeton University Press, 1966.

Barros Arana, Diego, *Obras Completas. Vol. IV: Nociones de Historia Literaria*, Santiago de Chile, Imprenta Cervantes, 1908.

Barthas, Jérémie, "Machiavelli in Political Thought from the Age of Revolutions to the Present," in John N. Najemy (ed.), *The Cambridge Companion to Machiavelli*, Cambridge, Cambridge University Press, 2010, pp. 256–73.

Bassani, L. M. and C. Vivanti, C. (eds), *Machiavelli nella storiografia e nel pensiero politico del XX secolo*, Milan, Giuffrè, 2006.

Baylin, Bernard, *Los orígenes ideológicos de la revolución norteamericana*, Madrid, Tecnos, 2012.

Ben Saad, Nizar, *Machiavel en France: des lumières à la révolution*, Paris, L'Harmattan, 2007.

Berlin, Isaiah, *Contra la corriente: ensayos sobre historia de las ideas*, Mexico, Fondo de Cultura Económica, 1992.

Bessio Moreno, Nicolás, "El sistema filosófico de Agustín Álvarez," in Agustín Álvarez, *¿Adónde vamos?*, Buenos Aires, La Cultura Argentina, 1915.

Bianco, José, *Mis lecturas*, Buenos Aires, Librería Mendesky-Augusto Sabourin e hijo, 1920.

Bianco, José, *Vida de las instituciones políticas*, Buenos Aires, Librería Mendesky-Augusto Sabourin e hijo, 1919.

Bireley, Robert, *The Counter-Reformation Prince: Anti-Machiavellianism or Catholic Statecraft in Early Modern Europe*, Chapel Hill, University of North Carolina Press, 2018.

Bobbio, Norberto, *La teoría de las formas de gobierno en la historia del pensamiento político*, Mexico, Fondo de Cultura Económica, 2012.

Botana, Natalio, *La tradición republicana: Alberdi, Sarmiento y las ideas políticas de su tiempo*, Buenos Aires, Sudamericana, 1997.

Botana, Natalio and Ezequiel Gallo, *De la República posible a la República verdadera*, Buenos Aires, Ariel, 1997.

Brading, David, *Mito y profecía en la historia de México*, Mexico, Vuelta, 1988.

Bruno, Paula, *Martín García Mérou: vida intelectual y diplomática en las Américas*, Bernal, Universidad Nacional de Quilmes, 2019.

Bruno, Paula (ed.), *Visitas culturales en la Argentina, 1898–1936*, Buenos Aires, Biblos, 2014.

Bruno, Paula, *Pioneros culturales de la Argentina: biografías de una época, 1860–1910*, Buenos Aires, Siglo XXI, 2011.

Bruno, Paula, "Un balance acerca del uso de la expresión generación del 80 entre 1920 y 2000," *Secuencia*, 68, 2007, pp. 117–61.

Buchbinder, Pablo, *Los Quesada: letras, ciencias y política en la Argentina: 1850–1934*, Buenos Aires, Edhasa, 2012.

Buchbinder, Pablo, ¿Revolución en los claustros? La reforma universitaria de 1918, Buenos Aires, Sudamericana, 2012.
Buchbinder, Pablo, "De la impugnación al profesionalismo a la crítica de la Reforma: perspectivas de la universidad," in Darío Roldán (ed.), Crear la democracia: Revista Argentina de Ciencias Políticas y el debate en torno de la República Verdadera, Buenos Aires, Fondo de Cultura Económica, 2006, pp. 260–1.
Buchrucker, Cristian, Nacionalismo y peronismo: la Argentina en la crisis ideológica mundial (1927–1955), Buenos Aires, Sudamericana, 1987.
Bustelo, Natalia and Lucas Domínguez Rubio, "Vitalismo libertario y Reforma Universitaria en el joven Carlos Astrada," Políticas de la Memoria, 16, 2015, pp. 295–310.
Calkivik, Asli, "Revisiting the Violence of Machiavelli," International Politics vol. 53, 4, 2016, pp. 505–518.
Carozzi, Silvana, Las filosofías de la revolución: Mariano Moreno y los jacobinos rioplatenses en la prensa de Mayo: 1810–1815, Buenos Aires, Prometeo, 2011.
Carozzi, Silvana and Maximiliano Ferrero, "El siglo XIX rioplatense y el ensayo liminar de una nación republicana," in Gabriela Rodríguez Rial (ed.), República y republicanismos: conceptos, tradiciones y prácticas en pugna, Buenos Aires, Miño y Dávila, 2016, pp. 227–44.
Carta, Paolo and Xavier Tabet (eds), Machiavelli nel XIX e nel XX secolo/ Machiavel aux XIXe et XXe siècles, Padua, Cedam, 2007.
Carta, Paolo, "Il Machiavelli di Angelo Ridolfi," in Angelo Ridolfi and Ugo Foscolo, Scritti sul Principe di Niccolò Machiavelli: a cura di Paolo Carta, Christian Del Vento e Xavier Tabet, Rovereto, Nicolodi, 2004, pp. vii–xxxiii.
Casares, Tomás, Conocimiento, política y moral: jerarquías espirituales, Buenos Aires, Docencia, 1981.
Castellani, Leonardo, "Introducción," in Ernesto Palacio, La historia falsificada, Buenos Aires, Difusión, 1939.
Catalano, Pierangelo, Costituzionalismo Latino: ricerche giuridique e politiche, Turin, Istituto Universitario di Studi Europei, 1991.
Catálogo de la Biblioteca, Mapoteca y Archivo del Ministerio de Relaciones Exteriores y Culto, Buenos Aires, Taller Tipográfico de la Penitenciaría Nacional, 1902.
Catálogo metódico de la Biblioteca Nacional. Vol. VI. Historia y geografía, Buenos Aires, Biblioteca Nacional, 1925.
Cattaruzza, Alejandro and Alejandro Eujanián, Políticas de la historia: Argentina, 1860–1960, Buenos Aires, Alianza, 2003.
Clarke, William, "Bismarck," The Contemporary Review, 75, January 1899, pp. 1–17.
Codesido, Lucas, El Ejército de Línea y el poder central: guerra, política militar y construcción estatal en Argentina, 1860–1880, Buenos Aires, Prohistoria, 2021.

Compagnon, Olivier, *Jacques Maritain et l'Amérique du Sud: le modèle malgré lui*, Villeneuve-d'Ascq, Presses Universitaires du Septentrion, 2003.

Conde, Francisco Javier, *Escritos y fragmentos politicos, Vol. I*, Madrid, Instituto de Estudios Políticos, 1974.

Conde, Francisco Javier, *El saber político de Maquiavelo*, Madrid, Instituto Nacional de Estudios Jurídicos, Ministerio de Justicia y Consejo Superior de Investigaciones Científicas, 1948.

Costa Pinto, António, *Latin American Dictatorships in the Era of Fascism: The Corporatist Wave*, London and New York, Routledge, 2020.

Croce, Benedetto, *Ética y política*, Buenos Aires, Imán, 1952.

David, Guillermo, *Carlos Astrada: la filosofía argentina*, Buenos Aires, El Cielo por Asalto, 2004.

De Mattei, Rodolfo, *Il problema della "Ragion di Stato" nell'età della Controriforma*, Milan, Ricciardi, 1979.

De Vedia y Mitre, Mariano, *Derecho Político General*, 2 vols, Buenos Aires, Kraft, 1952.

De Vedia y Mitre, Mariano, *Historia general de las ideas políticas*, 13 vols, Buenos Aires, Kraft, 1946.

De Vedia y Mitre, Mariano, *Curso de Derecho Político*, 2 vols, Buenos Aires, Biblioteca Jurídica, 1934.

De Vedia y Mitre, Mariano, *Programa de Derecho Político: carrera de abogacía*, Buenos Aires, Facultad de Derecho y Ciencias Sociales, Universidad de Buenos Aires, Imprenta de la Universidad, 1929 and 1944.

De Vedia y Mitre, Mariano (ed.), *Maquiavelo*, Buenos Aires, Facultad de Derecho y Ciencias Sociales, Universidad de Buenos Aires, 1927.

De Vedia y Mitre, Mariano, *Curso de Derecho Político*, Buenos Aires, 1926.

De Velasco, Recaredo F., *Referencias y transcripciones para la historia de la literatura política en España; la razón de estado; el tiranicidio; el derecho de resistencia al poder; bibliografía de la literatura política*, Madrid, Editorial Reus, 1925.

Del Lucchese, Filippo, *The Political Philosophy of Niccolò Machiavelli*, Edinburgh, Edinburgh University Press, 2015.

Del Lucchese, Filippo, Fabio Frosini, and Vittorio Morfino (eds), *The Radical Machiavelli*, London, Brill, 2015.

Devoto, Fernando, "Acerca de la clase dirigente como problema en el pensamiento de la derecha nacionalista argentina," in Carlos Altamirano and Adrián Gorelik (eds), *La Argentina como problema*, Buenos Aires, Siglo XXI, 2018, pp. 207–21.

Devoto, Fernando, *Nacionalismo, fascismo y tradicionalismo en la Argentina moderna*, Buenos Aires, Siglo XXI, 2002.

Devoto, Fernando and Nora Pagano, *Historia de la historiografía en la Argentina*, Buenos Aires, Sudamericana, 2009.

Di Stefano, Roberto, *Ovejas negras: historia de los anticlericales argentinos*, Buenos Aires, Sudamericana, 2010.
Di Stefano, Roberto and Loris Zanatta, *Historia de la Iglesia Argentina: desde la conquista hasta fines del siglo XX*, Buenos Aires, Grijalbo Mondadori, 2000.
Díaz de Vivar, Joaquín, *Ideas para una biología de la democracia*, Buenos Aires, La Facultad, 1937.
Dotti, Jorge, *Carl Schmitt en Argentina*, Rosario, Homo Sapiens, 2000.
Dotti, Jorge, *La letra gótica: recepción de Kant en la Argentina, desde el Romanticismo hasta el treinta*, Buenos Aires, Facultad de Filosofía y Letras, UBA, 1992.
Dotti, Jorge, *Las vetas del texto: una lectura filosófica de Alberdi, los positivistas, Juan B. Justo*, Buenos Aires, Puntosur, 1990.
Duarte, Ángel, "Los significados históricos del republicanismo," in Nicolas Berjoan, Eduardo Higueras Castañeda, and Sergio Sánchez Collantes (eds), *El republicanismo en el espacio ibérico contemporáneo: recorridos y perspectivas*, Madrid, Casa de Velázquez, 2021, pp. 9–23.
Duarte, Ángel, "Los republicanos del ochocientos y la memoria de su tiempo," *Ayer: Revista de Historia contemporánea*, vol. 58, 2, 2005, pp. 207–28.
Duarte, Ángel and Pere Gabriel, "¿Una sola cultura política republicana ochocentista en España?," *Ayer: Revista de Historia Contemporánea*, vol. 39, 3, 2000, pp. 11–34.
Elliot, John H., *Empires of the Atlantic World: Britain and Spain in America, 1492–1830*, New Haven, CT, and London, Yale University Press, 2006.
Entin, Gabriel, "Catholic Republicanism: The Creation of the Spanish American Republics During Revolution," *Journal of the History of Ideas*, vol. 79, 2018, pp. 105–23.
Esposito, Roberto, *Pensamiento viviente: origen y actualidad de la filosofía italiana*, Buenos Aires, Amorrortu, 2015.
Esposito, Roberto, *Confines de lo politico: nueve pensamientos sobre política*, Madrid, Trotta, 1996.
Estrada, José Manuel, *Obras completas. Vol. I*, Buenos Aires, Librería del Colegio, 1899.
Fernández-Santamaría, J. A., *Natural Law, Constitutionalism, Reason of State and War*, New York, Peter Lang, 2006.
Fernández-Santamaría, J. A., *Razón de estado y política en el pensamiento español barroco (1595–1640)*, Madrid, Centro de Estudios Constitucionales, 1986.
Ferrara, Orestes, *Maquiavelo*, Havana, Imprenta el Siglo XX, 1928.
Ferrara, Orestes, *La guerra europea: causas y pretextos*, New York, D. Appleton, 1915.
Fioravanti, Maurizio, *Los derechos fundamentals: apuntes de historia de las constituciones*, Madrid, Trotta, 2009.

Forte, Juan Manuel and Pablo López Álvarez (eds), *Maquiavelismo y antimaquiavelismo en la cultura española de los siglos XVI y XVII*, Madrid, Biblioteca Nueva, 2008.

Fuller, Timothy (ed.), *Machiavelli's Legacy: The Prince After Five Hundred Years*, Philadelphia, University of Pennsylvania Press, 2015.

Gallego, Julián, "De Heródoto a Romero: la función social del historiador," in José Emilio Burucúa, Fernando Devoto, and Adrián Gorelik (eds), *José Luis Romero: vida histórica, ciudad y cultura*, San Martín, UNSAM, 2013, pp. 165–84.

Gandarilla, Julio César, *Contra el yanqui*, La Habana, Imprenta y papelería de Ramela, Bouza, 1913.

García, Juan Agustín, *La ciudad indiana, sobre nuestra incultura y otros ensayos*. Preliminary study by Fernando Devoto, Bernal, Universidad Nacional de Quilmes, 2006.

García, Juan Agustín, "La actualidad de Maquiavelo," *Anales de la Facultad de Derecho y Ciencias Sociales*, vol. 3, series 3, Buenos Aires, 1917, pp. 99–102.

García Manrique, Ricardo, *La filosofía de los derechos humanos durante el franquismo*, Madrid, Centro de Estudios Políticos y Constitucionales, 1996.

García Mérou, Martín, *Libros y autores*, Buenos Aires, Lajouane, 1886.

Germani, Gino, *Política y sociedad en una época de transición*, Buenos Aires, Paidós, 1962.

Gerstle, Gary, *Libertad y coacción: la paradoja del gobierno estadounidense desde su fundación hasta el presente*, Mexico, FCE, 2017.

Gil Robles, Enrique, *Tratado de Derecho Político según los principios de la filosofía y el derecho cristianos*, Salamanca, Imprenta y Encuadernación Católica Salmanticense, 1909.

Gilbert, Felix, *Machiavelli and Guicciardini: Politics and History in Sixteenth Century Florence*, Princeton, Princeton University Press, 1965.

Giner de los Ríos, Francisco, *Estudios jurídicos y políticos*, Madrid, Imprenta de Julio Cosano, 1921.

Ginzburg, Carlo, "Pontano, Maquiavelo y la prudencia: algunas reflexiones más," *Anales de Historia Antigua, Medieval y Moderna*, 43, 2011, pp. 115–26.

Ginzburg, Carlo, "Maquiavelo, la excepción y la regla: líneas de una investigación en curso," *Ingenium: Revista de Historia del Pensamiento Moderno*, 4, 2010, pp. 5–28.

Goldman, Noemí and Ricardo Salvatore (eds), *Caudillos rioplatenses: nuevas miradas a un viejo problema*, Buenos Aires, Eudeba, 1998.

González, Juan Vicente, *Manual de Historia Universal*, Caracas, Rojas Hermanos, 1869.

González Blanco, Edmundo, *Introducción a El Príncipe: comentado por Napoleón Bonaparte*, Madrid, Ediciones Ibéricas, 1933.

González García, Moisés and Rafael Herrera Guillén (eds), *Maquiavelo en España y Latinoamérica (siglos XVI a XXI)*, Madrid, Tecnos, 2014.

González Prieto, Luis Aurelio, "La concreción teórica del partido único español franquista," *Revista de Estudios Políticos (nueva época)*, 141, 2008, pp. 41–68.
Gramsci, Antonio, *Notas sobre Maquiavelo, sobre la política y sobre el Estado moderno* [1949], Madrid, Nueva Visión, 1980.
Greenwood, Frederik, "Machiavelli in Modern Politics," *The Living Edge*, vol. 214, 2777, 25 September 1897.
Hale, Charles, *La transformación del liberalismo en México a fines del siglo XIX*, Mexico, Fondo de Cultura Económica, 2002.
Halperín Donghi, Tulio, *Las tormentas del mundo en el Río de la Plata: cómo pensaron su época los intelectuales del siglo XX*, Buenos Aires, Siglo XXI, 2015.
Halperín Donghi, Tulio, *Tradición política española e ideología revolucionaria de Mayo*, Buenos Aires, Prometeo, 2010.
Halperin Donghi, Tulio, *La República Imposible (1930-1945)*, Buenos Aires, Ariel, 2004.
Halperin Donghi, Tulio, *La Argentina y la tormenta del mundo: ideas e ideologías entre 1930 y 1945*, Buenos Aires, Siglo XXI, 2003.
Halperín Donghi, Tulio, *Vida y muerte de la República Verdadera (1910-1930)*, Buenos Aires, Ariel, 1999.
Halperin Donghi, Tulio, *Ensayos de historiografía*, Buenos Aires, El Cielo por Asalto, 1996.
Halperín Donghi, Tulio, *Proyecto y construcción de una nación (1846-1880)*, Buenos Aires, Ariel, 1995.
Halperin Donghi, Tulio, "Argentina: Liberalism in a Country Born Liberal," in Joseph Love and Nils Jacobsen (eds), *Guiding the Invisible Hand: Economic Liberalism and the State in Latin America*, New York, Praeger, 1988.
Halperin Donghi, Tulio, *Revolución y guerra: formación de una elite dirigente en la Argentina criolla*, Buenos Aires, Siglo XXI, 1972.
Hankins, James (ed.), *Renaissance Civic Humanism Reconsidered*, Cambridge, Cambridge University Press, 2000.
Harrison, Frederic, "The Modern Machiavelli," *The Eclectic Magazine of Foreign Literature*, vol. 66, 5, November 1897.
Hartz, Louis, *La tradición liberal en los Estados Unidos: una interpretación del pensamiento político estadounidense desde la Guerra de Independencia*, Mexico, FCE, 1995.
Hendrickson, David C., "Machiavelli and Machiavellianism," in Timothy Fuller (ed.), *Machiavelli´s Legacy: The Prince After Five Hundred Years*, Philadelphia, University of Pennsylvania Press, 2015, pp. 105–26
Herf, Jeffrey, *El modernismo reaccionario: tecnología, cultura y política en Weimar y el Tercer Reich*, Mexico, Fondo de Cultura Económica, 1990.
Hertford, C. H., "Mr. Morley and Machiavelli," *The Bookman*, July 1897, p. 92.
Hochner, Nicole, "Machiavelli: Love and the Economy of Emotions," *Italian Culture*, vol. 32, 2, 2014, pp. 79–84.

Hoipkemier, Mark, "Machiavelli and the Double Politics of Ambition," *Political Studies*, vol. 66, 1, 2018, pp. 245-60.

Holman, Christopher, *Machiavelli and the Politics of Democratic Innovation*, Toronto, University of Toronto Press, 2018.

Hornqvist, Mikael, *Machiavelli and Empire*, New York, Cambridge University Press, 2004.

Howard, Keith David, *The Reception of Machiavelli in Early Modern Spain*, Woodbridge, Tamesis, 2014.

Hulliung, Mark, *Citizen Machiavelli*, Princeton, Princeton University Press, 1983.

Ingenieros, José, *El hombre mediocre* [1913], Buenos Aires, Losada, 2001.

Ingenieros, José, *La simulación en la lucha por la vida*, Buenos Aires, Talleres Gráficos Schenone Hnos, 1920.

Iñurritegui Rodríguez, José María, *La gracia y la república: el lenguaje político de la teología católica y "El príncipe Cristiano" de Pedro de Ribadeneyra*, Madrid, UNED, 1998.

Irazusta, Julio, *El pensamiento político nacionalista, vol. 1. De Alvear a Yrigoyen*, Buenos Aires, Obligado, 1975.

Irazusta, Julio, *Memorias (Historia de un historiador a la fuerza)*, Buenos Aires, Ediciones Culturales Argentinas, 1975.

Irazusta, Julio, *La monarquía constitucional en Inglaterra*, Buenos Aires, Eudeba, 1970.

Irazusta, Julio, *Tito Livio: o del imperialismo en relación con las formas de gobierno y la evolución histórica*, Mendoza, Universidad Nacional de Cuyo, 1951.

Irazusta, Rodolfo and Julio Irazusta, *La Argentina y el imperialismo británico: los eslabones de una cadena, 1806-1933*, Buenos Aires, Tor, 1934.

Izaga, Luis, *Elementos de derecho político. Vol. 1*, Barcelona, Casa Editorial Bosch, 1952.

Jackson, Michael and Thomas Moore, "Machiavelli's Walls: The Legacy of Realism in International Relations Theory," *International Politics*, Vol. 53, 4, 2016, pp. 447-65.

Kahn, Victoria, "Machiavelli's Afterlife and Reputation to the Eighteenth Century," in John N. Najemy (ed.), *The Cambridge Companion to Machiavelli*, Cambridge, Cambridge University Press, 2010, pp. 239-55.

Kennedy, Ellen, *Carl Schmitt en la República de Weimar: la quiebra de una constitución*, Madrid, Tecnos, 2012.

Knoll, Manuel, "The Role of Emotions, Desires and Passions in Politics. Machiavelli's Political Psychology of Motivation," *Lo Sguardo: Rivista di Filosofia*, vol. 27, II, 2018, pp. 49-59.

Laclau, Ernesto, *On Populist Reason*, London, Verso, 2002.

Landi, Sandro, "Multitud, pueblo y populismo en Maquiavelo: un enfoque histórico," *Revista Argentina de Ciencia Política*, vol. 1, 27, 2021, pp. 1-28.

Landon, William, *Politics, Patriotism and Language: Niccolò Machiavelli's "Secular Patria" and the Creation of an Italian National Identity*, New York and Berne, Peter Lang, 2005.
Lastarria, José Victorino, *La América. Vol. 1*, Madrid, Editorial La América, 1917.
Lefort, Claude, *Maquiavelo: lecturas de lo político*, Madrid, Trotta, 2010.
Legaz y Lacambra, Luis, *Filosofía del Derecho*, Barcelona, Bosch, 1953.
Legaz y Lacambra, Luis, *Introducción a la Ciencia del Derecho*, Barcelona, Bosch Casa Editorial, 1943.
Legaz y Lacambra, Luis, *Estudios de doctrina jurídica y social*, Barcelona, Bosch, 1940.
Legón, Faustino, *Tratado de derecho político general*, Buenos Aires, Ediar, 1959.
Legón, Faustino, *Cuestiones de política y derecho*, Buenos Aires, Perrot, 1951.
Litvin, Boris, "Mapping Rule and Subversion: Perspective and the Democratic Turn in Machiavelli Scholarship," *European Journal of Political Theory*, vol. 18, 1, 2019, pp. 3–25.
López García, José Antonio, *Estado y Derecho en el Franquismo: el nacionalsindicalismo: F. J. Conde y Luis Legaz Lacambra*, Madrid, Centro de Estudios Constitucionales, 1996.
Losada, Leandro, "Conservadurismo y democracia en Argentina: formulaciones intelectuales y reflexiones políticas en el pensamiento liberal, 1912–1943," *Cuadernos de Historia Contemporánea*, 2022, 44, pp. 155–74.
Losada, Leandro, "El Derecho Político y las controversias acerca de la soberanía: Argentina, 1910–1940," *Cuadernos del Instituto Antonio de Nebrija - Revista de Historia de las Universidades*, vol. 24, 2, 2021, pp. 167–96.
Losada, Leandro, "Liberalismo y derechas en la Argentina, 1912–1943: apuestas interpretativas, posibilidades y límites," *Prismas: Revista de Historia Intelectual*, 24, 2020, pp. 219–25.
Losada, Leandro, *Maquiavelo en la Argentina: usos y lecturas, 1830–1940*, Buenos Aires, Katz Editores, 2019.
Losada, Leandro, "El ocaso de la 'Argentina liberal' y la tradición republicana: reflexiones en torno a los discursos públicos de Agustín Justo, Roberto Ortiz y Marcelo T. de Alvear, 1930–1943," *Estudios Sociales*, 54, 2018, pp. 43–66.
Losada, Leandro, "Soberanía y libertad: balances y diagnósticos de Mariano de Vedia y Mitre sobre el liberalismo (Argentina, 1920–1950)," *Anuario IEHS*, 33, 2, 2018, pp. 39–60.
Losada, Leandro, "Aristocracia y democracia: representación política y distinción social en la Argentina, 1810–1930. Un ensayo de interpretación," *Revista Economía y Política*, vol. 4, 1, 2017, pp. 5–36.
Losada, Leandro (ed.), *Política y vida pública: Argentina, 1930–1943*, Buenos Aires, Imago Mundi, 2017.

Losada, Leandro, "Las elites y los 'males' de la Argentina: juicios e interpretaciones en tres momentos del siglo XX," *Desarrollo Económico*, vol. 54, 214, 2015, pp. 387-409.
Lugones, Leopoldo, *La patria fuerte*, Buenos Aires, Luis Bernard, 1930.
Lugones, Leopoldo, "Elogio de Maquiavelo," *Repertorio Americano*, vol. XV, 19, 19 Nov. 1927. Originally published in *La Nación*, 19 June 1927.
Lugones, Leopoldo, "Historia del dogma," *Boletín de la Facultad de Derecho y Ciencias Sociales*, 1, I, 1921, pp. 1-112.
Macaulay, Thomas, "Machiavelli" (1827), in Thomas Macaulay, *Historical Essays*, New York and Chicago, C. Scribner's Son, 1921, pp. 382-423.
McCormick, John, *Reading Machiavelli: Scandalous Books, Suspect Engagements, and the Virtue of Populist Politics*, Princeton, Princeton University Press, 2018.
McCormick, John, *Machiavellian Democracy*, Cambridge and New York, Cambridge University Press, 2011.
McGee Deutsch, Sandra and Ronald Dolkart (eds), *La derecha argentina: nacionalistas, neoliberales, militares y clericales*, Buenos Aires, Javier Vergara, 2001.
Manent, Pierre, *Historia del pensamiento liberal*, Buenos Aires, Emecé, 1990.
Manin, Bernard, "Montesquieu, la república y el comercio," in José Antonio Aguilar and Rafael Rojas (eds), *El republicanismo en Hispanoamérica: ensayos de historia intelectual y política*, Mexico, Fondo de Cultura Económica, 2002, pp. 13-56.
Manin, Bernard, *Los principios del gobierno representativo*, Madrid, Alianza, 1998.
Mansfield, Harvey, *Machiavelli's New Modes and Orders*, London, Cornell University Press, 1979.
Maravall, José Antonio, *Estudios de historia del pensamiento español*, Madrid, Ediciones Cultura Hispánica, 1983.
Maravall, José Antonio, *La teoría española del Estado en el siglo XVII*, Madrid, Instituto de Estudios Políticos, 1944.
Maritain, Jacques, "The End of Machiavellianism," *The Review of Politics*, vol. 4, 1, 1942, pp. 1-33.
Martínez Paz, Enrique, *Sistema de filosofía del derecho* [1932], Buenos Aires, El Ateneo, 1940.
Mateos, J. Maury, *Ensayo de un estudio acerca de Nicolas Maquiavelo y principalmente de su obra El Príncipe*, Málaga, Tip. A. Castro, 1915.
Matienzo, José Nicolás, *Nuevos temas políticos e históricos*, Buenos Aires, La Facultad, 1928.
Meinvielle, Julio, *Concepción católica de la política* [1932], Buenos Aires, Cursos de Cultura Católica, 1941.
Mellado, Fernando, *Tratado elemental de Derecho Político*, Madrid, Manuel G. Hernández, 1891.

Mitarotondo, Laura, *Un preludio a Machiavelli: letture e interpretazioni fra Mussolini e Gramsci*, Turin, G. Giappichelli, 2016.
Mitre, Bartolomé, *Historia de San Martín y de la emancipación sudamericana. Vol. 1*, Buenos Aires, Imprenta La Nación, 1887.
Montero, Belisario, *Ensayos sobre filosofía y arte (de mi diario)*, Buenos Aires, Talleres Gráficos de Schenone Hnos y Linari, 1922.
Morley, John, *Machiavelli: The Romanes Lecture Delivered in the Sheldonian Theatre, 2 June 1897*, London, MacMillan, 1897.
"Mr. Morley on Machiavelli," *The Critic: A Weekly Review of Literature and the Arts*, vol. 28, 815, 2 October 1897, p. 185.
"Mr. Morley on Machiavelli," *Saturday Review of Politics, Literature, Science and Art*, vol. 83, 2171, 6 June 1897, pp. 619-20.
Mudde, Cas and Cristóbal Rovira Kaltwasse, *Populism: A Very Short Introduction*, New York, Oxford University Press, 2017.
Mussolini, Benito, "Preludio al Machiavelli," in Benito Mussolini, *Scritti e Discorsi*, I/1, Milan, Ulrico Hoepli, 1924.
Myers, Jorge, "Prólogo: El teórico de la libertad natural del hombre en el laberinto de la revolución americana," in Gabriel Entin (ed.), *Rousseau en Iberoamérica: lecturas e interpretaciones entre monarquía y revolución*, Buenos Aires, SB, 2018, pp. 9-23.
Myers, Jorge, "La ciencia política argentina y la cuestión de los partidos políticos: discusiones en la *Revista Argentina de Ciencias Políticas* (1904-1916)," in Darío Roldán (ed.), *Crear la democracia: Revista Argentina de Ciencias Políticas y el debate en torno de la República Verdadera*, Buenos Aires, Fondo de Cultura Económica, 2006, pp. 103-35.
Myers, Jorge, "La revolución en las ideas: la generación de 1837 en la cultura y en la política argentinas," in Noemí Goldman (dir.), *Nueva historia argentina. Vol. III: Revolución, república, confederación (1806-1852)*, Buenos Aires, Sudamericana, 1998, pp. 381-445.
Myers, Jorge, *Orden y virtud: el discurso republicano en el régimen rosista*, Bernal, Universidad Nacional de Quilmes, 1995.
Najemy, John N. (ed.), *The Cambridge Companion to Machiavelli*, Cambridge, Cambridge University Press, 2010.
Nállim, Jorge, *Transformación y crisis del liberalism: su desarrollo en la Argentina en el período 1930-1955*, Buenos Aires, Gedisa, 2014.
Pagden, Anthony, *The Uncertainties of Empire: Essays on Iberian and Iberoamerican Intellectual History*, Great Yarmouth, Variorum, 1994.
Palacio, Ernesto, *Teoría del Estado* [1949], Buenos Aires, Eudeba, 1973.
Palacio, Ernesto, *Historia de Roma*, Buenos Aires, Albatros, 1939.
Palacio, Ernesto, *Catilina contra la oligarquía*, Buenos Aires, Rosso, 1935.
Palti, Elías, *El momento romántico: nación, historia y lenguajes políticos en la Argentina del siglo XIX*, Buenos Aires, Eudeba, 2009.
Paludan, Phillip Shaw, "'Dictator Lincoln': Surveying Lincoln and the Constitution," *OAH Magazine of History*, Vol. 21, 1, 2007, pp. 8-13.

Patat, Alejandro, *Un destino sudamericano: la letteratura italiana in Argentina (1910–1970)*, Perugia, Guerra, 2005.
Payne, Stanley G., *El régimen de Franco, 1936–1975*, Madrid, Alianza Editorial, 1987.
Pettit, Philip, *Republicanismo: una teoría sobre la libertad y el gobierno*, Barcelona, Paidós, 1999.
Piñero, Norberto, *Política. El momento presente. Problemas sociales y políticos. Estabilidad de la constitución*, Buenos Aires, Menéndez, 1929.
Pocock, John G. A. *El momento maquiavélico: el pensamiento político florentino y la tradición republicana atlántica*, Madrid, Tecnos, 2008.
Pocock, John G. A., *Doce estudios*, Madrid, Marcial Pons, 2002.
Pocock, John G. A. *The Machiavellian Moment: Florentine Political Thought and the Atlantic Republican Tradition*, Princeton, NJ, Princeton University Press, 1975.
Portinaro, Pier Paolo, *La apropiación de Maquiavelo: una crítica de la Italian Theory*, Salamanca, Guillermo Escolar Editor, 2021.
Portinaro, Pier Paolo, *El realismo político*, Buenos Aires, Nueva Visión, 2007.
Posada, Adolfo, *Tratado de Derecho Político. Vol. I*, Madrid, Librería General de Victoriano Suárez, 1923.
Posada, Adolfo, *Teoría social y jurídica del Estado: el sindicalismo*, Buenos Aires, Librería de J. Menéndez, 1922.
Posada, Adolfo, *La idea del Estado y la guerra europea*, Madrid, V. Suárez, 1915.
Posada, Adolfo, *Principios de Derecho Político*, Madrid, Imprenta de la Revista de Legislación, 1884.
Prades Vilar, Mario, "La teoría de la simulación de Pedro de Ribadeneyra y el 'maquiavelismo' de los antimaquiavélicos," *Ingenium: Revista de Historia del Pensamiento Moderno*, 5, 2011, pp. 133–65.
Price, Russell, "L. Arthur Burd, Lord Acton, and Machiavelli," in John E. Law and Lene Østermark-Johansen (eds), *Victorian and Edwardian Responses to the Italian Renaissance*, London, Routledge, 2005.
Procacci, Giuliano, *Machiavelli nella cultura europea dell'età moderna*, Rome and Bari, Laterza, 1995.
Puigdomenech, Helena, *Maquiavelo en España: presencia de sus obras en los siglos XVI y XVII*, Madrid, Fundación Universitaria Española, 1988.
Quesada, Ernesto, *La evolución del derecho público (política y económica) según la doctrina spengleriana*, Buenos Aires, Universidad de Buenos Aires, 1924.
Quesada, Ernesto, *La enseñanza de la historia en las universidades alemanas*, La Plata, Facultad de Ciencias Jurídicas y Sociales, 1910.
Quesada, Ernesto, *Las doctrinas presociológicas*, Buenos Aires, Librería de J. Menéndez, 1905.
Quesada, Ernesto, *Bismarck y su época*, Buenos Aires, Peuser, 1898.

Quesada, Ernesto, *La época de Rosas*, Buenos Aires, Moen, 1898.
Quesada, Vicente, *La vida intelectual en la América española durante los siglos XVI, XVII y XVIII*, Buenos Aires, La Cultura Argentina, 1917.
Rahe, Paul (ed.), *Machiavelli's Liberal Republican Legacy*, Cambridge, Cambridge University Press, 2006.
Ramos, Juan P., *Fragmentos de vida*, Emecé, Buenos Aires, 1946.
Ramos, Juan P., *Ensayos hispánicos*, Buenos Aires, Institución Cultural Española, 1942.
Ramos Mejía, José María, *Rosas y su tiempo (1907)*, Buenos Aires, Emecé, 2001.
Reinsch, Paul, *World Politics at the End of the Nineteenth Century, as Influenced by the Oriental Situation (1900)*, New York, Macmillan, 1916.
Requena, Pablo and Ezequiel Grisendi, "Dos eventos de recepción densos en la Universidad de Córdoba: los homenajes a Oswald Spengler (1924) y Henri Bergson (1936)," in *Actas de las V Jornadas de Historia de las Izquierdas ¿Las "ideas fuera de lugar"? El problema de la recepción y la circulación de ideas en América Latina*, Buenos Aires, CeDInCI, 2009.
Rivarola, Rodolfo, *Escritos filosóficos*, Buenos Aires, Instituto de Estudios Filosóficos, Facultad de Filosofía y Letras, UBA, 1945.
Rivarola, Rodolfo, *Filosofía, política, historia: lecturas en la Facultad de Filosofía y Letras y en la Junta de Historia y Numismática*, Buenos Aires, Librería La Facultad de J. Roldán, 1917.
Rivaya, Benjamín, *Una historia de la filosofía del derecho española del siglo XX*, Madrid, Biblioteca Jurídica Básica, 2010.
Rivaya, Benjamín, *Filosofía del Derecho y primer franquismo (1937-1945)*, Madrid, Centro de Estudios Políticos y Constitucionales, 1998.
Rizzi, Miguel Ángel, "Teoría política de El Príncipe," *Nosotros*, X, vol. 22, 84, April 1916, pp. 153-8.
Rizzi, Miguel Ángel, *La lucha entre los grupos sociales*, Buenos Aires, Imprenta French, 1913.
Rock, David, *La Argentina autoritaria: los nacionalistas, su historia y su influencia en la vida pública*, Buenos Aires, Ariel, 1993.
Rodgers, Daniel T., "Republicanism: The Career of a Concept," *The Journal of American History*, 79, 1992, pp. 11-38.
Rodríguez, Jesús P., *Filosofía Política de Luis Legaz y Lacambra*, Madrid, Marcial Pons, 1997.
Rodríguez Aniceto, Nicolás, *Maquiavelo y Nietzsche*, Madrid, Imprenta de Fontanet, 1919.
Rodríguez Rial, Gabriela (ed.), *República y republicanismos: conceptos, tradiciones y prácticas en pugna*, Buenos Aires, Miño y Dávila, 2016.
Roig, Arturo Andrés, *Los krausistas argentinos*, Puebla, Cajica, 1969.
Rojas, Rafael, *Las repúblicas del aire: utopía y desencanto en la revolución hispanoamericana*, Buenos Aires, Alfaguara, 2010.
Roldán, Darío, "La cuestión liberal en la Argentina en el siglo XIX: política, sociedad, representación," in Beatriz Bragoni and Eduardo

Míguez (eds), *Un nuevo orden politico: provincias y estado nacional, 1852-1880*, Buenos Aires, Biblos, 2010, pp. 275-91.

Roldán, Darío (ed.), *Crear la democracia:* Revista Argentina de Ciencias Políticas *y el debate en torno de la República Verdadera*, Buenos Aires, Fondo de Cultura Económica, 2006.

Romero, José Luis, *Maquiavelo historiador* [1943], Buenos Aires, Signos, 1970.

Sabato, Hilda, *Republics of the New World: The Revolutionary Political Experiment in Nineteenth-Century Latin America*, Princeton, Princeton University Press, 2018.

Sabato, Hilda, *Buenos Aires en armas: la revolución de 1880*, Buenos Aires, Siglo XXI, 2008.

Sabato, Hilda, *La política en las calles: entre el voto y la movilización. Buenos Aires, 1862-1880*, Buenos Aires, Sudamericana, 1998.

Safford, Frank, "Politics, Ideology and Society in Post-Independence Spanish America," in Leslie Bethell (ed.), *The Cambridge History of Latin America, Vol. III: From Independence to c. 1870*, Cambridge, Cambridge University Press, 1985, pp. 347-422.

Sampay, Arturo, *Introducción a la teoría del Estado*, Buenos Aires, Politeia, 1951.

Sampay, Arturo *La crisis del Estado de derecho liberal-burgués*, Buenos Aires, Losada, 1942.

Sánchez Sorondo, *La revolución que anunciamos*, Buenos Aires, Nueva Política, 1945.

Sánchez Sorondo, Marcelo, *La clase dirigente y la crisis del régimen*, Buenos Aires, Adsum, 1941.

Sánchez Viamonte, Carlos, *Jornadas*, Buenos Aires, Samet, 1929.

Sánchez Viamonte, Carlos, *Derecho político (ensayos)*, Buenos Aires, Sagitario, 1925.

Sánchez Zinny, Eduardo F., *Fe de América*, Buenos Aires, Ayacucho, 1946.

Sanguinetti, Horacio, "La verdad acerca de la creación del Instituto de Enseñanza Práctica," *Academia: Revista sobre Enseñanza del Derecho*, 21, 2013, pp. 91-8.

Sarmiento, Domingo Faustino, *Facundo (1845)*, Buenos Aires, Emecé, 1999.

Sarmiento, Domingo Faustino, *Viajes*, Barcelona, Editorial Universitaria, 1997.

Sarmiento, Domingo Faustino. *Obras. Vol. XXII,* Buenos Aires, Imprenta Mariano Moreno, 1899.

Saz, Ismael, "Franco, ¿caudillo fascista? Sobre las sucesivas y contradictorias concepciones falangistas del caudillaje franquista," *Historia y Política*, 27, 2012, pp. 27-50.

Saz, Ismael, "Las culturas de los nacionalismos franquistas," *Ayer: Revista de historia contemporánea*, vol. 71, 3, 2008, pp. 153-74.

Saz Campos, Ismael, *España contra España: los nacionalismos franquistas*, Madrid, Marcial Pons, 2003.

Schmidt, Ronald J., Jr, *Reading Politics with Machiavelli*, New York, Oxford University Press, 2018.
Scichilone, Giorgio M., "Machiavellismo e antimachiavellismo nel pensiero cristiano europeo dell' Ottocento e del Novecento," *Storia e Política: Revista Quadrimestrale*, III, 1, 2011.
Segovia, Fernando, "El derecho entre iusnaturalismo, decisionismo y personalismo: Arturo Sampay lector de Carl Schmitt," *Anales de la Fundación Francisco Elías de Tejada*, 20, 2014, pp. 133–56.
Segovia, Juan Fernando, "Faustino Legón: del derecho natural al derecho constitucional," *Anales de la Fundación Francisco Elías de Tejada*, 17, 2011, pp. 83–136.
Sesma Landrín, Nicolás, "Sociología del Instituto de Estudios Políticos: un 'grupo de elite' intelectual al servicio del partido único y del Estado franquista," in Miguel Ángel Ruiz Carnicer (ed.), *Falange, las culturas políticas del fascismo en la España de Franco (1936–1975)*. Vol. 1, Zaragoza, Institución Fernando el Católico, 2013, pp. 253–88.
Sesma Landrin, Nicolás, "'La dialéctica de los puños y de las pistolas': una aproximación a la formación de la idea de Estado en el fascismo español (1931–1945)," *Historia y Política*, 27, 2012, pp. 51–82.
Sesma Landrín, Nicolás, "El republicanismo en la cultura política falangista: de la Falange fundacional al modelo de la V República francesa,' *Espacio, Tiempo y Forma*, Serie V, Historia Contemporánea, vol. 18, 2006, pp. 261–83.
Shalhope, Robert E., "Toward a Republican Synthesis: The Emergence of an Understanding of Republicanism in American Historiography," *William and Mary Quarterly*, 29, 1972, pp. 49–80.
Skinner, Quentin, *La libertad antes del liberalismo*, Mexico, Taurus-CIDE, 2004.
Smith, Norman H., "John Morley and Machiavelli," *Outlook*, vol. 56, 11, 10 July 1897, pp. 635–6.
Somos, Mark, "A Century of 'Hate and Coarse Thinking': Anti-Machiavellian Machiavellism in H. G. Wells' *The New Machiavelli* (1911)," *History of European Ideas*, 37, 2, 2011, pp. 137–52.
Speroni, Miguel Ángel, *Maquiavelo*, Buenos Aires, Santiago Rueda, 1971.
Spitz, Jean Fabien, "The Reception of Machiavelli in Contemporary Republicanism: Some Ambiguities and Paradoxes," in David Johnston, Nadia Urbinati, and Camila Vergara (eds), *Machiavelli on Liberty and Conflict*, Chicago, University of Chicago Press, 2017, pp. 309–29.
Stolleis, Michael, *Public Law in Germany, 1800–1914*, New York, Berghahn, 2001.
Strauss, Leo, *Meditación sobre Maquiavelo*, Madrid, Instituto de Estudios Políticos, 1964.
Suárez, José León, *Diplomacia universitaria americana: Argentina en el Brasil*, Buenos Aires, Escoffier, Caracciolo, 1918.

Suárez Cortina, Manuel, *Los caballeros de la razón: cultura institucionista y democracia parlamentaria en la España liberal*, Madrid, Genueve, 2019.

Suárez Cortina, Manuel (ed.), *Libertad, armonía y tolerancia: la cultura institucionista en España*, Madrid, Tecnos, 2008.

Suárez Cortina, Manuel, "El republicanismo institucionista en la Restauración," *Ayer: Revista de Historia Contemporánea*, vol. 39, 3, 2000, pp. 61–81.

Taborda, Saúl, *Escritos politicos: 1918–1934*, Córdoba, Universidad Nacional de Córdoba, 2008.

Taine, Hippolyte, *Historia de la literatura inglesa. Vol. II*, Madrid, La España Moderna, 1900.

Taine, Hippolyte, *Philosophie de l'art en Italie*, Paris, Germer Baillière, 1866.

Tanzi, Héctor José, "La enseñanza de Derecho Constitucional en la Facultad de Derecho de Buenos Aires," *Academia: Revista sobre Enseñanza del Derecho*, 17, 2011, pp. 85–112.

Tarcus, Horacio, *El socialismo romántico en el Río de la Plata (1837–1852)*, Buenos Aires, Fondo de Cultura Económica, 2016.

Tau Anzoátegui, Víctor, *Las ideas jurídicas en la Argentina (siglos XIX-XX)*, Buenos Aires, Perrot, 1977.

Terán, Oscar, *Vida intelectual en el Buenos Aires fin-de-siglo (1880–1910): derivas de la "cultura científica,"* Buenos Aires, Fondo de Cultura Económica, 2000.

Terán, Oscar, *Alberdi póstumo*, Buenos Aires, Puntosur, 1988.

Terán, Oscar, *Positivismo y nación en la Argentina*, Buenos Aires, Puntosur, 1987.

Vatter, Miguel E., *Between Form and Event: Machiavelli´s Theory of Political Freedom*, Dordrecht, Kluwer Academic, 2000.

Velasco Gómez, Ambrosio, "Republicanismo anticolonial y republicanismo nacionalista en el Renacimiento," in Moisés González García and Rafael Herrera Guillén (eds), *Maquiavelo en España y Latinoamérica: del siglo XVI al XXI*, Madrid, Tecnos, 2014, pp. 267–89.

Villari, Pasquale, *Maquiavelo: su vida y su tiempo*, Mexico, Biografías Gandesa, 1953.

Viroli, Maurizio, *Republicanismo*, Santander, Ediciones Universidad Cantabria, 2015.

Viroli, Maurizio, *De la política a la razón de Estado: la adquisición y transformación del lenguaje político (1250–1600)*, Madrid, Akal, 2009.

Vivanti, Corrado, *Maquiavelo: los tiempos de la política*, Buenos Aires, Paidós, 2013.

Von Vacano, Diego, "American Caudillo: Princely Performative Populism and Democracy in the Americas," *Philosophy and Social Criticism*, vol. 45, 4, 2019, pp. 413–28.

Von Vacano, Diego, *The Art of Power: Machiavelli, Nietzsche and the Making of Aesthetic Political Theory*, Lanham, MD: Lexington Books, 2006.

Winter, Yves, *Machiavelli and the Orders of Violence*, Cambridge, Cambridge, University Press, 2018.
Wood, Gordon, *The Creation of the American Republic, 1776–1787*, Chapel Hill, University of North Carolina Press, 1969.
Yanzi Ferreira, Ramón, "La enseñanza de Derecho Político en la Facultad de Derecho y Ciencias Sociales de la Universidad Nacional de Córdoba," *Revista de la Facultad*, vol. III, 2, new series II, 2012, pp. 177–98.
Zanatta, Loris, *Del estado liberal a la nación católica: iglesia y ejército en los orígenes del peronismo, 1930–1943*, Bernal, Universidad Nacional de Quilmes, 1996.
Zanca, José, *Cristianos antifascistas: conflictos en la cultura católica argentina, 1936–1959*, Buenos Aires, Siglo XXI, 2013.
Zarka, Yves-Charles, *Filosofía y política en la época moderna*, Madrid, Escolar y Mayo, 2008.
Zimmermann, Eduardo, "Constitucionalismo argentino, siglos XIX y XX: poderes y derechos," in Catherine Andrews (ed.), *Un siglo de constitucionalismo en América Latina (1917–2017)*, Mexico, CIDE-Secretaría de Relaciones Exteriores-Archivo General de la Nación, 2017, pp. 1–32.
Zimmermann, Eduardo, *Los liberales reformistas: la cuestión social en la Argentina, 1890–1916*, Buenos Aires, Sudamericana-Universidad de San Andrés, 1995.
Zuckert, Catherine H., "Review Essay: Machiavelli: Radical Democratic Political Theorist?" *The Review of Politics*, 81, 2019, pp. 499–510.
Zuleta Álvarez, Enrique, *El nacionalismo argentino*, 2 vols, Buenos Aires, La Bastilla, 1976.

# Index

Acton, J. E. E. D., 35
Alberdi, J. B., 17–22, 28, 30, 32, 41, 44n, 60, 92, 99, 116n, 122–3, 128, 133–4, 139, 145, 153n
Aquinas, Th., 70, 94, 97, 103, 128, 134
Aristotle, 35, 57, 97, 102–3
Astrada, C., 59–60, 62, 64, 69, 72, 74, 86–7, 89–90, 95–6, 103, 137, 144, 150n
authoritarianism, 3, 8, 17, 41, 68, 71, 74–6, 82, 85, 87, 90–1, 95, 112–13, 123, 133, 139, 146, 164, 167, 173, 178–9, 190n, 195–7

Baron. H., 83, 143
Benoist, Ch., 142, 144
Bessio Moreno, N., 135, 138, 150n
Bianco, J., 124–6, 128, 132, 150n
Burckhardt, J., 47n, 83, 130, 144, 153n
Burham, J., 152n

Carré de Malberg, R., 143
Casares, T., 56–8, 63–4, 109–14, 121n, 133, 137, 144–5
Cassirer, E., 58, 152n
Conde, F. J., 66, 75, 155–6, 162–8, 177, 182n
Croce, B., 152n

De Sanctis, F., 77n, 83, 142, 144
De Vedia y Mitre, M., 48n, 65, 73–4, 79n, 127–47, 165–6, 176, 183n, 185n, 197n
democracy, 2–4, 7, 31, 39, 67, 69, 71, 73, 82, 84–6, 90–3, 95, 97, 100–1, 103–6, 113, 121n, 123–4, 139, 140–1, 147, 154–5, 168, 173–8, 180, 193–5
Duguit, L., 61, 134, 146

Ercole, F., 142, 144

Fanfani, P., 142
Fascism, 3–4, 8, 41, 66–8, 70, 84–91, 94–5, 105–9, 112–13, 120n, 121n, 139, 141–2, 150n, 152n, 167, 182n, 192, 196
Ferrara, O., 49n, 65, 75, 153n, 172, 183n, 185n
Fichte, J. G., 37, 142

García Mérou, M., 25–6, 32, 88, 92, 122, 132–3, 165
García, J. A., 72, 74, 124
Gerber, C. F. V., 143
Gramsci, A., 75, 84, 102

Hegel, G. W. F., 37–8, 59, 68, 83, 107, 142

Ihering, R. V., 143
imperialism, 3, 7, 14, 32–3, 35, 37–8, 40–1, 49n, 51, 67, 75, 79n, 98–101, 118n, 122, 170–2, 193
Ingenieros, J., 41, 117n
Irazusta, J., 96–101, 103–4, 113–14, 118n, 119n, 139–40, 145–6, 153n, 177, 180

Jellinek, G., 143, 183n
Joly, M., 144

Kant, I., 72, 106, 116n, 121n, 150n,
Kelsen, H., 66, 152n, 160, 183n
Krausism, 134, 143, 156–7, 169

Legaz y Lacambra, L., 66, 75, 80n, 155–6, 159–61, 164–7, 182n, 183n, 184n
Legón, F., 56, 58, 62–3, 78n, 107, 112–14, 144, 152n
liberalism, 2–4, 6, 8–9, 13, 17, 22–3, 37, 39, 41, 51, 55–6, 60, 66, 68–70, 75, 82, 84–5, 89–93, 95, 97, 99–101, 103, 105–7, 109–15, 122–24, 130, 133–4, 139, 141, 145–7, 154–8, 163–5, 167–71, 174, 176–80, 190n, 191–6; *see also* anti-liberalism, 4–5, 7–8, 66, 70, 73, 82, 94–7, 99, 104, 109, 113–15, 145, 162, 167, 180, 184n, 192, 195–6
Lugones, L., 68–70, 74, 91–6, 102–3, 105, 109, 112–14, 116n, 117n, 118n, 123, 134, 137, 145–6, 150n, 152n, 165

Macaulay, T., 35, 48n, 130, 144, 148n
Machiavellianism, 7, 14–17, 19–21, 23, 29–30, 33, 38–41, 49n, 60, 63, 69, 78n, 87, 93, 103–4, 117n, 121n, 136, 152n, 161, 171–2; *see also* anti-Machiavellianism, 5, 8, 15–16, 20, 30, 42n, 44n, 45n, 75, 156, 165, 167, 171–2, 192, 196

Mariana, J., 16
Maritain, J., 55, 58, 104, 121n
Martínez Paz, E., 69, 72, 74, 86–7, 89–90, 95–6, 103, 107, 115n, 123, 140, 150n, 152n
Matienzo, J. N., 123
Maurras, Ch., 106, 109, 120n
Meinecke, F., 83, 143, 162
Meinvielle, J., 106–7, 112–14, 120n, 121n, 145
Menéndez y Pelayo, M., 130
Milanesi, G., 142
Montero, B., 25–6, 35, 46n, 48n, 150n
Morley, J., 33–6, 38, 40, 47n, 48n
Mosca, G., 70, 84, 102
Mussolini, B., 75, 84, 88–91, 108, 143, 152n

nationalism, 7, 14, 23, 32–3, 35–41, 49n, 51–2, 67–8, 70, 96–7, 104, 109, 119n, 122, 144, 153n, 158–9, 166, 171–2
Nietzsche, F., 47n, 68, 120n

Oncken, W., 130
Orlando, V. E., 142–3

Palacio, E., 70, 74, 96, 99, 101–4, 113–14, 119n, 139–40, 145–6, 165, 177, 180
Pareto, V., 70, 84, 102, 109
Passerini, L., 142
Piñero, N., 73
Plato, 97, 104, 135
political realism, 8, 30, 42, 51, 59, 62, 67–9, 74, 91, 94, 111, 139, 172
Polybius, 102, 139, 147
Posada, A., 39–40, 54, 68, 134–5, 144, 155–9, 161, 164, 166–7, 169, 172, 183n, 196

Quesada, E., 28–32, 41, 49n, 59, 68, 75, 92, 127, 132, 138, 142, 172, 185n

Ramos Mejía, J. M., 47n
Ramos, J. P., 126
Ranke, L. V., 83, 142

Reinsch, P., 38, 40
republicanism, 2–3, 8–9, 21–2, 34, 37, 41, 44n, 47n, 79n, 82, 85, 96–7, 100–1, 103, 105, 113, 118n, 136, 138–9, 141–2, 145–6, 153n, 154–5, 159, 162, 164, 167–71, 173–80, 184n, 185n, 189n, 190n, 192–5
Rizzi, M. A., 26–8, 32, 47n, 88, 92, 122, 133, 144, 150n
Rochau, L. V., 142
Romero, J. L., 62–5, 71, 74, 79n, 135, 137–41, 144–5, 151n, 152n
Rousseau, J. J., 6, 23, 89, 104, 106, 171

Saavedra Fajardo, D., 172
Sampay, A., 56–8, 63–4, 107–9, 112–14, 120n, 121n, 137, 144, 149n, 152n
Sánchez Sorondo, M., 70, 94–5, 99, 102, 118n, 120n, 150n
Sánchez Viamonte, C., 60–2, 86, 88–90, 95–6, 103, 123, 133, 140, 152n

Sarmiento, D. F., 17, 19, 21, 30, 36, 43n, 44n, 47n, 60, 87, 122–3, 128
Schmitt, C., 47n, 66, 80n, 83, 89–90, 109, 113, 121n, 152n, 160, 163, 182n, 183n
Spengler, O., 32, 59, 62, 86, 109, 115n, 120n
Suárez, F., 16

Taborda, S., 89–90, 95–6, 113, 140
Taine, H., 46n, 120n
thomism, 42n, 55–6, 71, 104–5, 107, 109, 114, 146, 160, 171
Tomassini, O., 83, 142
totalitarianism, 105, 107, 109, 114, 121n, 126, 195
Treitschke, H. V., 38–40, 54, 68, 83, 142, 144, 153n, 161

Villari, P., 26, 47n, 83, 142, 144, 151n
Villefosse, L., 142

Weber, M., 83, 163

EU representative:
Easy Access System Europe
Mustamäe tee 50, 10621 Tallinn, Estonia
Gpsr.requests@easproject.com

www.ingramcontent.com/pod-product-compliance
Lightning Source LLC
Chambersburg PA
CBHW051116230426
43667CB00014B/2606